ROUTLEDGE LIBRARY EDITIONS:
EDUCATION MANAGEMENT

Volume 7

STAFF DEVELOPMENT IN THE SECONDARY SCHOOL

STAFF DEVELOPMENT IN THE SECONDARY SCHOOL

Management Perspectives

Edited by
CHRIS DAY AND ROGER MOORE

Routledge
Taylor & Francis Group
LONDON AND NEW YORK

First published in 1986 by Croom Helm

This edition first published in 2018
by Routledge
2 Park Square, Milton Park, Abingdon, Oxon OX14 4RN

and by Routledge
711 Third Avenue, New York, NY 10017

Routledge is an imprint of the Taylor & Francis Group, an informa business

British Library Cataloguing in Publication Data
A catalogue record for this book is available from the British Library

ISBN: 978-1-138-48720-8 (Set)
ISBN: 978-1-351-04158-4 (Set) (ebk)
ISBN: 978-1-138-48785-7 (Volume 7) (hbk)
ISBN: 978-1-138-54533-5 (Volume 7) (pbk)
ISBN: 978-1-351-04126-3 (Volume 7) (ebk)

Publisher's Note
The publisher has gone to great lengths to ensure the quality of this reprint but points out that some imperfections in the original copies may be apparent.

Disclaimer
The publisher has made every effort to trace copyright holders and would welcome correspondence from those they have been unable to trace.

Staff Development in the Secondary School

MANAGEMENT PERSPECTIVES

Edited by
CHRIS DAY AND ROGER MOORE

CROOM HELM
London • Sydney • Wolfeboro, New Hampshire

Croom Helm Ltd, Provident House, Burrell Row,
Beckenham, Kent, BR3 1AT

Croom Helm Australia Pty Ltd, Suite 4, 6th Floor,
64-76 Kippax Street, Surry Hills, NSW 2010, Australia

British Library Cataloguing in Publication Data

Staff development in the secondary school:
management perspectives.
1. High schools — Great Britain —
Administration
I. Day, Christopher II. Moore, Roger
373.12'00941 LB2822.3.G7

ISBN 0-7099-0895-4
ISBN 0-7099-4539-6 Pbk

Croom Helm, 27 South Main Street,
Wolfeboro, New Hampshire 03894-2069, USA

Library of Congress Cataloging-in-Publication Data

Staff development in the secondary school.

Includes index.
1. High schools — Great Britain — Administration.
2. Departmental chairmen (High schools) — Great Britain. 3. School personnel management — Great Britain. I. Day, Christopher, ACP. II. Moore, Roger.
LB2822.3.G7S73 1986 373.41 86-16686
ISBN 0-7099-0895-4
ISBN 0-7099-4539-6 (pbk.)

Printed and bound in Great Britain by Mackays of Chatham Ltd, Kent

FOREWORD

The outline propoal for this volume was submitted by the joint editors at the very time when this Croom Helm series on education management was in conception. It was accepted with alacrity. The proposal gave promise of — and the completed text now demonstrates — an overriding concern with the practicalities of management in our secondary schools today.

There has been a tendency in the past to look upon books on education management as the product of the cloistered cell: written at a safe remove from the heat and dust of the arena of our schools. Such a charge cannot be levelled at those who have contributed to this volume, best described as practitioners and facilitators of education management, in schools, local education authorities and universities. All are widely experienced and write from the heart of that experience.

It is good to have contributions to a symposium of a reasonable length. Too often a collection of this kind whets the appetite without satisfying it. Nevertheless many of the chapters implicitly urge the reader to explore the topic in greater depth. To this end the chapter bibliographies are of value. There is no attempt to beat the reader about the ears with weighty tomes, but rather to indicate key texts which the contributor has found useful in the writing of the chapter and which the reader will undoubtedly find helpful in any further study of the topic.

This is a volume about education management issues present and future. it makes no pretence to bland solutions of the difficulties confronting our secondary schools in times of rapid change; but it does sound a note of confidence that educationists in all institutions will find welcome.

Cyril Poster

CONTENTS

ACKNOWLEDGEMENTS

We would like to offer our thanks and acknowledgements to a number of people without whose help this book could never have been produced. First and foremost to our authors who all agreed most readily not only to make a contribution but to stick to the briefs we gave them. Secondly the quiet but crucial encouragement we have received from the publishers, particularly Naomi Roth and Cyril Poster in his capacity as general editor of the series. Finally an especially big thank you to Linda Wightman for coping so admirably with the essentially humdrum but exacting work involved in preparing the manuscript for publication.

Christopher Day
Roger Moore

INTRODUCTION

Any book needs a clear justification. At the time of writing yet another in the veritable deluge of books about school management needs to be especially clear in its purposes. A collection of contributions by so many different hands with the inevitable variations in treatment requires particular care. We have tried, therefore, to collect clusters of original papers written from a number of different but complementary perspectives which together represent the major actors in the drama of school management.

The origin of the collection is a series of courses on school management which have been mounted by the In-service unit at the Nottingham University School of Education for something like a decade. The purpose of these courses is to promote immediate and tangible improvements in the management of schools. This essentially practical approach is underlined by the fact that the major influence in the processes of planning and implementation is exerted by senior teachers and advisers or inspectors from the three (and in some cases four) East Midlands LEAs who, together with colleagues from higher education, form the course planning teams. While such planning groups form the core of the tutorial support team for the duration of the course, other major contributors are, however, drawn from a much wider geographical and educational spectrum. It is not surprising then that the contributions to this book emanate from just such a broad spectrum and the perspectives of each of the partners in the management process - schools, LEAs and higher education - are represented. Teachers should be reassured that the largest group of contributors comes from the ranks of either currently practising heads and deputies or those who have recently held such positions. In addition there are notable contributions from LEA inspectors together with colleagues from industrial backgrounds. Of the traditional academics represented, one has been, until recently, a member of the team leading the National

Development Centre for School Management Training at Bristol. Short biographical notes on each contributor follow this introduction.

We asked this group to look at what seemed to be some of the most pressing current issues in the field of secondary school management and to focus particularly on human resource management, undoubtedly the most complex area of any manager's role. Thus the core of the book is sections 3 and 4 which contain five chapters concerned directly with the handling of staff. Appraisal as a concept has evoked a good deal of misgiving, mainly due to some quite natural misunderstandings as to its true nature and purpose. Certainly we would wish to argue that effective staff development cannot take place without first establishing where, in professional terms, the individual teacher, department or school is and just what personal, professional and institutional needs require to be met. John Berridge and David Trethowan, the one from the perspective of a particular LEA, the other from the viewpoint of an individual school, attempt to provide the necessary reassurance that appraisal can be positive and non-threatening (Chapters 6 and 7). However, there are still problems to be resolved for, as Christopher Day points out (Chapter 8) progress may be slowed by external constraints and inappropriate "top down" models which fail to recognise the crucial contribution individual teachers can make to their own development. Nevertheless, even allowing for such constraints, there are still considerable possibilities within the existing system given the necessary will. Ben Kerwood and Simon Clements provide us with a useful survey of these (Chapter 9) and against this general background it is particularly interesting to consider Brian Wakeman's case study of how action research techniques are utilised in his own school to the advantage of individual and institutional development (Chapter 10).

Good staff management only comes about as a result of the efforts of responsible professionals, themselves heavily involved in the hurly-burly of daily routine in the school and often in some doubt as to what they should be doing and how they should be doing it. Hence the contributions in Section 2 form an essential back-cloth to what follows. Inevitably the key role is that of the head, and here Frank Stoner gives us some valuable considerations of possible strategies to cope with change (Chapter 3) while Bill Flisher, using the experience of a sizeable number of actual heads and deputies, looks at the especially crucial pressures of time (Chapter 4).

Equally important, though less readily admitted, is the role of the middle manager. Recently a good deal has been written on the role of the pastoral head so we felt it might be useful to redress the balance by securing a fresh look at that of the subject head and hence Peter Ribbins' highly stimulating and original examination (Chapter 5). In Section 5 the emphasis moves to a consideration of the possibility that schools and industrial organisations have sufficient in common for the former to learn something from the latter. Here Paul Kibbey (Chapter 11) and Roger Moore and Maggie Pankhurst (Chapter 12) chart two different processes by which this might be achieved.

Finally, we felt that the discussions within these sections needed to be set within the broader national context. Hence in Section 1, Elizabeth Ballinger provides an overview of the definition and fulfilment of school managers' needs (Chapter 1) which is then juxtaposed with Joan Dean's analysis of the enabling policies to be pursued by the employing LEA (Chapter 2). Moreover, since rapid change is such a marked feature of the current educational scene and seems likely to be so for the rest of this century, we felt it vital to secure some perspective of the future. Thus in the final chapter Bob Moon looks forward optimistically, yet by no means unrealistically, to a system where, for the first time in history, teachers may be regarded as true professionals.

The fore-going paragraphs are intended to provide a flavour of the underlying assumptions and the structure of this book but, as an additional help to the reader, we have placed a short abstract of the contents at the head of each chapter.

Christopher Day
Roger Moore

THE CONTRIBUTORS

<u>Elizabeth Ballinger</u> taught in secondary schools for 20 years, becoming head of department and then taking on the role of professional tutor. She was a school-based tutor for 5 years in the PGCE division of the School of Education at Bristol University before becoming Senior Lecturer in Education Management at Bristol Polytechnic. She was then seconded to the National Development Centre for School Management Training when that body was established. Currently she holds a senior post at the Further Education Staff College at Coombe Lodge.

<u>John Berridge</u> taught biology and social sciences before becoming Head of Social and Careers Education and then Deputy Head of an 11-16 comprehensive school in Nottingham. He has since become an inspector with Nottinghamshire LEA where, in addition to general duties, he is responsible for personal and social education. He is particularly committed to the notion of a co-ordinated and progressive programme of personal and social education for all pupils within a comprehensive system.

<u>Simon Clements</u> has worked in schools, further education and for the BBC. After a period of ten years as deputy head and later acting head at Woodberry Down School, London, he was seconded for two years to The Centre for the Study of Comprehensive Schools as a field officer. This was followed by a period with BP where he carried out a survey on the briefing of industrialists working with education. He has written various textbooks and articles for schools.

<u>Christopher Day</u> is a senior lecturer and head of the In-service Unit in the School of Education of the University of Nottingham. Prior to this he worked in Primary and Secondary schools, initial teacher training, and as a local authority adviser. His research and teaching interests are in the professional learning of teachers, the management of innovation and change, and the role of the external consultant. Within this context he coordinates and manages a comprehensive programme of regional OTTO and 20 day management courses for heads and senior staff from secondary

and primary schools. Recent publications include 'A Survey on the Provision and Management of DES Regional Courses in England and Wales 1978-83' (DES/AISEIT, 1986), 'Managing Primary Schools' (Harper and Row, 1986) and 'Resourcing Management Courses' (NDC/University of Nottingham, 1986).

Joan Dean has worked as a teacher in primary and secondary schools and in further education, as lecturer in a college of education, as head of two primary schools, as Senior Adviser for Primary Education, and for the past thirteen years as Chief Inspector for Surrey. During this period she has written some twenty-four books, numerous articles for the educational press, has broadcast and appeared on television and has contributed to a number of national committees. Recent publications include 'Managing Secondary Schools' (Croom Helm, 1985). She was President of the National Association of Inspectors and Educational Advisers for the year 1971-2 and was awarded the OBE for her contribution to education in 1980. She is known in the field of management training for her work with Surrey teachers, which started in 1976. She is a member of the Steering Committee of the National Development Centre for School Management Training.

Bill Flisher is now Senior Secondary School Inspector with Nottinghamshire LEA. In addition to his previous teaching experience in schools and higher education, for many years he has organised and taught COSMOS, Middle Management, curriculum and methodology INSET courses. For six years he has been the LEA link inspector for the DES/Regional management courses for secondary heads and deputies organised by the School of Education, University of Nottingham contributing to the course books and lecturing. He was a founder-member of the Diploma Board of the Mathematical Association, a member of the DES funded Research Project Steering Committee and is now an External Moderator for the Diploma course. He has contributed several articles to educational and mathematical journals.

Ben Kerwood works in Oxfordshire as assistant education officer with responsibility for teacher in-service training. From 1983 to 1985 he was deputy director of the Centre for the Study of Comprehensive Schools, CSCS. Before that he contributed to the development of school-based secondments while himself on secondment to Oxford Polytechnic from his post as deputy head at The John Mason School, Abingdon.

Paul Kibbey joined Rank Xerox (UK) Ltd in November 1972 where he held a succession of management appointments in Personnel Operations, Industrial Relations and Corporate Affairs. He began his career with Hoover Ltd (1965-1968) and subsequently held personnel posts with Molins and Crane. His current appointment is Manager, Social Policy, in the International Headquarters of Rank Xerox Ltd. He is actively involved in industry-education liaison and is a member of the Department of Industry Education Technology Centre. He is a member of the CBI's Adult Training Committee and of the Charity Forum. He is General Administrator of the Rank Xerox Trust and assists RX operating companies here and overseas with their Social Responsibility programmes. In conjunction with Ruth Howell of UBI, Paul has developed the Rank Xerox/UBI partnership, which has produced a series of industry-based workshops and training courses for headteachers and others in education, and printed classroom material on 'The Office of the Future'. Paul also lectures on CRAC courses for teachers, undergraduates and sixth formers.

Robert Moon taught at Tulse Hill School, ILEA, before moving to Stantonbury, Milton Keynes, first as Deputy Head and then Head of Bridgewater Hall, one of the campus schools. He is currently Head of Peers School, Littlemore, Oxford. He has been Chairman of the Association for the Study of the Curriculum and from 1980 to 1985 was Deputy Editor of the journal "Curriculum". He acted as a consultant for Open University education courses between 1976 and 1981 and has written widely on educational issues. Most recently he has edited "Comprehensive Schools: Challenge and Change" (NFER/Nelson, 1983); (with Maurice Galton) "Changing Schools: Changing Curriculum" (Harper and Row, 1983); and "The New Maths Curriculum Controversy" (Falmer Press, 1986).

Roger Moore taught History, Humanities and General Studies in secondary schools for 16 years before spending 3 years in a college of education. He is currently in the School of Education at Nottingham University where an increasing amount of his time is taken up with organising and teaching on management courses. He is especially interested in the contacts and comparisons between school managers and their counterparts in commerce and industry. He is also involved in the evaluation of the TVEI Project in Derbyshire.

Maggie Pankhurst has the inestimable advantage of having worked both in education and industry before coming to her present post as Midlands Regional Liaison Officer for Understanding British Industry (UBI). A graduate in business studies and an accountant by training, she lectured in FE Colleges and then became Senior Training Officer with a firm of chartered accountants. While she is concerned generally with the problems of liaison between education and industry she feels it especially valuable that schools should be able to draw on the latter's accumulated experience in the field of management.

Peter Ribbins is a Lecturer in Educational Administration at the University of Birmingham. He has published many articles on a wide variety of aspects of the contemporary comprehensive school and is the co-author or co-editor of "Perspectives on Pastoral Care", "Education and Care", "Schooling and Welfare" and "Managing Education". He is one of the editors of the series "Studies in Pastoral Care and Personal and Social Education" (Blackwell) and is the founding executive editor of "Pastoral Care in Education". He is currently researching into the Careers' Service and also into the role of the subject department in the secondary school.

Frank Stoner worked as a deputy in an ILEA school and it was this, together with the experience of contributing to in-service courses, which developed his interest in the management of schools and especially the management of change. This was further strengthened by 6 years as head of Branston School and Community College, Lincoln, and a year's secondment as director of the Centre for the Study of Comprehensive Schools (CSCS) at York University. He is currently attached to the MSC as a member of the team of regional advisers for the TVEI Project.

David Trethowan, a Cornishman, became head of Warden Park School in West Sussex in 1973. It was then a secondary modern, due to go comprehensive the following year and subsequently to more than double in size. His previous experience includes eight years in the Royal Navy. This was followed by a two-year teacher training course and a further three years at university. He has led and taught on management courses throughout the British Isles, both in industry and education, is co-author of several books on management, and has produced many of the volumes in the "Management in Schools" series for the Industrial Society. In April 1983 he led the first One Term Training Opportunities at Oxford, and now advises on course structure and training techniques.

Brian Wakeman has been deputy head at Rotheram (11-16) High School, Luton, since 1980 and his responsibilities include curriculum and staff development, and evaluation. He has contributed articles on action research to several journals and books particularly in relation to personal, social and moral education, and has recently published 'Personal, Social and Moral Education - a Source Book' (Lion Publishing, Tring, Herts, 1984).

SECTION 1: ESTABLISHING CONTEXTS

Chapter 1

THE TRAINING AND DEVELOPMENT NEEDS OF MANAGERS: AN OVERVIEW

Elizabeth Ballinger

This opening chapter is concerned with the way in which the central task of managers - human resource management - may be best achieved. The author identifies as fundamental the problem of defining and meeting the needs of school managers. Needs vary according to different perspectives, for example, Government and DES, the LEA, school and the individual. She argues that needs can only be defined on the basis of the tasks (the 'what' of management) and the skills necessary for the achievement of those tasks (the 'how' of management), but that this is complicated because needs of the individual and the organisation inevitably change over time. The author suggests that needs may be met by both training for short term objectives ('on-the-job', 'near-the-job' and 'away-from-the-job') and longer term development (which can only be achieved by linking the growth of the individual with the development of the organisation. In presenting these two themes of training and development, and individual and organisational needs, the author highlights the need for managers who are highly skilled in the business of time management, interpersonal relationships and target setting and appraisal. These and other themes are examined in detail in the other chapters of this book.

1 Whose Perspective

The purpose of this overview of the training and development needs of those with managerial responsibilities in secondary schools is to bring together the various strands which need to be interwoven for effective learning. However, there is no ready agreement about what these strands are, or what the detailed outcome of successful development should be, so I shall design an outline map which others may detail or modify according to their own experiences and needs.

The first decision concerns the orientation of the map. Whose definition of training and development needs should predominate? Increasingly there are a number of parties who wish to influence both the nature and outcomes of management training and development. Some can use resource power and political clout to call attention to their views, others rely on professional judgement carried out in the context of accountability. Others are users or consumers of the services supplied. Each of these groups seems to have legitimate claims to be considered, but they can make contradictory demands in the formulation of training and development policy.

National education policy as embodied in Circular 3/83 and subsequent circulars gave priority through specific grant funding to the management training of heads and senior staff in order to improve the effectiveness of pupil learning.

However, the link between training, training outcomes and improved pupil performance remains an act of faith. Decisions about the content and methodology for 3/83 programmes were to be the field of the professional trainers, and money would be made available through LEAs, when particular courses or programmes had been approved through local consultative procedures. There was an expectation in 1983 when the National Development Council for School Management Training was founded that evaluated examples of "good practice" would be disseminated and that perhaps a model of effective development from training would emerge. Analysis of evaluation reports to date (Ballinger 1985) reveals a complexity of contexts and variables which makes a single successful model both highly unlikely and almost certainly undesirable.

Within national policy, the LEAs through their officers, and more usually their advisers, are required to participate in the local consultative arrangements. However, their contribution to the definition of the management training and development needs of the senior staff and their schools needs to be related to an LEA management development policy. At present few LEA management development policies exist to which training can be positively related. Most curriculum development concentrates, naturally, on its content and learning resources. Minimal attention is paid to the management implications, for LEAs, even when senior staff will be needed to support teachers through considerable changes in professional identity and methodology consequent on the changed student/teacher relationships inherent in TVEI, CPVE and, to a certain extent, in GCSE. LEAs therefore seem generally happy to allow the providing or training agencies to define the needs in terms of the staff development of individual managers rather than of the school or authority.

Another set of demands comes from parents and employers. The Hargreaves Report (1984) research appendices illuminate parental curricular values and expectations very fully, and were these to be translated into programmes for senior staff they would clearly be in tension with both national and LEA development policies. Employers, also while rightly making utilitarian demands on the education service, at present speak confusedly. They say they want to employ young workers with the right social skills and attitudes as well as relevant technical/professional skills and knowledge, and yet still emphasise at the point of selection the holding of academic qualifications designed for other objectives. However, they could help those in education define and clarify their objectives for management development.

Mediation between the school, its community and the elected members of the LEA is through the school governors. They at present play no part in defining management development needs, except as very rare members of county INSET committees.

If the views of the parties so far mentioned were to be brought together, there would at present be no consensus about training and development policy. Both in default of such a policy, and as a result of their own earlier efforts in the field, the providing agencies, the universities, polytechnics and regional management centres, have presented their own versions of what is needed. Though the comparative evaluation of 3/83 and 4/84 courses shows there have been some marked shifts in emphasis, there is still an uneasy relationship between what most providers are confident to provide and what senior managers in schools think they need.

It is the perspective of the latter, since they are the executives who are held accountable and those whose views in practice will determine what and how they are able to learn from management training and development activities, that I shall consider as determining the perception of needs.

2 <u>What needs</u>?

The needs of managers derive from the tasks they see themselves doing and the skills they need to do them. They may be alerted to their gaps in perception by others but the development of individual managers appears to be effective when it is based on the assumption that they are aware, or at least capable of becoming aware, of their own strengths and weaknesses, the stresses and rhythms of their particular jobs. By analysing what managers in schools say they do and the ways they succeed or fail in doing it, it becomes possible to develop a simple classification of tasks and skills which define areas for planning developmental responses. However, as Mintzberg (1980, 2nd ed) pointed out, the nature of the manager's day is such that its reality can be reflected by no calm detached model. (See Bill Flisher's chapter on time-task analysis.)

Because of the hectic pace of day-to-day management, one of the prime tasks of management in schools is often neglected: the setting of policy. Although each school now has its published list of aims, these are not a policy for action. Such a policy includes needs to be achieved, by whom, by when and with what resources, and, supremely, why? Answering the why question involves managers in schools making explicit their often conflicting educational values, the contribution of what they have learnt and therefore cherish from their own experience, and the deep-set and difficult to articulate 'ideal school' to which they would aspire (while simultaneously rationally denying its feasibility!) The price paid may be that planning is carried out superficially and incoherently, because of the lack of clarity not only about desired outcomes, but at times confusion about even the direction which needs to be taken. But setting both goals and direction are part of the task of the senior staff for overall school development, and for middle managers in relation to their sectional responsibilities. (See David Trethowan's chapter on appraisal and target setting for a detailed example of this.)

From overall policy decisions flow the further tasks related to implementing these policies. Detailed planning tasks will be considered later. Again, in the rush of events, and perhaps in the desire to avoid conflict, it may seem easier in the short term not to have explicit policies about implementation. yet there are overall questions of staff recruitment, development and promotion (even at present) which relate to meeting not only the present needs of the school, but its envisaged development. Planning the deployment of existing staff should occur in the light of this policy. Similarly, the phasing of school development, or sections of it, implies a policy for setting priorities not just on the immediate time scale, but to ensure adequate lead times for future longer-term change. The fact that LEAs are often unable to supply the necessary data which schools need for firm planning does not absolve managers in schools from responsibilities for setting priorities within probable constraints nor from a certain amount of contingency planning. Policies for the allocation of material resources, money, rooms and timetable time are also capable of a degree of rational development though they are often the focus of acute staff conflict as they become explicit. Avoiding ad hoc crisis management decisions in response to unpleasant pressure is a management development need. Carrying out effectively the tasks of policy making, then, I would argue is necessarily the prerequisite for managing the school.

The central service the school carries out is, of course, the education of its pupils, and so the major day-to-day tasks of managing the school must be concerned with the pupils and their curriculum. The management of the pupils is largely devolved to teachers in their academic and pastoral roles, and the way these roles interrelate to form the hidden curriculum of the school. Managers of the service, whether at middle or senior level, have a co-ordinating role ensuring that the progress of pupils is under observation. They may also be involved at critical moments of decision whether systematic in relation to growth through the school's opportunities and structures, or when there are major breakdowns requiring their additional experience or resources or power. The tasks of managers in managing pupils, in their managerial as opposed to their teacher role, may not be as significant as they claim, but it is an intensely time-consuming one, especially for middle managers, and one to which all other tasks can very easily be represented as coming second. This is not a popular view but sharpens the issue of what <u>managers</u> are expected to manage. The answer 'pupils' may be a response to a genuine fundamental school policy; often it is in ignorance or neglect of other essential managerial tasks.

The management of the curriculum, on the other hand, does create tasks which depend on their success in influencing other staff in their own classrooms to implement an agreed policy, subdivided into particular syllabuses. Operating the procedures for teaching which will command the necessary consent, and supporting staff, pupils, and parents through new curriculum approaches again involves answering the why, what, who, when and with what questions. In addition, it involves questions of human relationships which may not so far have been considered, and which do not always smoothly coincide with the organisational relationships which would enable the school most efficiently to educate its pupils. (Christopher Day highlights the importance of the affective dimension in his chapter on staff development.) So opportunities for managerial flexibility and a willingness to manoeuvre within priorities are further needs to which the school has to learn to respond, either by taking the initiative or reacting to pressure. The extent to which managers need to become involved in the detail of the curriculum in order to appreciate its implications for the wider system varies with the scope and nature of the issues under consideration. The costs of change, psychological as well as in material resources, can destabilise a school to such an extent that it creates major managerial problems. Managing the curriculum therefore requires in addition to the tasks of analysis and planning, an ability to anticipate how much change the school can assimilate, or, if change is externally imposed, how the security of

Managing material resources in comparison would become a rational allocation task were it not for the fact that these decisions are often the focus and expression of unarticulated and unresolved problems arising from the human relationships. They make an acceptable professional arena for surfacing the organisational discontent and low morale which often results from unsatisfactory interpersonal relationships. However, it should not be assumed that all conflict about resource management should be interpreted as displacement activity. Resources can be managed well or badly, systematically and sensibly, or on an ad hoc crisis basis where decisions are reversible under even greater antagonism or pressure.

A major decision, therefore, which managers must make in defining their needs in this area is the extent to which they are prepared to set up a <u>system</u> of material resource allocation, staff and pupil time, rooms, grounds, money, which is rational, open and defensible in terms of school practice and priorities both internally and externally. Since senior managers in practice have very little power and manoeuvrability they must also decide how far they wish to use resource allocation as a power mechanism, their major means of direct pressure. Resource allocation is also one of the few major quantifiable areas for which the Head can be most visibly held to account, and (s)he may need considerable confidence in the professional integrity and support of colleagues before making the whole area one of open discussion and participation.

Managing the external relationships of the school becomes increasingly important a task area as the individual becomes more senior. Most senior staff are concerned in differing degrees with three kinds of external relationships, those with other professionals, inside and outside education, those with the politically involved (party or otherwise), and those with the consumers of the service, primarily parents and employers. The nature of the relationships between the school and other professionals is undergoing rapid changes, as is the understanding of the boundaries of their respective roles. The increasing flow of DES documents and guidelines, the role of HMI and the ambiguity of their relationship with the DES is increasing the direct impact of central thinking on schools. This in turn is affecting the role of the LEA both in extending its demands on the school to respond to local guidelines, initiatives and returns and in simultaneously decreasing its ability to underwrite in resource terms the good practice it wishes to promote. Managers have to decide how far they will willingly mediate externally imposed policies and act as a buffer between their staff, LEA and national pressures. Additionally, schools increasingly need to work with specialists from the medical, paramedical, career and social services to implement in particular the 1981 Act. Although these latter tasks are usually delegated to operation by a few managers, all teachers need to be informed and involved, since attitudes to them are an important component of the hidden as well as the pastoral curriculum.

Relationships with professionals, however, set tasks within a degree of professionally consensual practices. The demands of parents and employers on the school can be spasmodic, about breakdowns as well as development. The task of managing relations with these interest groups who usually act individually rather than corporately concerns therefore setting up routine, positive communication networks, including the use of local media, so that there are opportunities for discussion between the school and those concerned with its processes and outcomes, mainly in relation to individual pupils. Corporately the parents may of course bring pressure to bear on the school through PTAs. Since the 1980 Act they have been able to do so through participation on governing bodies. The nature of this participation can change over time depending on the way in which heads view their respective roles and give them the opportunity to develop. If so, then the task of managing this relationship for the good of the school as the Head sees it becomes another area for action.

The final major area of managerial tasks is monitoring and evaluating the extent to which those decisions made at the level of policy have been translated into action through the four major process areas, the management of pupil learning and the curriculum, the management of human resources, the management of material resources and the management of external relations. Again, the task is not simply one of setting up systems but of establishing the relationships which will enable the systems to operate satisfactorily. Monitoring and evaluating is an area of increasing sensitivity and visibility. The present demands of the Secretary of State for a system of staff appraisal, combined with the increasing activities of the Audit Commission in its search for value for money means schools are already under a two-pronged demand to establish their criteria for effectiveness and to display evidence that they are meeting those criteria. With such external pressure, easily perceived as threatening, will senior staff, inexperienced by and large in handling appraisal techniques or evaluation methodology inside their own schools, see this area as one of welcome development for themselves? Sensitivity about using such approaches is increased by the growing politicisation of the unions at school level who fear, or say they fear, that they have more to lose than gain from increased monitoring.

Good managerial practice nevertheless demands that the progress of the school, and of the individuals, pupils and staff alike, be regularly reviewed against the goals of the school. Such a review may legitimately lead to modifications in a number of ways. Most radically, it may lead to a redefinition of strategic policy either overall or in a particular area of management. It may retain the goals while deciding that the structures or operational processes are at present inappropriate. It may reveal that actual working relationships, organisational or interpersonal, are incompatible with existing goals or structures or both. It may well reveal that progress is being impeded by a lack or misallocation of resources. Finally it should reveal the present strengths and weaknesses of individuals and identify the potential and limitations for individual and organisational growth. This point will be further developed in the next section.

One set of needs for the training and development of managers will emerge then from the analysis of what they do. The diagram on page 19 summarises the management tasks into which activities can be classified. The three circles should be seen as having different time cycles. The central one, policy-making, is relatively long term and slow-moving. The middle ring is fast-moving, the ever-changing day-to-day life of the school as it operates its policies in practice. The outer one accompanies its predecessor as it monitors continuing activity, and extends its time span and rhythm as it evaluates through periodic review the success of central policy. It would seem that managing these dimensions alone creates sufficient tasks for a training and development programme. Yet they comprise only the 'what' of management: the 'how' is at least as important.

3 What Skills?

'How' is more effectively revealed in action than by description and the needs it reveals for training are probably better handled directly through practical workshops than through intellectual analysis. Even so, in order to clarify what the objectives for such training might be, I am proposing to classify the skills required by managers into three major sets, although in operation they flow in and out of each other.

The first set of skills arise from focusing on people. The whole of the previous section emphasised that without satisfactory relationships it would be difficult to operate the task areas of management effectively. These interpersonal skills appear to need three intertwining dimensions if individuals and groups are to collaborate successfully. They can be distinguished as leadership skills, sharing skills and supporting skills. Leadership skills are perhaps best seen in terms of an appropriate

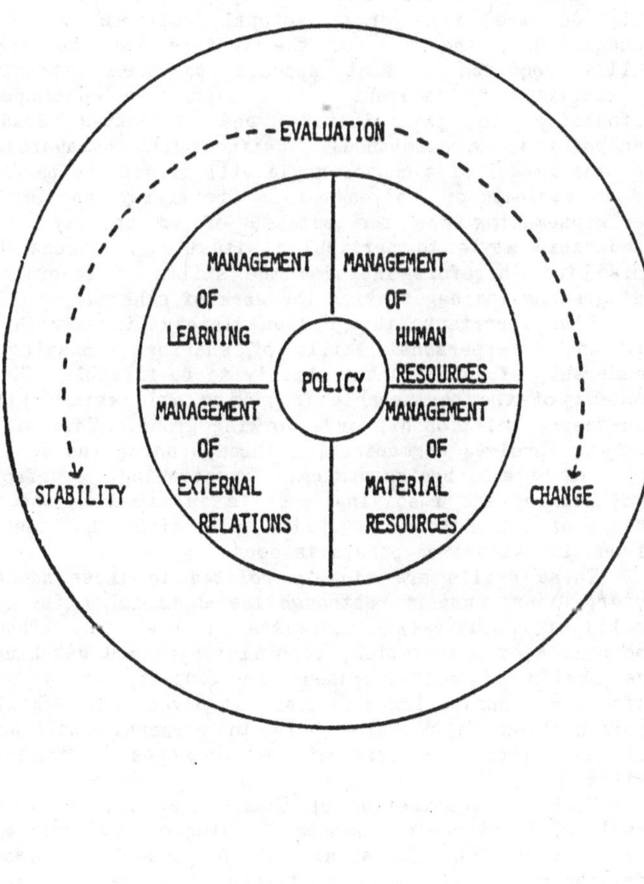

The Classification of Management Tasks

response to managing a combination of three factors, the task to be done, the people available to do the task and the context with which the people execute the task, rather than based upon a single and simple model of ideal leadership behaviour.

Appropriate leadership skills will be related to the personalities of the teachers and their colleagues, the nature and ethos of the organisation, and the tasks to be performed. Professor Charles Handy (1984) has succinctly outlined the four organisational cultures which shape fundamentally the role of the leaders and therefore the skills required. What appears to need enhancing is flexibility of leadership style along the continuum from autocratic to participative and delegated leadership according to circumstances, combined with an awareness of how the impact of a chosen style will affect the performance of a variety of colleagues. Creativity and effective decision-making are the outcome of an ability to mould leadership style to particular situations. Leadership of this kind therefore includes the skills of co-ordinating, integrating and negotiating the work of others.

Also important, though less visibly linked with power, are the interpersonal skills of sharing. Sharing, like leadership, focuses on the ability to be flexible. Here the context of the partnership is giving and taking, within a one-to-one relationship or a working group. This effective sharing involves communicating through using the skills of, for example, brainstorming, questioning, confronting, synthesising and resolving. It is in managing the interchange of professional attitudes and actions that the impact of one individual on others is seen.

These skills are closely related to those needed for interpersonal support, although the emphasis on the quieter skills of communication increases in this area. These are the skills of observation, both listening and watching, and the skills of self-awareness and empathy which lead to effective counselling. Also involved are skills of confrontation in relation here to personal attitudes and actions rather than primarily to ideas as in the sharing skills.

From the combination of these three sets of interpersonal skills, those of leading, joining and supporting, come the skills of judgement which underpin successful decision-making and implementation. Judgement calls on personal attitudes which, though not immediately amenable to training and development, can nevertheless be articulated and reviewed in sympathetic, positive and challenging relationships with others.

The second major set of managerial skills needed relate to administrative effectiveness. These tend to be more easily defined, analysed and learnt. First come the cluster of skills related to the detailed planning. These include the skills of breaking down decisions into their component actions, and executing them logically. Detailed planning involves learning how to assemble relevant information, filter out unnecessary data, clarify actions and outcomes for those who will carry them out, acquire and monitor the use of resources, set deadlines and coordinate the activity into the wider work of the school. These are detailed skills requiring accuracy, clarity of understanding and firmness of purpose.

These skills are translated into the actions through the skills of effective organisational communication, in addition to the kinds of interpersonal communication skills already listed. Organisational communication may be written or spoken, directly or by telephone. The writing of reports, analyses and discussion papers is a necessary skill for all senior managers, to be able to express oneself with clarity, brevity and relevance, all communicated in acceptable language and format. The oral communication skills needed by managers to make an impact at a variety of meetings include in addition to those required for written presentations an ability to understand, anticipate and respond to the needs of the audience, to establish good non-verbal communication, through eye contact and use by the voice, and to use visual aids if appropriate. The controlled, reasoned presentation of a case in committee combines the use of leadership and administrative skills.

Again, at the individual work level, the administrator needs techniques to control the flow of paperwork. This has two aspects, its physical control at any given moment and the use of other people in facilitating its progress. Physical control involves setting up systems of classification, storage and retrieval, and organising working patterns so that systems are implemented. The optimal use of secretarial or other support staff in handling correspondence, returns and reports depends on how a feasible administrative structure has been established, and an appropriate use of the skills these staff possess.

Much of the discipline of a successful administrative system is the result of another set of skills, time management skills. These include the skills of setting priorities, regulating engagements and meetings, controlling acceptance of tasks, phasing work and knowing when to leave things undone! Systematic methods of allocating work, chasing progress and updating diaries save time, although managers in schools as in all organisations will still be constantly subjected to unpredictable interruptions to planned work.

Effective time management, however, enables individuals to pay some attention to an increasingly important area to which they need to develop skills, that of managing stress

pre-requisite for promotion. Development needs are then perceived in terms of the imagined scope of the new post rather than based on the experience of the opportunities and constraints of the existing one. The need for courses pursued in hopes of future prospects tend therefore to be selected on different criteria from those applying to developing increasing effectiveness to meet present demands.

This is one aspect of developmental needs. The other is the development of the school itself over time, and the changing demands this makes on its managers. If the task of managers is to endeavour to see that the school's goals are achieved through the combined efforts of the staff, then managers and teachers alike must accept some responsibility for developing to meet the needs of the school and not just for their own individual ends. In order for this to occur, the school needs a clear development policy so that individuals can see the probable nature of their changing contribution to it. In addition, within this overall school development policy, there needs to be a coherent management development policy to enable managers collectively to contribute more effectively through carrying out the variety of management tasks with increasing management skills as detailed in Sections 2 and 3. The development of the individual manager for the school's needs is the first stage; the development of individual managers into the more effective collaborative management of the school in all its aspects is the ultimate goal of this second aspect of developmental needs over time.

5 The relationship of training to development

The basis for this section is a distinction between training and development which although the result of an arbitrary boundary nevertheless clarifies differences in responses to the needs so far analysed. I would argue that most development, and the most powerful forms of development, take place on-the-job. Managers who are effective and capable of becoming more effective improve their performance most significantly through the experience of handling the demands of their particular positions both on a day-to-day basis and as they shape their contribution over longer periods. Similarly, the management of the organisation is enhanced as individual managers actually learn to work together consciously setting, implementing and evaluating developmental goals for the school. I start the consideration of the nature of training, therefore, with a plea that the importance of development through work on-the-job should not be ignored because it requires no further organisation by senior managers. Doing the job is itself sufficient of a professional stimulus of individuals to meet the perceived personal and professional growth needs of individuals at certain stages. As such it should be accepted as one legitimate organisational response to needs identified through an 'appraisal for staff development' process.

In addition to this response, however, additional developmental activities are required. Where those are relatively short-term, sharply focused and with identifiable outcomes, I shall define them as training. I shall consider other planned interventions in the normal process of developing on-the-job which may be longer-term, more diffuse in their goals, or perhaps only partly of immediate relevance, as development. Both training and development, by these definitions, may occur on-the-job, near-the-job or away-from-the-job. My purpose now is to concentrate on the availability of training responses to the levels of needs identified in the preceding sections, and to mention other forms of development only briefly.

Training on-the-job comes from two major activities, coaching and counselling. Although they are conceptually distinct, in practice it is difficult to undertake coaching without counselling, although not all counselling has to be related to coaching. Assessment should play no part in coaching, and its relationship to an appraisal system needs sensitive handling. The purpose is to gain detailed feedback on performance from a skilled and trained colleague in order to acquire greater standards of competence and achievement. The subsequent discussion of observed performance almost invariably contains elements of the second activity, counselling. The second activity becomes set in a wider context, assessing reaction to deeper issues which impinge on particular performance and relationships.

Counselling, whether between peers or in some kind of superordinate-subordinate relationship, is a major force for managerial development on-the-job, and therefore one which needs to be allocated both the priority and the resources of time and congenial surroundings to become an effective management tool. Many of the needs derived from the six task areas can be met by other managers giving time, both informally and as part of a planned development policy to talking their colleagues through problems and opportunities. Counselling is particularly helpful in enabling managers to manage other people more effectively.

Effective counselling also requires many of the skills mentioned in the interpersonal skills section, and where surely these are identified as needing improvement, then the appropriate development response may be near-the-job skills training. All near-the-job training is so defined because it arises from demands to be met in the present job which the individuals or other senior staff feel are at present being inadequately fulfilled, or are being carried through at disproportionate psychological or resource costs. This kind of near-the-job developmental response needs to be sharply focused, therefore, on the identified needs of specific individuals or groups. Depending on the nature of the needs and the number of people involved, training can either be brought into the school by using an outside consultant or by going out to a short-term clearly defined training activity. Effective training in these skills areas will involve workshops and simulations in order to give opportunities for practice. At times, skill training will involve the acquisition of particular techniques in order to structure later action. The internalisation of such techniques will take longer than the training period and the individual will need to be supported back on-the-job by the organisation, a point of crucial importance.

The acquisition of techniques in the form of near-the-job training is relevant for most of the administrative skills as well as to some of the interpersonal ones. In relation to many administrative skills, success through training in techniques is demonstrably visible as an outcome in a very short period. However, many of these skills are often perceived as trivial, and managers are often reluctant to discipline themselves either to acquire or use the techniques which improve performance and reduce stress dramatically, quite particularly in areas of organisational communications and effective committee work.

One other form of training near-the-job which proves developmentally powerful is action learning. It is included in this training programme section because to be effective it needs the disciplined use of an analytic model initially and the kinds of group interpersonal skills which may themselves need to be acquired for if the action learning methodology is to be adopted. Action learning enables members of the set to bring to bear their expertise in counselling to members with the management of the selected problem or area for development. Unlike other training activities so far mentioned, it requires quite a long time-span, though the purpose is closely defined and the desired outcome of the methodology, <u>not the solutions or actions to be adopted</u>, are clear from the outset.

Finally, the school may 'buy' off-the-job training, using the term to describe specific, skills-based, visible outcome activities. Since these will be externally provided for a wider target group, provided as a response to a common managerial need rather than for a known group of individuals, the probability of their making the desired impact is less than the two earlier approaches. However, they are available as chosen organisational responses, often LEA promoted, and all the school has the energy to provide given the other demands on its managers' energies.

The development of managers, on the other hand, while embracing and drawing on some of the training techniques and activities so far mentioned, is more extensive. Essentially it is the intertwining of professional and personal growth in the context of the developing organisation. It is not realistic, therefore, to expect short courses, for example, of the 3/83 type, to achieve broad developmental goals. What needs further investigation is whether secondment for a term or a year could or could not be expected to lead to such development. Evaluation from some (though by no means all) OTTO courses reveal that they have given considerable personal refreshment, some personal and professional reorientation, but little directly developmental in terms of organisational impact because all the thinking and planning has been carried out off-the-job. However, it may be too early to look for such results. Even more remote from making an impact on the development of managers in their schools have been long full-time accredited courses which though stimulating and intellectually demanding do not call on the same kinds of expertise and abilities as are required for successful day-to-day management.

The provision of training and development responses is limited by a number of factors, some of them based on lack of resources, some of them based on the psychological readiness to learn. If schools or LEAs are to set up effective training and development programmes, then they need to clarify their own view of what the realistic boundaries of this development are.

At present, one of the greatest difficulties revealed by analysis of current evaluation reports is the lack of expertise in providing a range of learning opportunities in response to a wide spectrum of needs. There are many people who can transmit the latest information and thinking about developments within the education system, and this is a necessary ingredient for some sorts of developmental work at institutional level. There are fewer, though still considerable, numbers of people available who can enable the learner to use this knowledge or these new concepts to formulate developmental plans, particularly at the curriculum level. However, few of those at present leading 3/83 type programmes have a sufficient overview of the managerial demands in terms of staff support and development, resource management and political boundary management to enable individual senior staff to see and plan for the implications of curriculum development as part of an overall school developmental process. The greatest lack of expertise within the education system for management development at present appears to be in specific skills training, the need for which was argued in detail in earlier sections. It is becoming increasingly apparent that those courses which attempt to provide this element in the portfolio of learning responses are finding that their most effective and skilled trainers have to be brought in from the industrial and commercial sector.

Alongside present gaps in terms of the responses which the providers can provide are limitations in the support available for those undergoing training and development - whether on-the-job, near-the-job or away-from-the-job. Lack of time is the reason most usually given for being unable to provide the on-going support which may be through discussion, changes in organisational structures or procedures, or resource reallocation. However, another component of this lack of commitment to follow-up support is the lack of confidence many of those in supportive positions have in their ability to contribute usefully to the situation. The research findings emerging from Sussex indicate, however, that much of the effect of courses evaporates unless there is positive support before and after the particular developmental activity.

Support provided before the activity shapes the perception of what the course is intended to achieve. Lack of clarity about the kind of outcome it is hoped the programme will achieve imposes another kind of boundary on the kinds of learning that individual staff seem able to assimilate. This is why the role relationships and expectations of the partners in the training/development process (Ballinger, 1985) need to be understood and agreed. Thus the nature of the intended results of the provision can be defined in general terms for the purpose of designing the learning and the participant can be oriented to the experience (s)he is about to have. In particular, if there is to be effective transfer of learning, then the integration of the development of the individual with the development of the school becomes an explicit area of concern, action and follow-up support.

The learner needs such overall clarity of purpose, role and outcome in order to perceive what is available for enhancing managerial effectiveness. It is apparent to all who teach that one of the greatest limitations on learning is not intellectual ability but lack of motivation or readiness to learn. Providers of training and developmental activity therefore need the active cooperation of the learner, those who are sponsoring the learning, both the school and the LEA, and those who are providing the learning opportunities, so as to promote a readiness and openness to learn. Since there are many countervailing forces to openness and trust in a learning situation, a planned approach to and realistic appreciation of the boundaries of learning would seem to be an integral part of the management of the development and training process.

6 Ways of learning

The learning needs of individual managers are most effectively met when the providers can make use of a repertoire of approaches in their planned activities.

Though our experience teaches us that different pupils learn in different ways, the transfer of this experience to planning courses for adults is not always readily apparent in their design. I shall briefly refer to three dimensions of the learning process as it affects the setting up of learning activities. What follows should be taken as referring to the context of learning for increased managerial effectiveness, and is not necessarily as useful in relation to adult learning for other purposes.

The first dimension of this learning relates to an overview of the sequence through which individual learners seem to need to go in order to affect their managerial performance. It has three phases, each sub-divided. The order of the phases appears to me to be unfailingly sequential, the ordering of events within the phases more flexible and responsive to a variety of variables. The first phase is the attention phase during which individuals become aware of learning needs, either through internal reflection or through external stimulus, and start a search for new knowledge, concepts or skills to meet these needs. Coming across new information is often the external stimulus which raises the consciousness of need. This phase of paying attention to the new awareness of a need to learn leads into the second phase, where the learner discriminates between available choices of information and responses while formulating intention for action. This intention phase may vary considerably in time and the intensity of the demands it makes on the learner, but if it is disproportionately short in relation to the complexity of the situation, then the outcomes of intentions will not be effectively translated into action. The intention phase is a testing out phase in terms of such factors as congruence with internal and school values, feasibility in terms of existing structures, procedures, resources and readiness to change, and preliminary 'sounding board' discussions with trusted colleagues to explore the initial reactions of others. A sufficient level of favourable responses, internal and external to the individual, will lead on to the final phase, the action phase, where the learner implements the outcomes of the two previous phases and incorporates on-the-job, possibly on a trial basis, a commitment to develop some part of himself, school or both. Training and development programmes need to reflect which of these phases form the basis of their action, and to what extent they can and should attempt to respond to all three within their time and resource limitations.

Similarly, taking the framework used by David Kolb (1979) for the analysis of experiential learning, course designers can estimate which parts of the learning cycle they are targeting in particular activities. Kolb sees the learning cycle as consisting of four processes, concrete experience, reflective observation, abstract conceptualisation, and active experimentation. This learning is a constantly recurring cycle, but individuals tend to have preferred parts in that cycle to enable them to learn for particular purposes. If the purpose of the learning is unclear, then it follows that the kind of learning activity needed to stimulate it is also unclear, with evidence outcomes in terms of ineffective course or activity design.

In addition, as Kolb goes on to explore, individuals have preferred learning styles which are superordinate to particular learning purposes, and part of the dilemma for providers of learning is to create a learning climate in which different learning styles are seen as legitimate and catered for at the design level. Honey and Mumford (1982) explore the same territory from a slightly different angle, and describe the needs of individual learners in terms of four preferred learning styles, those of the activist, the reflector, the theorist and the pragmatist. It is important that course designers decide whether they are going to encourage participants to widen their response by learning from a variety of learning approaches, or to reinforce and make use of those with which the learners are already comfortable. It is the problem again of assessing to what degree change is both desirable and realistic in the context of working in a particular situation with a known group of people towards a specific outcome. In addition, an understanding of how people learn and prefer to learn is also a managerial skill. Without some conscious reflection on the process during training and development activities, it can be assumed that other people learn in the same style which the manager himself prefers, with consequent loss of effectiveness in getting changes embedded into the actions of others in the school.

7 Summary

I have attempted in this brief overview of the management development and training needs of senior staff in secondary schools to achieve two purposes. The first is to analyse the sources of need as deriving from the tasks managers have to do and the skills they need to do them. The second purpose is to review the kinds of training and developmental responses that are available to meet the identified needs, emphasising that the providers of such responses also require managerial and pedagogic expertise for the design, implementation and evaluation of the effectiveness of what they have set up.

Throughout, I have called attention to the greater need for clarity of role, purpose and outcomes in the perceptions of all the partners in the network of school development. There have been some shifts in emphasis and a few shifts in practice shown in the responses to the management training of senior staff since 1983. Much remains to be done, and the subsequent chapters of this book detail why and what remains to be achieved as well as successes already visible on a small scale.

References

Ballinger E A (1984a) Final Report on the Development of a Governing Body 1981-1984, National Development Centre for School Management Training, Bristol

Ballinger E A (1984b) Headship in the 80's: an evaluation report of a 20 Day programme, National Development Centre for School Management Training, Bristol

Ballinger E A (1985) An Interim Analysis of Available Evaluation Reports on Basic and OTTO Programmes, National Development Centre for School Management Training, Bristol

Handy C (1984) Taken for Granted? Looking at Schools as Organisations, Longmans/Schools Council

Hargreaves D (1984) Improving Secondary Schools, Report to the Inner London Education Authority

Honey P and Mumford A (1982) Manual of Learning Styles, Honey Publications

Kolb D, Rubin I, McIntyre J (3rd edition 1979) Organisational Psychology: an experiential approach, Prentice Hall

Mintzberg H (1980) (2nd edition) The Nature of Managerial Work, Harper and Row

Chapter 2

MANAGEMENT AND THE ROLE OF THE LEA

by Joan Dean

In this chapter, Joan Dean provides an LEA perspective on the need for more systematic provision of management training. She argues that local authorities, as employers, must be responsible and accountable for the quality of their workforce, and that management training at all levels is part of this accountability. She stresses the need for LEAs to have an agreed management policy based on a regular and systematic assessment of in-service needs; and that this policy must be represented by a comprehensive programme of management development which itself reflects a partnership in planning between LEAs, schools and higher education institutions. Built into such programmes would be systems of appraisal, record-keeping and evaluation. Finally, she advocates training for advisers as well as headteachers in which the links between training and implementation, preparation and support, are integral to the course design.

Recent years have seen the development of training programmes for headteachers and other senior staff in schools following the publication of Circular 3/83 which set out the arrangements for management training and for the National Development Centre. Now that these programmes are under way it becomes increasingly evident that if training senior staff in schools is to be fully effective, it should be seen not only as part of a professional development programme but also as part of a total LEA management training policy and programme which involves not only teachers with management roles in schools, but the officers and advisory services of the LEA and to some extent Members and Governors. Although this paper is specifically concerned with management training at secondary level, much of it applies more widely. The processes of management are interrelated at every level and a manager at any point in the system needs those senior and those junior to him/her to have a shared understanding of these processes if (s)he is to be able to use this knowledge to the full.

LEA Accountability

The development of management training might be seen as part of the larger concern with the accountability of public services. Local authorities are big spenders; the heads of secondary schools carry a considerable responsibility and it is not unreasonable to expect the education service to demonstrate that it is employing its resources to the best effect. This means not only having clear educational aims but managing each part of the service so that those aims are achieved to the optimum extent. This requires both the skills of relating to people and also the skills of management.

The LEA is also the employer. This brings a responsibility to see that employees develop in their work, acquiring and maintaining the skills for the tasks they have to undertake.

The responsibility to be accountable and to develop employees are complementary parts of the LEA's task. They are reflected in practice at all levels and may sometimes conflict, as can be seen in the ambivalent views of teachers towards appraisal of performance. Teachers find appraisal for development attractive but appraisal to identify outstanding teachers or for calling incompetent teachers to account much less so. It is possible that teacher reaction to the latter may make it difficult to provide the former.

The LEA discharges its responsibilities for accountability and for development in various ways.

In the first instance the spending of public money is the responsibility of the publicly elected councillors forming the local education committee who delegate responsibility for the running of the education service to the CEO and his colleagues. He in turn delegates to heads of schools and colleges with something of a parallel system of delegation to governors.

A good deal of the accountability process devolves upon the advisory services who straddle the LEA's responsibility to account for its spending and that for development. The last ten years or so have seen a considerable shift in emphasis on the part of many advisory teams towards the inspection aspect of their role and in some authorities there has been a separation of the inspectorial role and the advisory one.

Management tasks and activities

The list which follows notes the groups of management tasks for which training may be needed. (A fuller version of this list is given in Dean, 1985.)

1 The articulation of aims, objectives and policies agreed by the school community and arrangements for their implementation.

2 The management of learning involving the articulation of the curriculum, the grouping of pupils, the deployment of staff etc.

3 The management of the school as an organisation, including care and discipline, personal and social development, day to day administration, the management of resources including financial control, and care of the building and environment.

4 The management of people. Almost all aspects of management involve managing people in one way or another, but there is a particular need to learn to manage situations, communication of various kinds; staff development and linking school and community.

5 Evaluation and assessment.

We can go on to consider the nature of the provision of activities related to management training for which the LEA may be responsible. The provision should include:

1 An explicit statement of LEA management policy which covers all employees. Heads and staff in secondary schools will be part of this.

2 Regular assessment of the in-service needs of the teachers including their need for management development. This might be expected to take into account:
   a) National developments
   b) The needs of the LEA
   c) The needs of the individual school and groups (e.g. years, departments) within the school.
   d) The needs of individuals at all levels.

3 A programme of management development stemming from the policy, for all those requiring it. It should include:
   a) An adequate system for the selection and appointment of senior staff, regarding this as complementary to the overall programme of development.
   b) A programme of induction for all teachers newly in management roles.
   c) A programme of specific training for management.
   d) Consideration of ways in which management skills can be developed as part of everyday work and encouragement to seek out and use such opportunities.

4 The preparation of those about to attend management courses and detailed follow-up with them in their schools.

5 An appraisal system which applies at all levels and involves individual interviews with all employees.

6 A pattern of record keeping which enables everyone concerned to see the overall development of the management programme.

7 Evaluation of the management programme.

These points can be examined in more detail.

1 **An explicit statement of LEA management policy.**
This policy should cover all aspects of management including the ways in which teachers learn as part of their everyday work. It might specifically include:

a) Elements designed to help heads and other teachers in management roles to meet the aims and policies of the LEA and improve its institutions.
b) Opportunities for individual development in which the management needs of the post a person holds are analysed with him/her and a personal programme developed to run alongside a broad, more general programme. This suggests a need for a system of appraisal and counselling.

Any management training programme should have elements of these two purposes, but it should be remembered that they are strongly linked. Very often a programme designed to teach specific skills related to the tasks of management will provide opportunities for course members to consider inter-personal skills and to look at wider issues and develop their thinking through discussion with colleagues and the tutorial staff of the course.

Within the individual secondary school there also needs to be an all-embracing policy which interlinks with the LEA policy.

The LEA task here is to see that schools develop an appropriate programme using opportunities within the school to aid development and it should try to provide whatever support a school seems to need. This is most likely to be a function for the advisory team, whose members may be talking through with the head and senior staff the needs of their colleagues and the ways in which these can be met, perhaps by linking together schools with similar needs. For example, in one LEA, small groups of secondary schools whose heads worked together on the

County management courses have come together with the advisers in their area to plan and carry through training programmes for middle management in their schools.

The LEA is also responsible for seeing that the overall policies for management training and information about the programme communicated to all those who may be affected. In schools this task might be expected to be undertaken by the head and senior staff who are also in a position to relate LEA views and policies to the schools policies and views.

2 **Regular assessment of in-service needs**

Some needs are visible to everyone and if provision is made there will be an enthusiastic response with teachers needing no persuading to take part. There are a number of management training needs which come into this category. For example, most people in management roles in schools welcome training in the techniques of interviewing.

It becomes more difficult when the authority sees needs which are not seen or felt by teachers, as for example, when there is a reorganisation resulting in specific in-service needs which the teachers concerned may not be aware of until the reorganisation has actually taken place. Or there may be a situation where an unpopular decision has been made by the Education Committee which results in in-service needs and teachers may not wish to appear to support the decision.

This kind of problem also exists in the management development field at an individual level where the teacher concerned is happy with his own performance and thinks he has little to learn, while his colleagues have very different views. A good deal of work is often needed with such people in looking at the application of what might be learned to the person's work and in helping him or her to apply it.

Such problems are in the first instance the responsibility of head and school, who must be expected to do everything possible to help the teacher concerned to see his own deficiencies. It may then become a case where help is needed from the LEA, as part of a programme which may eventually lead to disciplinary action. Where heads are concerned it must be a task for the LEA working alongside the governors.

In general, however, most heads and teachers in senior and middle management are well aware of the management demands of the secondary school and the need to acquire management skills. Many middle managers will see training opportunities as a hope in a situation where promotion prospects have diminished.

Needs can also be normative. If one LEA provides an induction programme for all probationers, the LEA next door may be pressed to do likewise. Provision of this kind is likely to be well received.

The LEA's assessment of management needs in secondary schools has in many places progressed no further than assessing the training needs of heads and deputies. This is only the beginning of a programme so far as the secondary school is concerned. A teacher starts with the need for management skills within the classroom and then needs the opportunity to undertake increasing responsibility and training as (s)he becomes more senior in service.

Regular assessment of needs will not only indicate the perceived needs and the actual needs but should also help the LEA to decide on priorities.

3 **A programme of management development**

This should include:

a) An adequate system for selection and appointment of senior staff seen as complementary to the overall programme of development.

The LEA's management programme should be more than a commitment to training and follow-up. The appointment of heads and senior managers in schools is also part of the overall LEA development programme and should be seen as complementary to other parts of the programme.

The recently published Post Project Report (Morgan et al 1983) on the appointment of heads of secondary schools, suggests that the process is often somewhat haphazard, although many LEAs have recently reviewed their practices, partly as a result of the findings of the study. While this is partly the problem of involving all the people who need to be involved, there is nevertheless a good deal to be done to ensure that the selection process involves matching candidates to the tasks which the job entails as well as ensuring that the person appointed has the right experience and personality.

The appointment process allows the governors and the staff of the LEA to find out a good deal about individual candidates if the arrangements for the interviews are adequate. This information might be regarded as the starting point for an individual development programme for the person appointed. It will identify strengths and weaknesses and suggest areas where (s)he may need help and training.

Exactly the same is true in appointing staff to the individual school. For the head and any senior staff involved in appointment, the information which is revealed through the interviews and other time spent with candidates become the starting point for the in-service programme for the successful candidate. The LEA, through its advisory service, can encourage this.

b) A programme of induction which is available to new employees at all levels.

In a paper given to the NFER Annual General Meeting in 1982, Dick Weindling and Peter Earley described some of their findings about the experience of new heads of secondary schools with particular reference to their relationships with LEA staff, which they are currently studying. Their findings suggest that the following activities were particularly valued:

i) Opportunities to visit the school to meet the staff and obtain information during the term preceding the taking up of the appointment.
ii) Preliminary visits to the local or main LEA offices to meet staff and obtain information.
iii) Visits from officers or advisers fairly early in the first term to establish a point of contact.
iv) Some form of induction course, possibly before taking up the appointment.
v) A handbook of LEA procedures and other information.
vi) Contact with advisers and officers during the first year in office.
vii) Guidance over such issues as the suspension of pupils.
viii) Regular heads' meetings with LEA staff.
ix) A close relationship with another head or heads and possibly some form of mentor system.
x) The existence of heads' support groups.

There was also evidence that new heads often felt a sense of professional isolation. It would seem that the way in which new heads are received into their LEA is an important element in creating the kind of ethos within the LEA which encourages individuals and schools to develop. Similarly the way new teachers are received into their schools is important in creating a climate for professional development.

c) A programme of specific training for management which is concerned with people at all levels. This should include the following elements:

i) A statement of broad objectives for the programme as a whole and for the various parts of it.
ii) A coherent, published pattern of courses, seminars, study groups and other similar activities, some of which are held within schools and some elsewhere. These should enable everyone who needs to do so to consider some aspects of

management in depth, over a period. This should enable teachers to look at how theoretical knowledge might inform practice and provide an opportunity for them to acquire and practice management skills. There should be a time scale for the programme as a whole and for elements within it.

iii) The provision of a sufficient range and breadth of courses to allow people at different stages over a period to select elements which meet their needs.

iv) A pattern of counselling and advising which helps individuals to assess their own needs and plan and implement their own development programme with support from others.

v) Some opportunity within the programme overall and within individual courses and activities for a negotiated element, selected by the course members in the light of their perception of their needs.

There are management demands of different kinds at all levels from the classroom management skills of the subject teacher to the skills which involve carrying a group of adults through a particular development. There should also be some specific provision by the school for the needs of its staff.

Consideration of the development needs of their staffs and how these might be met should be part of the training programme for heads and senior staff in schools, which is then followed-up in the school after the course is over.

The programme of management education offered needs to meet the following broad aims.

i) Helping individuals to maintain or improve their management performance in their current post.

ii) Identifying people who have management potential.

iii) Training people for possible promotion, thus ensuring succession.

There are problems about iii) because of the lack of current promotion prospects for teachers. Involvement in training for promotion can easily be seen as a promise of promotion, however much there are statements to the contrary, and disillusioned teachers are unlikely to give of their best. It is wise to be careful about arranging courses designed to identify future leaders and those with management potential, remembering that there are a good many capable people who will not achieve the promotion they might. It is probably wiser to work at training people to undertake their present role effectively and to include in all such courses some material which could be seen as not only useful for the current role, but also offering some training for promotion.

The business of identifying people with potential in the course of their current work is something which everyone in management needs to undertake. Headteachers and local authority staff, usually advisers, normally have a mental list of people whom they see as possible candidates for promotion. It is now more important than formerly that the head and the adviser get to know the work of such people, so that the knowledge is available when promotion is considered and the right person is appointed to the right post.

It is essential that LEA staff have the opportunity to work with the local providers to consider the content and teaching strategies of management courses, their arrangement and which heads and other teachers will be seconded to attend each one. The kind of opportunity offered will depend on the area from which the course draws but all the LEAs concerned with a course should be involved in discussion of this kind. Most people would acknowledge the value of involving heads in such planning but if advisers are to play a proper part in the follow-up procedure it would seem important that they are represented in such discussions and it may also be valuable for the administration to be involved.

Each LEA also has to decide on the best way to involve heads and other teachers in the planning of courses. Most courses now involve some heads as course tutors, usually those who have followed a course of preparation and these heads are likely to be the people who will be most knowledgeable about what is involved.

However, it will also be valuable to involve some heads who are not in the forefront in the planning process, who may represent those heads who need convincing that they need a course. There should also be some people chosen by their colleagues rather than the LEA.

What seems to be needed is some kind of advisory committee which can work with the course providers and the LEA representatives to advise those responsible for the actual running of the courses. It is the responsibility of the LEA to see that such opportunities are provided.

d) Consideration of the ways in which management skills can be developed as part of everyday work.

We have already noted that a good deal of management development takes place as a result of the experiences a teacher is given in the course of his daily work in school. Opportunities for taking responsibility can be widely shared. Teachers may gradually be given opportunities for leading groups of adults concerned with a particular task. Discussions about possible changes or developments can be used as an opportunity for learning for those involved and so on.

In many industrial settings, there is concern to train people for succession. This is not normally considered in education and yet there are some schools where the informal opportunities offered to staff ensure that when a post is advertised there will be some knowledgeable c ndidates from within the school. One school, for example, appoints deputy heads of year to assist heads of year on a voluntary basis as an opportunity to get to know the work involved. The post is held for a year, and is treated as part of the development programme of the school, with the heads of year having a responsibility for training their colleagues. When a head of year post becomes vacant in this school or elsewhere, there are thus a number of teachers who have already had some experience of what is involved. It is of course, important to set this firmly in the context of training and to give this aspect of the work priority. It should not be seen as a means of getting work done on the cheap.

4 Preparation for course work and follow-up

One common finding among those who have been involved in management training is that if it is to make a difference in the schools, it needs to involve a much wider range of activities than the courses themselves. There must be a bridge from training to its implementation. It is important that those applying for management training or invited to attend a course, should have some idea of what is involved, including the idea that there should be direct follow-up in the school. This is likely to involve some evaluation within the school in order to see what can be used from the course.

It is also a common finding that training for middle management is more successful if those in the senior posts in the school from which a teacher comes have experienced similar training. A head of department following a management course needs to be able to use his/her learning in the schools. (S)he needs de-briefing by the head or deputy immediately after the course and then opportunities to discuss the implementation of some of the ideas (s)he has acquired, with further discussions about how the work is progressing. If the head and deputy have no experience of similar courses they will be less able to undertake the support and de-briefing role effectively. This kind of activity meeds to be touched on at least as part of courses for heads.

This suggests that bridging activity should be an integral part of the programme for management training needing to be clearly delineated with time allowed for it. Within the school this will gradually emerge as more and more heads undergo training, particularly if everyone concerned agrees that it is important for top and middle management to be expected to discuss his/her experience with someone and plan forward. Some help may be available from outside for this activity but the main thrust of it needs to be within the school.

There is also the question of who de-briefs the head and works with him or her to implement what has been learned. Within the school many heads are likely to use their senior staff to discuss the application of what they have learned and some heads will have individual governors who have a good deal to offer. Outside the school, the most likely people to undertake this activity would seem to be local advisers, providing they have the training, experience and knowledge to gain the confidence of the heads concerned. Someone in the general advisory role who already knows the school should be able to act as a sounding board and talk through the various ideas which a head thinks might be possible and go on to support him or her in working them out on the ground and evaluating progress.

This suggests that advisers, like heads, need training for this role and this should include not only training in management and advisory work but also training in counselling skills, which are an essential part of the adviser's daily work.

Traditionally advisers have been in much the same position as heads. It has been assumed that someone who has been a successful teacher of children will become a successful manager of adults. It is similarly assumed that a successful teacher and manager in school will be a successful adviser. Neither of these assumptions stands up to scrutiny. The roles of the head and other senior managers in the school are distinct from those of teachers although there is much common ground. The role of an adviser is also different from that of a manager in school and in both cases new skills and knowledge have to be acquired.

The need for training has now been recognised for headteachers, but not yet for advisers. Much of the expertise of today's advisers comes from working with more experienced colleagues and this is valuable but advisers, like heads, need courses specifically designed for them. Such courses need to cover a good deal of ground and in the context of management training the adviser needs training in the kind of support role that heads will need to complement externally based management courses.

In some LEAs this kind of training has been in being for some time. There have also been a number of national courses run by the National Association of Inspectors of Schools and Educational Advisers and the DES which have been concerned with general advisory skills. Without such training some advisers may be respected for their ability to draw on their own experience and that of others, but may not have the skills and knowledge to support heads in this way.

Support of this kind might also be offered by those responsible for training courses. Some of the course providers will have the advantage of being independent of the authority and a head may prefer this. The difficulty about this at the present time would seem to be the size of the overall task of training. At this stage of the national training initiative the provision of courses is taking a great deal of time and it is possible that those acting as tutors will be too involved with the actual courses to involve themselves in the preparation and follow-up procedures which probably need to be as time-consuming as the course. This situation will change when the bulk of heads have undergone a courses and the programme will be concerned with far smaller numbers of newly appointed heads.

The current pressures of time create a problem for whoever acts in the bridging role. An adviser trained for this work has the advantage of knowing the school and there is a good deal to be said for LEA involvement of this kind, but the staffing of most advisory services and the number of demands being made of them at present may make it difficult for advisers to do as much of this work as they would wish. This is partly a matter of where priorities are placed. It would seem to offer a valuable way of helping schools to move forward.

5 **An appraisal system**

Alongside the training programme and work on appointments, the LEA needs some form of appraisal scheme which is available for everyone employed in the service. The word 'appraisal' may have a variety of meanings, but one interpretation likely to be generally accepted defines it as the process of assessing individual performance against the job requirements.

The introduction of appraisals for teachers has been proposed both by the Secretary of State for Education and by the employers. The white paper 'Teaching Quality' (HMSO, 1983) includes the following statement:

> The Government welcome recent moves towards self-assessment by schools and teachers, and believe these should help to improve school

> standards and curricula. But employers can manage their teachers only if they have accurate knowledge of each teacher's performance. The Government believe that for this purpose formal assessment of teacher performance is necessary and should be based on classroom visiting by the teacher's head or head of department, and an appraisal of both the pupils' work and of the teacher's contribution to the life of the school. They therefore welcome the interest currently shown among employers and the teachers' associations about the career development of teachers ... The Government believe that those responsible for managing the school teacher force have a clear responsibility to establish, in consultation with their teachers, a policy for staff development and training based on a systematic assessment of every teacher's performance and related to their policy for the school curriculum. (HMSO, 1983)

The Secretary of State has also put forward the idea of a two year porobationery period for headteachers, and this too involves the process of evaluating performance.

The employers, the local authorities, would like to see a teacher appraisal scheme in which:

a) Increments are linked to teacher performance and career development.
b) Outstanding teacher performance is rewarded by accelerated progression up the scale.
c) Increments are withheld from teachers whose performance is unsatisfactory.

Difficulties arise over what the aims of appraisal may be. Teachers themselves and many others would welcome a scheme which concentrated on the development of individuals but not one which affected pay and prospects. It would seem difficult to combine these purposes since the teacher being appraised will have a very different attitude to the exercise according to whether the intention is development or whether salary or even job depends upon a satisfactory outcome. A system which appeared to threaten would make it more difficult for a teacher to see the exercise as supportive. The NUT, in particular have stated that they are opposed to a scheme that is linked to pay.

Most heads do a certain amount of appraising informally in order to deploy staff and in order to provide information when a teacher is serving the probationary period or is a candidate for promotion. The introduction of an appraisal scheme is a formalising of what is already in existence in most schools and is a full programme in a few others, and involving the teacher in the process. Presented in this way it looks a trifle less threatening whatever depends upon it.

The purpose of appraisal needs to be clear to everyone involved. There would seem to be a number of possible reasons for appraising the work of teachers:

a) To help teachers improve their classroom performance.
b) To identify outstanding teachers and teachers who are failing in order to identify where help is needed and those who might be future candidates for senior posts or those who have something to contribute to the development of other teachers.
c) To assess career potential and advise the teacher about career possibilities.
d) To provide an opportunity for praising what is good and dealing with unsatisfactory aspects of each teacher's work.
e) To provide the teacher with an opportunity to ensure that others know what (s)he is doing and for expressing views.
f) To provide the appraiser with additional knowledge about what is happening, enabling him or her to have a view of the department or school as a whole.
g) To give an opportunity for the head or head of department to influence the thinking of each teacher and to be influenced by each teacher's views.
h) To provide information for the satisfactory completion of probation and for writing confidential reports for teachers who are candidates for promotion.

If a staff appraisal scheme is to work well, there need to be certain conditions present at the beginning. The following should be considered:

a) There should be a measure of consensus about values among those involved. Differences should be recognised and the views of each party considered and respected.
b) There needs to be an atmosphere of trust. Teachers being appraised need to be confident that the information they give will not be used for purposes other than those agreed, without further consultation.
c) Those involved need to be open-minded. The opportunity for learning is not only there for the person being appraised but also for the person doing the appraising.
d) The teacher's self-image is important. A teacher with a poor view of his/her own work, will find it difficult to use the experience of appraisal in positive ways.

e) The organisational climate of the school needs to be positive, concerned with helping teachers to give of their best and with helping each person to develop his/her full potential.
f) A clear job description is needed for each teacher. This provides agreed objectives against which performance can be assessed.
g) The possible outcomes of appraisal should be clearly given at the outset. In particular teachers need to be aware of the use likely to be made of the information gained.
h) Both parties need to prepare for the meeting. It is therefore necessary for there to be agreement about the ground to be covered.

It is likely that appraisal will be most successful in improving performance where the teacher has some control over the appraisal. A recent article in TES (Virgiania Makins, TES, 1985) described the practice in one school where a staff working party agreed that the teacher should decide on the parts of his or her performance to be reviewed and how the information would be used.

This is undoubtedly a way of making the whole proceeding less threatening and this has many advantages in terms of development likely to be made. The difficulty is that some teachers may not be willing to tackle their own weak points and it may be difficult for the head or other senior member of the staff to help someone who insists that all is well. This kind of problem needs to be tackled both within the school and with support if necessary from the LEA.

Appraisal is another name for evaluation and this is very properly part of every teachers' work. The teacher in the classroom is continually assessing how pupils are doing, what they have learned and where the difficulties lie. Senior staff and heads will also be considering the success of the curriculum overall and the abilities of the teachers. There may also be occasions when an individual teacher or a group of teachers decides to make a more formal evaluation of the work they have been doing.

If appraisal is to be successful, each teacher needs to assess him or herself by way of preparation. The person doing the appraising also needs to see the teacher at work in the classroom. Many LEAs have published check lists of various kinds for the use of schools and there is much to be said for a school agreeing the areas in which teachers might be expected to undertake self-evaluation. There is also much value in groups of teachers building their own check lists.

In one school, where the head held a regular review meeting with each member of staff, he sent out a paper to everyone he was due to see which starts by saying:

> The purpose of this document is to create a framework for our review of your work in such a way that it creates:
> a) an opportunity for you to think through and evaluate your aims, objectives and practices.
> b) an agenda for us to work together on a programme of development and consolidation over a period of time. (Robertson, 1982)

He then goes on to provide questions and ideas for the teacher to consider. These include not only questions designed to help the teacher to look at his or her own work, but also some questions which would encourage the teacher to consider other aspects of the life of the school which might be improved eg "How far do our 'systems' enable and support each teacher ... and give every individual self esteem as a result of his/her contribution".

The LEA's role in all this would seem to be that of ensuring that there are people within each school who have the capacity and skills to undertake this work and seeing that each school actually has a programme of appraisal. One LEA, for example, asks annually for a statement from every head about the way in which appraisal is being carried out in his/her school. This leaves schools free to decide how best to carry out the process but ensures that they think about it.

There is a further area in which the LEA has a role in dealing with the problems which will inevitably arise from an appraisal programme, particularly if the programme is one which affects salary or could lead to possible dismissal. It is a considerable responsibility where such decisions are left to one individual, but any cross-checking by other senior staff would add to the considerable time already needed for appraisal. There will certainly be cases where the judgement of the individual will be called in question where the LEA will be expected to act as arbiter. It seems possible that the advisory service would have a part to play here with a further appeal procedure involving elected members as a final court of appeal at a later stage.

The LEA will also have to take on the final decisions about teachers who appear to be failing and while the bulk of the evidence will be provided by the school, the advisory service will also need to provide evidence and both school and advisers will need to demonstrate that the teacher concerned was given every possible chance to improve. Many LEAs now have experience of such cases and it has proved very difficult to provide evidence which the DES find acceptable, let alone industrial tribunals.

6 **A pattern of record keeping showing the overall development of the management programme**

A programme of management development which includes both specific training and opportunities to develop management skills and knowledge as part of everyday work, is likely to involve different people in different patterns of training. In an LEA where there is a programme for middle management, another for deputy/senior teacher level, and yet another for heads there may be repetition. Sometimes this will be profitable, but on other occasions may be time wasting. There is therefore a need for good records of who has undertaken different forms of training and had different kinds of experience. Such information might very properly be taken into consideration when making appointments.

It is not easy to keep this kind of information at LEA level although with computers easily available it would be quite possible. There would seem to be much to commend asking teachers to keep a much fuller record of their experience and in-service training, perhaps suggesting that every year a teacher contributes to his or her record a statement of the work (s)he has done during the year and the in-service experience undertaken.

7 **Evaluation of the management programme**

The LEA needs to evaluate the provision for management training formally and informally. Informal assessment of any training initiative goes on all the time it is taking place and after it has finished with various people seeking for positive outcomes. The problem about overmuch reliance on this kind of evaluation is partly that it tends to be guided by the views that the person judging has about management training and partly the problem that the most effective training for management will not be easily visible because it should affect a person's work by affecting his or her thinking. These are not reasons for avoiding evaluation, even if this were possible, but a statement of the need for care.

All major initiatives of this kind should be more formally evaluated from time to time, partly in order to satisfy demands for accountability but also because this is the best way to maintain high standards and the necessary flexibility. Evaluation may be carried out by various people and in various ways. The providers of the course will themselves wish course members and others to provide some feedback on how effective the training has been and it may be that the LEA should undertake this as part of its own evaluation of the programme as a whole.

In general it is more likely that evaluation will be unbiassed if it is independent of those involved in the training itself and while it may properly be commissioned by the LEA as employer, there is much to be said for evaluation by independent evaluators. It is interesting to note in this context that Sweden, where a national programme for management training has been in being for some years, evaluators were invited from other countries to assess the effectiveness of what had happened. (Described in a paper presented by Mats Ekholm in Strasbourg in 1980.)

The advisory service will inevitably play an important part in evaluating the programme whether formally or informally. Advisers are in and out schools and they talk to teachers and headteachers, both hearing views and observing effects in action. HMI are also in a good position to reflect what is happening as a result of training.

What seems to be needed is a broad plan for evaluation which makes use of the various pieces of evidence which are available and also undertakes a periodic programme of more formal assessment of different aspects of what is offered. If the programme is well thought out it may be possible to use the services of higher degree students and even to second teachers to undertake this work with assistance from appropriate higher education establishments. Some evaluation may also be directly commissioned.

Conclusion

These are specific roles for the LEA. The programme will also be affected for better or worse by the attitudes of officers, advisers and members. Where an LEA is really behind the programme and where many of those running the service have knowledge of the nature of the training offered, there is likely to be greater effect than where there is little encouragement.

The LEA may thus be seen to have an important role in seeing that its employees, in this case heads and staffs of secondary schools, receive appropriate training for their roles and actually put this into practice at school level. While a good head, like a good teacher, will do well whatever the context, most heads, like most teachers, are more likely to do well if the context is supportive. This means that LEAs need to offer not only opportunities but also positive encouragement and support to teachers developing the skills of management. They also need to try to create the kind of climate within the authority which is open, flexible, creative and supportive.

References

Dean J (1985) Managing the Secondary School, Croom Helm Ltd

Ekholm M (1980) Evaluation of In-service Education of Teachers in Sweden - Results and Aspects of Future Evaluative Activities, Universitetet I Linkoping, Sweden, 1980

HMSO (1983) DES Circular 3/83,

HMSO (1983) Teaching Quality, (White Paper), Secretary of State

Makins V (1985) Luxury or Threat, Times Educational Supplement, 15.3.85

Morgan C, Hall V, Mackay H (1983) The Selection of Secondary School Head Teachers, (The Post Report), Open University Press

Robertson G (1982) Draft Outline of Tutorial Review, Headmaster, Newquay Tretherras School

Weindling R and Earley P (1983) The Management of Secondary Schools - LEA Support for New Heads, Paper presented to the NFER Annual General Meeting, December 6, 1983

SECTION 2: THE PRACTICALITIES OF ROLE: WHAT SCHOOL MANAGERS ACTUALLY DO

Chapter 3

MANAGING THE SCHOOL: THE ROLE OF THE HEADTEACHER AT A TIME OF RAPID CHANGE

Frank Stoner

This personal account of experience starts from the premise that heads must accept that the effective management of change is one of their most important tasks. Within a context of ever increasing pressures they must extend their knowledge of "self" before proceeding to the enabling of individual staff development and motivation. A team approach to decision-making and the evaluation process is seen as a vital prerequisite to the introduction of the crucial principle of partnership which involves not only staff at all levels in the school but also the other interested parties - "the stakeholders" - in the wider community.

Introduction

Just before he died, W C Fields, the Hollywood comedian, was found by a friend reading the Bible. "What are you doing?" enquired the friend. "Looking for loopholes" replied Fields. Whilst not wishing to pursue the deathbed analogy too far there is a certain similarity to the position of the head at a time of rapid change; notably that the search for both educational bible and associated loopholes is likely to prove equally unsuccessful. Change is with us and needs to be managed; loopholes are few and probably inappropriate. The educational bible has yet to be written and we are faced instead with a series of documents emerging in ever-increasing number and complexity "... like Irish signposts, too many, too difficult to read and with a tendency to confuse, they achieve the reverse of their intention, namely uncertain and dangerous immobility. Those who know the way don't need them; those who need to know can't understand and are uncertain and afraid" (Brighouse, 1985).

Perhaps the headteacher can turn to modern-day equivalents of the Temple at Delphi for help, to management theory and practice from other spheres of activity, or to the MSC? Even here the likely response will be to reflect the Delphic inscription "Know thyself" and probably to add, as Charles Handy (1984) would have us do: "Know thy institution for good measure".

So there is no bible and there are precious few loopholes. Add to those the burdens produced by the traditional isolation of the headteacher and the associated insularity of the school; include strongly repetitive calls for closer public accountability, and throw in for good measure repetitive and lengthy periods of industrial action and you have a cocktail recipe for headship more akin to Molotov than champagne.

The temptation for headteachers in such circumstances is to react in ostrich fashion despite the attendant vulnerability of that position. The intention of this chapter is to suggest that there are other options. Although the commentary on managing change is necessarily general, examples of practice are included which have been drawn from the author's own experience as a headteacher and also as Director of the Centre for the Study of Comprehensive Schools, York, in 1983/84. The successful practice observed over the six years (and indeed the observation of less successful practice from which considerable learning has resulted) suggest firmly that the challenge of change is being met, often head-on and that common strategies do exist of value to headteachers, wherever they find themselves.

Before considering the strategies for managing change this chapter attempts to explore the nature of the changes that are affecting schools and the context in which they are occurring, including the changing role of the headteacher. The chapter itself does not claim to contain the biblical solution sought by W C Fields, but it does make three important assumptions:-

1 That a prime role for heads is to ensure that all change is managed effectively.

2 That to achieve 1 all headteachers will be obliged to tap into as wide a range of expertise and experience as possible and that this means primarily making full use of the available talents of the school or college staff.

3 That for most of us change is threatening, and we are likely to set up barriers or resistance to it, especially where there is an element of risk involved.

John Locke stated the situation very precisely in "An Essay Concerning Human Understanding": "New opinions are always suspected and usually opposed without any other reason but because they are not already common." Spike Milligan is the unlikely source of a way out of the difficulty:

Things that go bump in the night
Should not really give one a fright
It's the hole in each ear
That lets in the fear
That, and the absence of light.

How then, to bring up the light and distinguish accurately what we hear? Whatever strategies are adopted to manage change the counsel is for the avoidance of isolation. The head who sets out alone is at best demonstrating over-confidence for, as T H Huxley put it, "If a little knowledge is dangerous where is the person who has so much as to be out of danger?" (or at worst courting disaster). A closer look at the context of change sharpens the focus of the counsel.

The context of change

Even the most superficial look at the educational scene of the 1980s cannot fail to spot that change is with us, that the pace of change even within the most traditional of our schools is on the increase and that the agents for change are now more numerous, often more vociferous and occasionally very much more powerful than before. Who or what are the agents for change and how do they affect the context in which schools have to work?

Mention will be made later (see Day's chapter) of the deluge of curriculum advice which has appeared over the last ten years. In this the DES, HMI and some LEAs have been considerable providers and within their publications the shift towards at least a common and possibly even a centralist curriculum is clearly observable. But they have not been alone; TVEI, CPVE,YTS - they and others have forced their way onto the curriculum stage and now represent important and legitimate stakeholders in the curriculum debate over what are appropriate education experiences for young people between the ages of 5-18. Like them or not, their influence along with that of other similar managing agencies is likely to be with us for a very long time.

What of other stakeholders? Further and higher education and the Examinations' Boards do more than lobby their case powerfully; indeed many would argue that the influence brought to bear by such bodies could be better described as a stranglehold - but they remain with us and cannot be lightly dismissed. The introduction of GCSE, whether welcome or not, represents further influence in this field. What about parents and governors? In the call for greater school accountability their voices have grown stronger and the shape of their partnership within the school management has changed - not always to the comfort of the head and staff. The strengthening of parental choice and the reshaping of governing bodies consequent to the Taylor report have sharpened the interface between school and community, obliged schools to become more market-orientated and brought their own special pressure for change upon heads and teaching staff.

And so it is with students themselves. Despite continuing confusion over their role in our schools (are they co-workers, raw material, customers?) and little real development nationally in terms of student participation in school management, student pressure for change has grown until its strength has become irresistible. Mass unemployment and the development of national training schemes beyond 16 (effectively raising the "leaving age" by one or now two years for the great majority of young people) have contributed strongly to their closer questioning of what is on offer in the school curriculum, its relevance and appropriateness. Observation of experiential and off-site learning for a minority of students in schools has encouraged a lobby for similar opportunities by the majority. Realisation that traditional examination passes are no longer enough to ensure future employment coupled with increasing student knowledge that employers are looking for skills rarely developed in traditional examination syllabuses (for example, initiative, team attitudes, and interpersonal) has produced its own pressure for change - very often in the form of student disaffection via disruptive behaviour and truancy.

Beyond the school a rapidly shifting employment picture, changes in social attitudes both within and outside the family, the effect of technology upon access to education via video, Prestel and Teletext, increasing leisure time for all age groups both in and without employment - all add to the confusion of the context of change in which schools find themselves.

Ironically the schools themselves are still, very largely, organized in a very traditional way and working through a curriculum little changed to meet the challenge of the 1970s and 80s let alone that of the millennium - small wonder that heads call for help, that loopholes are sought within non-existent biblical texts and that the common cry from headteachers has become: "It's a very different job now to when I started ten years ago".

The changing role of the headteacher

So what about the cry? A rationalization of underachievement? A prepared excuse for likely poor performance? Or a realistic assessment of the situation? Certainly, whatever else has changed the expectations of the stakeholders have done so bringing additional pressure to bear on the head. Hall, Mackay and Morgan (1983) reporting on their research project on the role of headteachers comment:

> The significant change has been in the expectations of a growing number of groups of what the role should encompass and how it should be performed.

They go on to state that:

> Changing the multiplying expectations is only one aspect of the perceived complexity of the job. The sheer quantity of tasks to be performed and the multi-dimensional quality of the myriad inter-personal relationship are others.

Increased pressure for public accountability brings a particularly sharp focus to the headship role, its complexity and contradictions. For the headteacher, traditionally isolated from the staff and rarely enjoying anything much stronger than an ambivalent relationship with the LEA, it has become not enough to answer simplistically "I shall be the leading professional" or "I will concentrate on management" or "I shall ensure the school is smoothly administered". She or he is obliged to respond to all of these and to seek a balance across them to meet the needs of the particular institution. In this work confusions which exist over terminology such as management, leadership and administration are not helpful.

Everard (1984) argues "there are no widely accepted definitions, no clear dividing lines between management, administration and leadership. Management does not and should not imply the naked exercise of power, nor the subservience of anyone managed nor insensitivity nor the renunciation of human values. However, it does mean a readiness to grasp nettles and take unpalatable decisions.

He continues:

> Leadership qualities are indispensable to the effective manager since the manager holds responsibility for motivating the people in his or her charge.

Handy (1984) argues that schools would be wise to shun the word manager "because it does confuse and combine the two very different requirements of leadership and administration. Schools need both but they can seldom be done by the same individual ... To combine the two roles in one person is an invitation to stress".

Role uncertainty or even confusion, together with raised and changing expectations, create pressures and increase the challenge to the headteacher. Over-response to pleas for strong leadership may produce the counter criticism of autocracy, desire for charisma may lead to accusations of administrative anarchy, and even the use of the term manager may, in some academic circles, have "perjorative overtones; it may present a threat to autonomy and professional values by conjuring up ideas of ruthless authoritarian bosses and its use to describe the major part of the headteacher's role may tend to distance her or him from the body of the teachers from whence initially all heads are recruited" (Everard op cit).

Harry Secombe, describing Spike Milligan's appearance at their first meeting in North Africa during the Second World War, noted that "he was wearing a German helmet, an Italian tunic and British boots". Asked "Why?" he replied "I don't believe in taking chances". A joke, of course, but some strong messages, too, for any similar attempt by a head to be everybody's ally could so easily backfire resulting in a salvo of shots from perhaps three directions at once to be followed by a hasty and probably undignified retreat.

A changing context, a changing role, increasing pressure for change within schools and, to date, the additional problem of hierarchical, fragmented and closed school organisations in which the provision of a setting for well-managed change may at best be difficult and at worst well nigh impossible - what strategies are there available for heads to enable them to manage the situation effectively? What ideas are around which will help heads not only to work more efficiently but also to restore the sense of enjoyment and professional satisfaction many claim are now missing from their jobs? Are there ways ahead which will enable heads to grapple with the challenges and be able to measure achievement at the end of the process?

National evidence suggests "Yes" and the examples from practice which follow support the evidence. The examples have in common the need for headteachers to recognise that their role is corporate rather than isolate, team rather than individual, sharing rather than secretive, open rather than closed. They argue collectively that central to the idea of managing change is the issue of creating an organisational climate, as observed by Halpin (1966) within an institution capable of responding to change. Six strategies are suggested to help in the creation of a receptive and productive climate and the suggested text for the reader belongs to Francis Bacon: "He that will not apply new remedies must expect new evils" rather than Plautus, "Keep what you have; the known evil is best".

Recognising and sharing role difficulties

In "Taken for Granted" Charles Handy (1984) argues that schools are difficult to run. They differ essentially from other more conventional organisations because of:

1 Their multi-purpose nature which is often reflected in lengthy statements of declared aims and objectives.

2 The limited amount of time devoted to management within the school compared with teaching time.

3 The amount of role switching required of teachers on a daily basis and especially for the head.

4 Confusion over the precise role of the students. Are they workers, clients, products?

Although Everard (1985) challenges the Handy assertion that No 1 above is peculiar to schools - "Companies aims are pluralistic and a manager's objectives often logically inconsistent" - both underline not only the difficulties of school organisation but also the relatively low capacity of the management system for effecting change.

Headteachers know this only too well, but only recently has any concerted effort been made to assist heads to meet the challenge more effectively via local and national training schemes. This has happened via such agencies as the LEAs and the National Development Centre for School Management Training at Bristol. The development of the INSET provision nationally has highlighted not only the difficulties heads face in their work but also the inadequacy of much of the thinking and practice of what the training needs are and what the training process should be.

If there are heads who feel their role is straightforward and relatively easy to manage - let them stand up. But the total of headteacher colleagues who have failed to analyse just what <u>is</u> difficult about the role, and never attempted to ensure that immediate and LEA colleagues are aware of the difficulties, is legion.

The strategy being suggested is not that heads should go out simply to seek comfort, solace and an everlasting supply of tissues from colleagues. On the contrary, the needs of colleagues may be greater than their own. It is simply challenging headteachers to consider whether they have taken enough trouble to share with all the stakeholders positively and thoughtfully the nature of the task in which they are involved, to check that there is a clear understanding of the role of headship. How far, for example, are governors invited to share the challenge of change rather than simply expected to receive reports of its attendant difficulties? How much are staff, even senior staff, allowed to share in understanding the real nature of the head's work on a regular, partnership basis rather than obliged to guess at what goes on behind closed doors? How much better informed would the community beyond the school be, including the media, if heads took time to explain how their role is changing, what pressures for change exist and to invite participation and debate in what is happening?

The call is for more effective communication about the role of the headteacher both within and beyond the institution. This requires a greater sharing of all aspects of the job, success and failure, achievement and under achievement, perks and cop outs, warts and all - not in a way designed to elicit tacky sympathy from any source but in a genuine attempt to involve all working colleagues and partners in the role itself.

A recent Industrial Awareness Conference held in a Lincolnshire secondary school brought twelve industrial colleagues into the school as tutors for two days. At the close one of the industrialists commented, "I now know what it means to be a teacher and just how demanding a job it can be. My views about the current pay dispute have been substantially altered as a result - you have my support now".

Here participation led to greater understanding. A similar message is there for heads, too - that their ability to carry out the role, and especially at a time of rapid change, will be substantially enhanced if that role is fully understood by all who have a stake in what is going on in schools. To do that effectively the headteacher must firstly pay attention to the Ancient Greeks.

Know yourself

That much abused and often misused inscription on the temple at Delphi retains its relevance for the headteacher at a time of rapid change. Responses to the need for change fail or only partly succeed for a variety of reasons (eg failure to diagnose properly, inadequate planning, a piecemeal approach to the problem, absence of effective evaluation). In almost every case the reasons have a particularly human face - eg where the staff as a whole feel no sense of involvement or ownership of a new development. Very often the root cause of difficulty lies in the headteacher's failure to come to terms with the "yourself" of the inscription and the all too frequent mismatch between self and the organisation.

The situation isn't surprising. If change is threatening for all of us then close examination of ourselves as people and in role as heads might well be considered at best hair raising and at worst potentially destructive.

Is it possible, however, that the threatening nature of self analysis or appraisal has been overstated? Ask just about any teacher what she or he is doing and part of the response will almost invariably include a degree of self-criticism, ideas for improving the scheme, project or lesson and plans to put those ideas into practice. Although no clear consensus emerges from the report on underachievement in London's secondary schools (ILEA, 1984) its author bravely concludes that "the admission of a problem is a first and most important step towards a solution". In this instance the conclusion reached reflected the agreed view of pupils, teachers and parents and was the stronger for the collective appraisal involved.

There are times when a head must be seen to be courageous as a decision maker; there is an equally strong argument for equivalent courage in the field of self-analysis and analysis of the organisation of which (s)he is part in order that the match is good for organisational health, and one of cultural unity rather than clash.

In "Helping Schools Change" Harold Heller (1984) develops the FOCUS model for use by staff in schools, including the head. Participants use questionnaires from which a matrix of four quadrants is produced. These report on the temperaments, cultures and repertoires of behaviour within the organisation. At the simplest level the individual head is able to investigate his or her own perception of personal behaviour, temperament and institutional culture. More importantly if a team of staff are involved, the personal perceptions can be matched against those of colleagues - thus enhancing knowledge of self and organisation.

The FOCUS Model represents one way through the analysis jungle for heads. Others include:-

1 <u>The Buddy Approach</u>: Here a colleague from within the school or Authority is charged with the particular task of assisting the head to keep her or his role under scrutiny. The relationship needs to be one of trust and not necessarily friendship, honesty, truthfulness and high professional integrity. Meetings need to be regular rather than ad hoc and no punches should be pulled. The agenda can be as wide-ranging as trust allows.

2 <u>The Use of Non-threatening Consultants</u>: Perhaps from within user-friendly organisations such as CSCS, colleagues from other schools, higher education or authorities, or alternatively via colleagues from another field of work, eg industry. So often the "fresh view" highlights the overlooked problem; more satisfyingly it produces a new approach to solving particular problems.

3 <u>The "Culture Investigation"</u>: In "Taken for Granted" Charles Handy (1984) applies his work on how organisations function - through their own organisational ideas or cultures - to schools. The four cultures described by Handy - club, role, task and person - are translated to the school setting, and heads encouraged to investigate their own cultural predilections. The conclusions drawn are that schools are often a mix of all four cultures. Getting the right mix at the right time should help school success and the instrument provides a useful analysis tool for the head willing to engage in the business of analysing self and institution. Once again it is an activity which needs to be shared and worked at with colleagues.

Space does not permit the inclusion of more examples of similar opportunities open to heads for establishing a clear understanding of "self" - in theory and practice. In this field the work of the Industrial Society and the Careers Counselling Development Unit are useful sources. Common to all is the need for personal courage to face the analysis involved. The outcomes could well lead to more consistent success within strategy three to which we now move.

Developing shared values, aims and objectives

Sir John Betjeman, writing about new buildings in Bath, makes us stop and think about the values, aims and objectives of our schools and warns us against unthinking acceptance of other people's designs.

> Official designs are aggressively neuter,
> The Puritan work of an eyeless computer.

"Ten Good Schools" (HMI, 1977) commented upon the commonality of clear aims and objectives in the ten schools described. New syllabus construction in the GCSE examination demands clearly stated aims and objectives. For the busy head the danger is to yield to the temptation of adopting other people's objectives, of bud-grafting onto a rootstock without checking on the match of species. The Irish signposts mentioned earlier may give confusing directions; they may also be guilty of misdirection if interpreted too literally.

The argument is not against the consideration and use of established practice, advice and experience from elsewhere - far from it. The argument is for development of shared aims and objectives by all the educational stakeholders, and this represents a crucial strategy for headteachers in their attempts to manage change.

David Trethowan (1983) who writes elsewhere in this book poses the question, "Who determines the aims of a school?" and goes on to state that:

> Schools belong to society at large, not to any group within society ... and teachers clearly have responsibilities to society as well as to children and to each other ... decisions on the structure of the school system and on the type of curriculum required are community decisions.

Included in the community are pupils, parents, teachers, employers and governors, but none of the existing groups has the right to decide these matters alone.

The central issue is a willingness - and in this instance the collective willingness of the whole staff - to accept shared responsibility for the values, aims and objectives of the school. This sharing of responsibility not only takes place within the school but also involves those beyond the school gates. Once again we are dealing with trust, openness and partnership; we are talking about the rejection of the hardy school line, "*We* know; we are the professionals", and its replacement by something which reflects the partnership of interests which should be the reality of schools in the 1980s.

At a recent Education/Industry Conference in Oxfordshire an industrialist declared:

> The trouble is our expectations of young people at 16 are so different from schools. Our cultures are so very different.

The debate sharpened, expectations of teachers and industrialists attending were drawn up and compared - and found to be so similar as to deny the earlier assertion. Common ground was found through words such as adaptability, flexibility - and common objectives forged.

A headteacher anxious to re-define the role of his heads of house collected examples of role definitions from other schools and LEAs, sifted, selected and wrote down a new definition. It was tried out on a head of house colleague who read, silently, and commented: "That seems to cover everything" - and left saying she had an important appointment.

In the first example common ownership was discovered through working in partnership. In the second, potentially stronger partnership was lost by the head removing all possible contribution by a colleague, by denying potential ownership of the role declaration. And the institution was weaker as a result.

DES/LEA initiatives now require schools to declare curriculum aims and objectives. The moment is opportune to ask heads to what extent have all the stakeholders been involved in the process so far - and will be in the future.

What about the pupils, parents, governors, industrialists and other representatives of the wider community beyond the school - has an opportunity been afforded to them to contribute their perspective on what a school should be offering? Hargreaves (ILEA, 1984) suggested that the contribution of parents to the partnership of interests involved in improving pupil achievement is "the cornerstone of a school's success" and in suggesting new initiatives, eg "a think-tank for home-school relationships", called upon schools to be more welcoming. Too often "There's no time"; "They don't understand"; "They're not interested" - are the attitudes adopted by schools whose declared aims often include "the full participation of parents" and the "personal growth of the students".

For the headteacher at a time of rapid change, strategies to forge shared values, aims and objectives need to be a priority. Time is limited - but what might be taking valuable time that is less important? "They" may not understand - but if so it is often because of the poor flow of information which has so far been released from within traditionally closed schools.

Interest in education is strong nationally and not simply in schools. Given the context of change discussed earlier, to miss the opportunity now of developing new aims for the future with all our partners is courting disaster. Where to start? Why not at the beginning establish clearly where we are and where we want to go - simple rules for managing change but ones which are all too often overlooked.

Developing the individual

> Heads have the ultimate responsibility for the performance and reputation of their schools, taking into account the wide variations between schools of intake and social background. Their basic resource in doing so is the teaching staff with whom therefore their relationship is of paramount importance. (Frith, 1985)

The author reminds us sharply of the responsibility heads have for the development of teaching staff. Too often we overlook just how much even a casual remark may affect that development. A simple "Good Morning. How are you?" depending upon delivery and context may be the most crucial thing said by a head during the day. The spotting of uncertainty in a colleague's approach to you, observation of the personal agenda hidden in phrases such as "I'm not sure I should be telling you this" or "Have you got a minute?" - all example a key area for heads to consider in their search for strategies to manage change effectively. We need to be concerned for the individual - but not just within school.

Donald Frith's underlining of the importance of the staff as key resources is irresistible. But colleagues beyond the school, governors, parents and the pupils themselves also represent essential resources and the head's relationship with them, too, is of "paramount importance". The argument is for the development of caring and valuing within the organisation, for good organisational health in the field of inter-personal relationships throughout and beyond the school - and it is crucial that the head sets the tone in this field.

The valuing of individuals for themselves and the valuing of their potential or actual contribution as individuals or in teams is a well resourced area of research into which any headteacher should be able to dig effectively and easily. Sadly, it is all too often at best an overlooked or at worst ignored strategy in our schools with "I haven't got time for that sort of stuff" being a common excuse heard. I would argue that we ignore the development of improved inter-personal skills at our peril, for if the personnel resources available to heads within and beyond the school gate are to be effectively mustered then enhancing the motivation of the individuals and groups concerned is of vital importance.

Consider yourself as an example. Unless you are exceptional you enjoy being praised; criticism may be acceptable to you but it will still niggle and possibly hurt. Temper it with a seasoning or a balance of praise and the bitterest pill is easier to swallow. We all enjoy being on the receiving end of skilled inter-personal contact and protest strongly if badly treated by our GP, solicitor or boss. We enjoy "positive stroking" and are motivated by it; we cherish inter-personal warmth and are moved to share it when it is received. We feel strengthened by appraisal when it has been carefully, purposefully and professionally handled and especially when there has been a sense of partnership and mutual respect in the discussion. If such experiences are good for heads, then why not try harder at creating more opportunities for them to be enjoyed by colleagues? Most of us would claim that we do, of course, and would criticise what is written in this section as "Old hat", "Heard it all before", "We've been doing that for years". But have you? Work by the Industrial Society in the field of motivation quite clearly demonstrates that senior staff in both industry and education consider their motivational ideals to be different and often superior to those of their subordinates. What does that say about the attitudes which we adopt, both overtly and covertly, to our colleagues?

How carefully do you structure review/evaluation meetings with individual staff or teams of colleagues to ensure balanced discussion of the successes as well as the failures of a particular scheme, or include an evaluation of the merits of having tried even though total success was not achieved? (See Trethowan's chapter.) How many meetings with members of the pupil body invite the question, "What do you think is the best thing to do/What is your opinion" - rather than the common statement - "Listen carefully to what I am going to tell you". How far do we value the potential contribution of young probationary staff so often bursting with new ideas and enthusiasm and almost certainly amongst the best read and up to date in the field of educational writing?

How much trust do we really put in colleagues working enthusiastically in a working party or study group or have we decided, as so often happens, just what will happen before the working group even gets started? How often do the words, "Thank-you" feature in your working vocabulary each day? Are you brave enough to adopt an American Principal's approach by agreeing with all staff that, during the next week or month, all will choose somebody to value they have undervalued before - and do it?

Of course there are dangers. Overstroking can be as misleading as no stroking at all. At Stantonbury, Geoff Cooksey, the former Principal, relates that a policy of "Inter-personal Warmth" whilst benefiting from becoming "Persistent" did need eventually to be declared "Non-possessive" for very obvious reasons. George Carnie's motivational exercise does lead to some colleagues feeling very embarrassed by a positive flood of additional warmth -the embarrassment being enlarged by the realisation of just how many people must have undervalued them before! And the skills - which can be learned - can become mechanistic, automatic and therefore lose credibility. We are all familiar with the friendly greeting delivered through clenched teeth.

In "Taken for Granted" Charles Handy (1984) draws attention to the importance given by HMI in "Ten Good Schools" to creative and committed staff and the role of dedicated leadership in the development of such staff. He goes on to make an interesting cross-reference to Peters' and Waterman's (1983) analysis of the most successful business organisations in America. They end their review of excellent organisations:

> These organisations create environments in which people can blossom, develop self-esteem and otherwise be excited participants in the organisation and in society as a whole.

The differing cultures of school and industry therefore come together via common strategies for the development of the individual. Enabling people to blossom as individuals is, then, a key strategy for heads to develop at a time of rapid change. Nurturing the new-found energies and enthusiasms which result in team situations is the setting for the next section.

Team tactics

> Cross-Patch
> Draw the latch
> Sit by the fire and spin
> Take a cup
> And drink it up
> And call your neighbours in.

The nursery rhyme describes the sulking child; it also gives a clue to a further strategy for the head faced with rapid change. If the major resource available to a head to meet the challenge of change is the staff of the school, the questions to be answered must be "How well am I involving the whole staff in the exercise of managing change?". How often and appropriately do I "call my neighbours in?".

It is not my intention to suggest that all staff have to take part in every decision made; rather that all staff should have an opportunity to contribute, to dissent, to develop a sense of ownership, to produce ideas and have a chance to test them out in appropriate settings. The argument is for participation through working parties, task or action groups, or sub-committees that have clear objectives and a confidence that what they have been charged to do matters, will be listened to and will contribute to the pool of available expertise.

The sense of involvement is in itself energising, and the practical activity of such groups will often produce much "learning by doing" for group members. The notion of "team spirit" developed often produces the drive and determination needed to carry through the agreed policy - with the energy of the team doing the driving rather than the somewhat limited pedal power of the individual.

Anthony Jay's April, 1980 article in "The Observer", "Nobody's Perfect but a Team Can Be" reflects the work of Belbin and others in this field. Clearly identifiable team members such as the whizz-kid, the steady plodder, the knocker of ideas, the loyal company slave feature widely in team literature. We've all met them or worked by them at some time. Individually they may drive us mad. But give them a role in a team and they could help to knock the opposition for six. Chairman, Shaper, Team Worker, Finisher and others are described, strengths and weaknesses analysed, team role described, and team construction debated.

A different approach to team tactics is well illustrated by the work of John Adair (1973) in his Action Centred Leadership Model. Developed first in the armed forces services and later in industrial settings, it identifies the team approach as a crucial element in the role of the manager. Balancing task, team and individual needs to ensure success is doomed to failure if inadequate attention is paid to anyone of the three elements, and in the case of the team to its construction, objectives, plan of campaign, sense of confidence and ownership and ability to evaluate.

The development of Quality Circles presents an alternative approach. A quality circle is a small group which meets regularly and voluntarily to identify, analyse and consequently solve work problems. The theory was developed in the UK and the USA in the 40s and 50s but it was the Japanese who implemented and refined it as a technique in more recent years. The circle, five to ten strong, suggests solutions to managers, and if adopted should be involved in the implementation of them. The Quality Circle philosophy is based on certain assumptions; firstly that virtually everyone has the ability to solve problems at work in an imaginative and creative way (the individual is therefore valued) and secondly that the potential of most people is only partly used.

It is no accident that the three organisational examples chosen to illustrate team tactics have industrial origins, for part of the broader argument of this chapter is that our school organisations should be open enough to seek and take advice from other cultural sources. There are obvious dangers involved, and imitation is the worst form of flattery. Handy warns us strongly that, in adopting the methods of large business organisations, schools may well be adopting theories and methods of management that are already out of date. But as with motivation if there is new expertise to be tapped by the application of team skills to our schools then heads can ill afford to ignore them.

The team approach need not and should not stop short with the teaching staff. Why not student teams, governor teams, parent teams, teams that represent all three - indeed reflect as far as possible all the stakeholders described earlier?

At my former school the work of governors, sub-committees for curriculum and staffing, finance and buildings has generated ideas, action, greater understanding and therefore respect for the organisational demands of a school and a sense of partnership of particular value at times of stress. Via the work of the sub-committee, notably within the area of curriculum review, has come the development of appraisal of what is going on and a sense of corporate responsibility for the changes seen to be essential for the future: in a nutshell strength through proper accountability.

Back again in an industrial setting, the aim of a conference of school-link officers employed by an international company well-known for its strong links with education, was to produce an action check list to ensure good practice in the education-industry partnership. The work of the fifty conference members explored areas of common concern between schools and industry, reviewed successful <u>and</u> unsuccessful practice. Individual and team action plans were drawn up which, using the Senior Liaison Manager present as rapporteur, were shared at the end of the day. A composite of these was quickly seen to be quite appropriate as the aimed-for check list for good practice. Conference members left happy at the end of the day. All had been involved, all had contributed, all present had a sense of ownership and a feeling of personal involvement with not only the outcomes of the day but the development of company policy. They had enjoyed teamwork, enjoyed trust and were anxious to assist implementation. The individuals, the team and the task ended the day well balanced, the quality circle happy, the teams well motivated and valued. The manager ended the day very well resourced.

In his autobiography, Louis XIV claimed that, "Good Government stems primarily from the application of common sense to a sufficient number of facts. Bad Government arises from natural predilections, from wanting to please this or that friend or from accepting advice without weighing it". The dictum remains good advice for the head. It becomes even better advice if the sifting of facts and the weighing of advice is done by as wide a range of co-workers as possible both within and beyond the school -in teams, working groups, sub-committees - but above all in partnerships.

Partnership - for better or worse

The development of the individual and the team within the school setting will have only limited effect upon the successful management of change if the organisation remains isolated and insulated from the world outside. Good organisational health will not be achieved behind closed doors and the head's attempt to manage change effectively requires the strength of broad partnership rather than the weakness of narrow isolation. The argument was cogently put by David Hargreaves at the CSCS National conference in July, 1985 when he called for closer and more effective partnerships between, amongst others:

1 Parents and school
2 Teachers both within and between schools
3 Teachers and pupils
4 Pupils
5 Schools/LEA and higher education, notably in teacher education and secondment
6 Industry, commerce and education

Handy (1984) argues for closer partnership of a different kind - that between the school and the customer: "Accountability in the education system often means the school explaining what it is doing to its customers rather than asking its customers whether and when they are satisfied". Schools should ... "identify their customers; talk to them, listen to them and find out what they need and want, lean over backwards to deliver it and monitor the results continually".

Bill Stubbs, Chief Education Officer, ILEA, argues strongly that "The head's contribution at the school boundaries is vital to its well-being - the ambassadorial role". Thomas Carlyle was blunter, "Isolation is the sum total of wretchedness to man".

Developing shared objectives, encouraging individuals and teams and recognising the legitimate claim of all the stakeholders demands the building of effective partnerships. Whilst no one can expect the head to be the leading or simply an active partner in all developments the argument for at least responsible shareholder status is strong.

Hargreaves suggests that immense benefits would accrue from stronger partnerships between teachers (the sharing of expertise), pupils (cooperative learning), and teacher-pupil (development of negotiation and assessment skills). What about the possible advantages of comparative partnerships for heads? Why not partnership <u>between heads</u> -opportunities for the sharing of experience, mutual counselling and two-way consultancy. On the latter little sharpens the focus on your own institution more than the obligation to consider and advise upon the problems of another.

Between head and staff - opportunities for a more open school, greater sharing of information, development of trust and the establishment of institutional strength necessary to survive the demands of success as well as the stress of crisis.

Between heads and local industrialists - opportunities to share expectations of the education service, investigate alleged cultural divides, compare management strategies and problems, to become more informed and therefore better resourced for informing others.

Between heads and media - a chance to discover that the need for successful marketing is common to both, and that by-lines are as much a necessary currency for heads as for the journalist.

Partnerships, like marriage, should not be entered into lightly; they need to be worked at, they require give and take, sharing and a preparedness to concede to a partner's point of view. They can be highly threatening and when they break down the public and private heart-searching and even grief can be severe. Partnerships are risky; in business they may involve unlimited liability and the same could be true in schools. They do involve the loss of autonomy without the loss of final responsibility; they demand a shift to real democracy away from even benevolent or paternal autocracy. But partnerships can and do bring strength, the satisfaction derived from sharing, increased resources for tackling difficulties, and the joy of achieving common objectives. For the headteacher, building partnerships is likely to represent a crucial safeguard against the slide into at best safe, cosy, orthodoxy and at worst institutional lassitude and personal demoralisation.

Partnerships will provide but they demand contribution and especially from the headteacher. In Idries Shah's book "The Wisdom of the Idiots" in which the Sufi philosophers' thinking is reported, Kitab-I-Ami-Dana writes:

> The Chief takes less than he is given
> And gives more than he has taken

Appropriate words, perhaps to describe the quality of contribution heads need to make if the partnership strategy for handling rapid change is to achieve success.

Endpiece

When asked "How do you like children?" W C Fields replied "Fried". In writing this chapter I have taken it for granted that the reader's attitude towards young people is somewhat more sympathetic and that, at the end of the day, it is the young people who matter most in our schools and colleges. In arguing for heads to consider appropriate strategies for the management of change, we need to remember those who are central to the issue whatever the nature of the changes that beset and besiege us.

James Hemming (1977) commenting upon education today, writes, "In a fascinating way, all roads seem to lead in the same direction ... The movement is from the impersonal to the personal, from domination towards partnership, from the piecemeal towards integration, from isolation into the world". The strategies in this chapter are, I hope, in tune with this view. They certainly argue for an organic rather than mechanistic approach to school management, for building upon partnership rather than personal whim, for the development of the open rather than the closed mind and institution. In a nutshell they call upon heads to CARE, SHARE and DARE. Perhaps, too, in seeking to improve the headteacher's ability and confidence to manage change, we also seek a restoration of that most crucial element in the equation - job satisfaction. As with John Betjeman reflecting, in his bath, on his schooldays - so with the head, too?

> As with my toes I reach towards the tap
> And turn it to a trickle stealing warm
> About my tender person comes a voice
> An inner voice that calls "Be fair, Be fair"
> It was not quite as awful as you think.

References

Adair J (1973) Action Centred Leadership (McGraw Hill)

Brighouse T (1985) in TES, August

Everard K B (1984) Management in Comprehensive Schools. What Can Be Learned from Industry) CSCS (2nd ed), University of York

Everard K B (1985) The Management of Schools: An Industrialists View SHA Review, July

Frith D (ed)(1985) School Management in Practice Longmans

HMI (1977) Ten Good Schools: A Secondary School Enquiry HMSO

Hall V et al (1983) Defining Headship: An Impossible Task SHA Review, July

Halpin A (1966) Theory and Research in Administration Macmillan, New York

Handy C (1984) Taken for Granted? Understanding Schools as Organisations Longmans

Handy C (1985) What Culture is Your School: Patterns of Leadership SHA Review, July
Handy C (1985)
Heller H (1984) Helping Schools Change CSCS, University of York
Hemming J B (1977) in Annand J B (ed) Education for Self Discovery Hodder and Stoughton
ILEA (1984) Improving London's Schools
Peters T J and Waterman R H (1983) In Search of Excellence Harper and Row
Trethowan D (1983) "Industrial Means to Educational Needs" in Contributions, Summer, CSCS, University of York.

Chapter 4

HOW HEADS AND DEPUTIES USE THEIR TIME - A TIME-TASK ANALYSIS

Bill Flisher

The chapter elaborates on one of the major constraints upon staff development: the pressure of time on heads and deputies. Taking self-management as his particular theme, the author of this chapter argues that the effective management of self is a necessary precondition for the effective management of others. Using evidence from a time-task analysis which was devised by the author and colleagues who were members of planning teams for two regional in-service courses for heads and deputies in the East Midlands, he argues that the long hours and pressures from a variety of external and internal sources cause senior managers to tend towards reactive rather than proactive management strategies. The author suggests that there is a need for scheduled time for critical reflection and for in-service work which actively assists senior managers in the day-to-day handling of time, task and relationship.

Heads and deputy heads of secondary schools are undoubtedly very busy people. They certainly have no difficulty in filling their working hours and a great many - very often too many - hours outside the school day as well. But what do they actually do? A study of their job specifications does not help very much in trying to establish how they actually spend their time. Job specifications are not task specifications and they usually give no identifiable picture of the daily round, and little indication of any order of priority that might be applied to the various areas of responsibility listed. Anyway, job specifications do not help the researcher in the case of heads because they frequently do not have them (Morgan and Hall, 1982), although this does not stop them writing long and detailed job specifications for their deputies. It seems that whilst the head's job is thought to be so well known that it is not necessary to put it on paper, it is considered essential to spell out the large number of different responsibilities carried by his deputies. It would be interesting to explore why this difference between heads and deputies should exist, but as we are concerned with what heads and deputies actually do and not with their job specifications, we shall not pursue it here. The assumption in this chapter is that if one wants to discover how senior managers spend their time, what activities they undertake, when, how often and with whom, then it is necessary to devise a strategy which focuses on tasks and times rather than on responsibilities and accountabilities.

The context

As part of the DES Regional INSET provision, the School of Education of Nottingham University has for some years organised one year part-time management courses for deputy heads in secondary schools in three LEAs in the region and, more recently, has mounted similar courses for secondary heads. The planning teams consist of two headteachers from each of the three participating LEAs, who also act as tutors for the course, together with an inspector or adviser from each of the LEAs. The planning teams are led by members of the School of Education staff who act as Course Directors. Quite by chance the author was the only member common to the planning teams for both the headteacher and deputy headteacher courses. This, as will become apparent, was a piece of good fortune at least so far as the strategy for investigating how deputy heads and heads spend their time was concerned.

The teams planning the courses for the deputy heads have been supplemented in recent years by a deputy from each of the LEAs who had been a member of a preceding course in order to provide a "consumer viewpoint". These deputies have been full members of the teams and have contributed very substantially to the planning of the courses. Each of the courses is planned on a three module basis, each LEA sub-group taking on the initial responsibility for planning and leading one of the modules. The draft programmes for the modules, together with substantial module resource booklets, are then discussed by the full planning team, modified, refined and cross referenced to each other to form a cohesive whole. The modules each consist of one residential period of two or three days, when mixed county group work is the major element, and several days of local county group work led by the headteacher tutors, often school-based with course members visiting or working in each other's schools in twos or threes. The courses are strongly experiential in nature. From the introduction of the DES initiative Circular 3/83, the deputies' courses have been of 20 days duration, and while those for heads have been slightly shorter, both continue to run over a one year period.

It is reasonable to argue that in developing management skills with heads and deputy heads there is a logical progression from the management of self to the management of people and finally to the management of systems. It would seem to make sense that managers need to have strategies for ordering their own priorities and managing their own activities and time, before they can effectively manage those of others. Without successful use of the skills involved in these areas, it is difficult to see how they can begin to manage systems successfully simply because systems are run by people. Thus in 1982, in preparation for the 1983/4 courses for both heads and deputies, the planning teams decided to begin the courses with activities concerned with the exploration of self-management including the management of time.

Planning the time-task analysis: the process
The two planning teams, one for the deputy headteachers' course and the other for the headteachers' course, separately discussed various ways of recording the activities of the course members over a period of time. The keeping of detailed diaries in which activities undertaken and the times at which they occurred, together with their durations had attractions, the main one being that such diaries could give clear indications of what had actually been done and when. There are, however, several disadvantages. One is that keeping such a diary is a time consuming process which, if undertaken within the working day, is itself a substantial activity which necessarily distorts the overall picture. Another disadvantage is that if the diary is completed after working hours then it depends too much on fallible memory. A further, and related, source of inaccuracy is that there is a high risk of unconscious distortion when activities the recorders dislike can loom too large in their thinking and therefore also in their recording. This would interfere with the intention of sensitising the recorders to what they actually did and the time taken to do it. The diary method would also make it difficult to categorise the activities in a way suitable for analysis and comparison.

As the discussions progressed it became clear that whatever method of recording were to be adopted it should be one that would be practical, would not significantly distort the pattern of the day and would be acceptable to the course members. At about the same time it was realised that the pattern of the day and the pattern of the week might well be important aspects of the exercise. The patterns would identify any clustering of particular activities and also identify pressure points where many things seem to be happening at once - a potential source of stress. Thus it was decided to use a schedule for each of the five days of a working week divided into time periods set against a list of activities. This decision gave rise to further questions; should the duration of each activity be recorded and if so how, and what activities should appear on the schedule?

At this point it was realised that it would be too much to expect that course members should time each activity. (For example, there are obvious difficulties in reprimanding a pupil whilst operating a stop-watch!) Consequently it was decided to record not the durations of the activities, but their frequencies; thus the record would be of how often the head or deputy did certain things, not for how long he or she did them. It was decided, therefore, to record the activities of each day as they occurred in half hour periods of time during the day. An activity which took place during a half-hour period would be marked by a tick in the corresponding time period column. If an activity overlapped two consecutive time intervals it would be recorded by a tick in both the relevant columns. An added advantage of this method would be that data collected would be readily amenable to analysis by computer. As it turned out the decision to operate in this manner was a good one precisely because it focused on the variety of activities undertaken and on the frequent changes between one sort of activity and another totally different sort. John Buckley (1985) reports that "the head's work can be described as 'a frantic succession of disconnected activities' and further 'the head is subject to considerable personal stress'". It would be reasonable to suppose that if a parallel piece of research on deputies were to be carried out it would show many similarities to heads in this respect.

The planning groups were well aware that when obtaining data by any form of questionnaire the questions asked are inevitably to some extent idiosyncratic and can, and usually do, introduce bias. The planning groups could see no way of avoiding this, but nevertheless wanted to obtain a reasonably accurate picture of how heads and deputies used their time over a period of one week. The planning groups undertook "brainstorming" sessions, producing lists of activities for the schedules which the author attempted to categorise under broad headings. He then asked three or four heads and deputies not involved in the courses to produce a list of activities they frequently found themselves undertaking. These, too, were categorised and collated with the outcomes of the "brainstorming", and a further list was produced. In the case of the deputies' course the consultant deputy then refined the questions and recategorised them into broadly related groupings. These categories were only to make it easier for the course members to find their way around the schedules; they were not to be used for calculating sub-totals of frequencies of activities because it was realised that in the context of the investigation this would give rise to numerical values of very doubtful validity.

It was suggested at this point that the list of activities could be divided into just two categories; those things the heads or deputies chose to do and those things that they felt compelled by demands from others to do. This was an interesting idea and provided a clear indication of the feelings of the head-tutors and the consultant deputies on the planning groups that the demands made on their time were rapidly increasing and their area of choice about how they use their time was rapidly decreasing. However, the main purpose of the investigation was to sensitise the course members to how they actually used their time, whether from choice or otherwise, and additionally to explore the decisions they made about their priorities and their freedom to do what they felt was desirable. In other words they were being asked to consider the degrees to which they were being pro-active or re-active. The planning teams rejected the suggestion that "demanded" and "chosen" should be the only two categories on the grounds that the extent to which senior managers have choice or are under constraints would be an excellent area for exploration in the working groups which were to follow the presentation of the analyses of the returns during the first working day of each of the courses. In the event this turned out to be a good decision.

The final selection of activities was drawn up bearing in mind that the question being explored was not "What did you do during the week?" but rather, "What actions did you take during the week and at what times?". It was essential to avoid including activities expressed in general terms so far as this was possible. For example, "administration" was not used in the list of activities because it gives no indication of what is being administered or by what process - use of the telephone, filling in forms, writing letters, negotiating with staff, or whatever. Administration is not an activity in itself. The criterion underlying the choice of activities to put in the list was, "Is this something a head or deputy would enter into his timed diary if he had used that method of collecting the information?". For example, entries like "Meeting of heads and advisers at the Teachers' Centre", "Had a chat with the head of maths about study skills", "Completed LEA questionnaire on careers education", "Chaired heads of year's meeting", would be likely to appear and therefore it was terms indicating these types of activities that were included in the schedule.

A small group of heads and deputies not involved in the courses and in different schools, were asked to complete a draft schedule. The deputies were asked to do it for just one day, but the feedback from this trial suggested that a longer period would be more useful and therefore the heads completed their schedules for a whole working week. The completed schedules were discussed with these trial groups and further modifications were then made to the titles of the activities listed in the schedules to incorporate the improvements suggested. Also, a trial analysis of the completed schedules was undertaken to see what sort of patterns might ultimately emerge to give a basis for some initial thinking about how the data collected could be processed and presented. It turned out that the responses from the three heads and three deputies involved in the trial correlated very closely indeed with the full exercise conducted with over 30 heads and 40 deputies.

The next problem to be tackled was the placing of the week of the time-task schedule within the school year. The courses began with three-day residential periods around the middle of September and the presentation of the analyses was to be on the first day in order to give impetus to the theme of "self-management". The planning teams were painfully aware that the first fortnight of the academic year is never a "typical" period in a school's annual cycle. However the dates of the first residential period were determined by the availability of halls of residence at the University and could not be changed. It was also argued with some force that the last two weeks of the summer term were even less "typical" than the second week of the autumn term. More than one of the head-tutors made the very telling point that it is well-nigh impossible to talk of any week in the annual cycle as being "typical". In the end the decision was made to place the exercise for the deputies in the second week of the autumn term, which also had the merit that it would be fresh in the course members' minds on the first days of the courses when the analyses of the data collected would be presented. The heads undertook their exercise in the third week of June preceding the course which was thought to be as typical a week as one was likely to find for them.

A booklet of pre-course tasks and related reading matter, including substantial extracts from the Surrey Inspectorate's booklet "Using Your Time", and instructions concerning the time-task analysis, together with five blank schedules was sent to each course member a few weeks before the start of the courses. The instructions for the deputy heads' course are given in fig. (1). Those for heads were essentially the same. The schedule for the deputy heads' course is given in fig. (2) and that for the heads' course in fig. (3).

Although there were a few obvious differences in the items listed in the two schedules the similarities were many and highly significant. It is worth noting that the schedule for the deputies was drawn up in its final form by one of the consultant deputies and agreed by the others and by the head-tutors, whereas the schedule for the heads was devised by the member of the inspectorate of one of the LEAs in conjunction with heads. Thus independently the two groups chose very similar lists for the sort of activities that form the daily round of both heads and deputies. This suggests that in terms of tasks performed, as distinct from roles and responsibilities, heads and deputies do much the same things. The completed schedules showed the extent to which they did them with similar frequencies and in similar ranking orders.

Some differences between the lists are to be expected; for example, most heads and deputies teach but, in general, deputies teach appreciably more often than heads do. Also, attendance at Governing Body meetings is expected of most heads, but few deputies are governors and only rarely do they attend Governing Body meetings in any other capacity, though they may occasionally have reasons for discussing things with governors in an informal way. Similarly it is heads who relate to politicians, whether or not they are also governors, rather than deputies and perhaps it is these two areas of activity, dealing with governors and politicians, that the special position of heads is most significant.

The heads' schedule includes "unwelcome interruptions" but no specific reference to telephones, whereas the deputies in the planning group felt that "answering telephones" is an activity that is very significant to them. It is certainly true that deputies in large schools tend to be people whom other teachers frequently need to contact in order to obtain information or help with a problem, or a decision, and inevitably a response is wanted immediately. The internal telephone is the obvious line of approach. Heads are much less often the recipients of such demands for attention, but more often the initiators of telephone contacts both within and outside the school. As an inspector the author is well aware that if he receives a call from a school it is most likely to come from the head, whereas if he makes a call to a school to obtain specific information or for an appointment, for example to see a probationer, discuss the timetable or enquire about a curriculum development project, he will most often want to speak to the appropriate deputy. It was argued earlier that our perceptions of the time we spend doing certain things depend on our attitudes to those tasks and here it would seem that the use of the telephone is of less significance to heads than to deputies because, by and large, heads use it by choice, but deputies most often have to react to it with a fair expectation that it will cause some sort of interruption to their current task, or simply bring them more work.

Fig. (1)

The task analysis is designed to obtain a crude picture of a Secondary Deputy Head's working week, in particular, to indicate any significant pressure points. It is recognised that the chosen days may not be typical, but even so, a "snapshot in time" will undoubtedly be of interest.

Please complete the attached tick charts for the week beginning Monday, 10th September, 1984. Just put a tick in the appropriate time column against any activity (or activities) which you undertook during the half hour periods. This does not imply that the activity lasted throughout the half hour period, only that it occurred during it. There will probably be several ticks in some of the columns. A fresh chart is provided for each day of the week.

We will want to analyse your returns on a group basis to find common elements. Please therefore use only the list of activities given, making judgements about the "category of best fit" if a particular activity does not exactly match any of those listed. When complete, please add the number of ticks in each row and column and enter in the total row and column. Then return to:

Name

Address

Please send by first class post to arrive not later than Monday, 17th September, 1984.

Please remember:

1 To put the date on each chart in the space provided
2 To add up both the "across" and "down" totals
3 To check that the totals in the bottom right-hand box agree
4 To send the completed, totalled, analysis forms to the above address by Monday, 17th September, 1984 in order that it can be included in the computer analysis of all members' forms. This analysis will be used on the first day of the first residential element.

It would be easy to make flippant remarks about the inclusion of "thinking" as an activity for deputies but not for heads, but the temptation will, with some effort, be resisted. The explanation is really to do with the question of perception again. "I've not had a moment to think all day" is probably not entirely true but it is what many deputies feel as they look back on a day spent rushing around reacting to a large number of demands on them for some sort of action to be taken. On the other hand it is

Fig 2: Time-Task Chart (Deputy Heads)

		Before 8.30	8.30- 9.00	9.00- 9.30	9.30-10.00	10.00-10.30	10.30-11.00	11.00-11.30	11.30-12.00		12.00-12.30	12.30- 1.00	1.00- 1.30	1.30- 2.00	2.00- 2.30	2.30- 3.00	3.00- 3.30	3.30- 4.00	4.00- 4.30	4.30- 5.00	5.00- 5.30	5.30- 6.00	After 6.00	Raw totals	
Normal day to day activities	Teaching																								1
	Assembly																								2
	Preparing for lesson/ assembly																								3
	Marking																								4
	Reading correspondence																								5
	Answering letters																								6
	Answering telephones																								7
	Administrative demands from outside (e.g. Form 7)																								8
Meetings with groups of people	Top management																								9
	Pastoral management																								10
	Subject management																								11
	P.T.A.																								12
	Parents																								13
	Other																								14
	Scheduled meetings outside school																								15
	Ad hoc meetings of groups in school																								16

Fig 2 (continued)

Discussions with individuals (in person or by 'phone)	Pupils																								17
	Teachers																								18
	Ancillary staff																								19
	Governors																								20
	Inspectors/advisers																								21
	L.E.A. officers																								22
	Parents of individual pupils																								23
	Careers officers																								24
	E.W.Os.																								25
	Other support agencies																								26
Staff development	Unplanned within school																								27
	Planned within school (including preparation)																								28
	Outside school (including preparation)																								29
Other activities	Forward planning/ organisation																								30
	Thinking																								31
	Extra curricular activities																								32
	Emergencies - fire, flood, illness, etc.																								33
	Moving around school to exercise a presence																								34
	Column totals																								

Fig 3: Time-Task Chart (Heads)

Week beginning ______________________

Day ______________________

	ACTIVITIES	PRE 8.30	8.30 -9	9- 9.30	9.30 -10	10- 10.30	10.30 -11
Forward planning/organisation							
Administrative demands from outside (e.g. Governors)							
Dealing with routine mail							
Unwelcome interruptions							
Teaching							
Preparing for lesson/assembly							
Taking assembly							
Marking							
Scheduled meetings with groups in school	Top management						
	Pastoral management						
	Subject management						
	P.T.A (including committee)						
	Parents						
	Governors						
	Others (specify)						
As above outside school	Obligatory						
	Voluntary						
Ad hoc meetings with groups in school							
Discussion with individuals (in person or by telephone)	Pupils						
	Teachers						
	Ancillary staff						
	Governors						
	Inspectors/advisers						
	L.E.A. officers						
	Politicians						
	Parents of individual pupils						
	Careers officers						
	E.W.Os.						
	Other support agencies						
Staff develop-ment (INSET)	Planned within school						
	Unplanned within school						
	Outside school						
Emergencies (e.g. fire) handled yourself							
Extracurricular activities							
Walking round school							
	TOTALS						

Fig 3 (continued)

County ______________________________

11-11.30	11.30-12		12-12.30	12.30-1	1-1.30	1.30-2	2-2.30	2.30-3	3-3.30	3.30-4	4-4.30	4.30-5	5-5.30	POST 5.30

easier for heads to put up the "Engaged" signal on their doors or tell their secretaries they are not to be disturbed for an hour and thus give themselves time to tackle problems in relative tranquility. This is a luxury that deputies rarely enjoy, and is possibly why they wanted "thinking" included in their schedule, presumably to demonstrate how little time they could find for it.

This discussion of the differences between the two schedules illuminates a deliberate omission in the form of time-task analysis adopted. The completed schedules showed what was done and how often, but not why the activities were undertaken. They gave no indication of the extent to which the heads and deputies initiated the activities that occupied them or alternatively undertook those activities in response to some demand made upon them. The suggestion here is that, by the nature of their jobs as commonly understood, heads are more likely to perform the listed tasks in a pro-active way and deputies in a re-active way. This proposition gave rise to much discussion in the working groups that followed the presentation of the analyses which appear below. What the proposition does not mean is that in their functions as distinct from tasks, heads are always initiators and deputies always reactors.

Analysis of data

Background

Analyses of the completed schedules are shown in figs (4) and (5). It is interesting to compare the results for the three counties which differ significantly in geography, sociology and educational philosophies and practices. Counties A and B both have large areas of concentrated industry including mining and manufacturing, and major cities with the usual inner-city problems but also large areas of rural countryside in which secondary schools are widely separated and serve well spread out catchment areas. Both are fully committed to comprehensive education but between them they have virtually every possible form of organisation. County C is geographically very large with little heavy industry, its most obvious industry being agriculture. It has few large towns and its average population density is low. Secondary education is provided by a small number of comprehensive schools in the vicinity of the city, but elsewhere mainly by a traditional selective system including a fair number of schools which by current standards are very small. These have only one deputy head and in them the term "Senior Management Team" must have a very different meaning from that understood in larger schools.

Fig 4: Frequency of Activities - Heads

	ALL		LEA A		LEA B		LEA C	
	RANK	%	RANK	%	RANK	%	RANK	%
Discussion with individual teachers	1	16.0	1	16.5	1	16.0	1	13.2
Forward planning and organisation	2	9.5	3	8.6	4	7.4	2	9.1
Discussion with individual ancillaries	3	7.9	2	11.3	5	6.5	6=	6.1
Walking round the school	5	7.3	4	6.7	2	8.9	5	6.7
Dealing with routine mail	6	6.4	5	6.6	7	5.6	4	7.1
Teaching	7	5.0	9	3.2	6	6.2	6=	6.1
Administrative demands from outside the school	8	3.6	7	4.3	13	2.5	8	5.3
Scheduled meetings of top management	9	3.1	12	2.5	8	4.2	12	2.5
Scheduled meetings out of school - voluntary	11	2.8	8	3.6	11	2.9	15	2.2
Extra curricular activities	15	2.2	24	1.1	9	4.0	17	2.0

Fig. 5: Frequency of Activities - Deputy Heads

ACTIVITIES	ALL		LEA A		LEA B		LEA C	
	RANK	%	RANK	%	RANK	%	RANK	%
Teaching	1	17.5	1	16.1	1	15.3	1	20.7
Discussion with individual teachers	2	11.9	2	13.9	2	12.9	2	9.6
Discussion with individual pupils	3	7.9	3	9.7	3	8.4	4	6.0
Forward planning and organisation	4	7.1	5=	5.5	5	7.3	3	8.1
Moving around the school	5	6.6	7	5.4	4	8.0	5	5.8
Answering the telephone	6	5.2	4	6.1	6	5.2	7	4.4
Preparing lessons or assemblies	7	4.9	8	5.2	9	4.7	6	4.9
Discussion with ancillary staff	8	4.5	9	5.0	8	5.0	11	3.6
Thinking	9	4.1	12	2.2	7	5.2	8	4.3
Administrative demands from outside school	10	3.6	5=	5.5	10	3.2	13	2.8
Meeting of top management	11	3.5	10	4.0	12	3.0	9	4.0

Figures 4 and 5 above show 11 selected activities for the complete groups of heads and deputies to enable the upper quartiles of 9 activities for each LEA to be shown separately and compared.

<u>Note</u> The percentages were calculated by totalling the number of ticks for the week for each LEA and for all three combined and expressing the number of ticks against each activity as percentages of these totals. The ranks were then obtained by ranking these percentages in order of magnitude.

Comparison of heads' and deputies' completed schedules

Comparison of the tables shown in figs (4) and (5) is interesting because of the similarities between them. Apart from "teaching", which ranked first with the deputies but only seventh for the heads, which is not surprising since few heads teach as much as their deputies, the rankings are very close indeed, as also are the percentages of ticks for items of equal ranking. This similarity between the tasks undertaken by heads and the tasks undertaken by their deputies and the frequencies with which they undertook those tasks raises all sorts of questions which are of interest to those concerned with the role, functions and tasks of members of senior management teams in secondary schools, and we shall explore some of them later.

The activities which show the greatest differences are "discussions with individual ancillaries" which ranked 3 for the heads but only 8 for the deputies and "dealing with routine mail" which ranked 6 for the heads and as low as 14 for the deputies. In the first case the assumption is that the individual ancillaries with whom the heads talked with were probably the school secretaries, whereas the deputies would usually reckon to have less frequent contact with them but be more likely to be talking with librarians, laboratory technicians etc. The second case is quite predictable. Heads do have a large amount of routine mail to deal with, much of it being quite properly directed rapidly to a more appropriate member of staff or to the waste paper basket. The head's office is the school's clearing house for mail. Most of it is, therefore, filtered out long before it reaches the deputies.

The telephone item is also interesting. It was said earlier that the deputies on the planning group wanted the item "telephone" included because they felt strongly about it. In the event it would appear that they were proved right because a ranking order of 6 is high and is above, for example, "preparing lessons or assemblies", and "administrative demands from outside". This last item needs explanation bearing in mind the argument earlier in this chapter which suggested that administration as a heading would not be included. The important point here is that the emphasis is on "demands from outside", eg staffing returns,

returns concerning school meals numbers, analyses of public examination results and the seemingly endless flood of paper from area office and County Hall, and questionnaires from researchers, leaders of national or local projects and so on. One has to ask if it makes sense that highly paid professionals like heads and deputies should so often spend time personally dealing with matters like these. Most of the examples above are surely cases for secretarial rather than professional action.

When this point is put to heads and deputies there are usually two responses; firstly that the secretaries are not professionally competent to undertake these tasks and secondly that the secretaries are heavily overworked and it would be unfair to ask them to undertake them. The obvious answer to the first response is that the secretaries will remain unable to undertake the tasks if they are not taught how to do them. On the second point it is a source of continuing amazement that many LEAs seem to be so ungenerous in the provision of secretarial staff in secondary schools. To argue, as is often done, that secretaries cost the Authority money is to obscure the poor cost effectiveness of using the time of heads and deputies for doing secretarial work. This is, of course, a totally hidden cost in terms of money, though the cost in terms of the heads' and deputies' time which should be available to do more important things is another matter entirely.

But heads and deputies must accept some of the blame for this misuse of their valuable time. It is established folk-lore that when promoted to a new post people often tend to hang on to those things they are good at doing even if they are not entirely appropriate in the new situation. Teachers who are good at organisation and administration become promoted to middle management jobs in which they develop and extend those skills, and then, having gained a good reputation for efficiency and reliability along with other qualities and skills, become deputy heads. Once in their new jobs, very different from anything they have done before, they naturally find security in an initially insecure new world by continuing to do those things on which their reputation is largely based. They then go through the same process as they become heads. We shall return to this matter of the retention of redundant skills later on. It is an important issue for management staff in all walks of life because it is in human nature to seek comfort in doing things we like doing and know we are good at doing instead of facing a task we find unwelcome or threatening. We are guilty of self-indulgence and of dodging the important issues. The amusing thing about this behaviour is that we then complain that we could not get round to tackling the really important job because the things we chose to do got in the way. (Note the 'Games Educators Play' in

Christopher Day's chapter.) This is as true of inspectors as it is of heads and deputies - even they are human, despite popular mythology.

County differences

Some of the differences in the geography and educational practices of the three counties are reflected in the rankings of several of the activities. Heads in the three counties spent approximately the same amount of time teaching, but in County C "marking" ranked as high as 9th, in County B it was 18th, and in County A only 25th. This strongly suggests that in the smaller schools in County C the heads' teaching was largely in the main-stream of the curriculum, whereas in the other two counties it was either in areas like sixth form general studies or in covering for absent staff. The deputies in County C taught some 30% more than their colleagues in the other two counties. This suggests both a greater need for the top management to contribute to main-stream teaching in smaller and/or selective schools and fewer management tasks needing to be done which would otherwise reduce the teaching time available to them. A consequence of this is that deputies in such schools may gain only limited experience of the management role and could therefore be disadvantaged when they seek further promotion.

Discussions

The frequency of informal contacts between top managers and other members of the school staff (both teaching and ancillary) and with individual pupils is related to the complexity of the school structure, the management style adopted (or imposed) and opportunities being available. Taking together the three items relating to discussions it is clear that heads in County C talked less often with colleagues and pupils than did those in Counties A and B, and the deputies as much as 30% less frequently. This may be related to their much heavier teaching commitments but perhaps also to a greater degree of delegation of tasks to other teachers, whether by choice or necessity. In a great many schools too much responsibility for discussion, negotiation and decision-making concerning pupils is passed upwards to deputies and heads by members of staff who either have not been clearly given the responsibility themselves or who, having been given it, choose not to exercise it. Ideally negotiations should be carried out and decisions taken at the lowest possible level, ie the point at which the need arises. In schools this means, for example, that form tutors should handle the vast majority of matters concerning pupils in their care, be they disciplinary, academic, domestic or whatever. Only rarely should they feel the need to refer upwards to the head of year or house and even then only those cases which are well outside their experience or of a very serious nature. Far too often minor problems arrive at the pastoral deputy's door as first point of call instead of the ultimate, by-passing the head of year or head of house en route. Sadly, these are then much too frequently dealt with by the deputy instead of being sent back to the form tutor or pastoral head to handle. The heads and deputies in County C were, perhaps, more on the right lines than those in the other two counties in this respect, though whether by choice or necessity it is impossible to say.

Administrative demands from outside come to schools from both central and local sources. At a given time in the year the majority of demands from central sources are likely to be much the same for all secondary schools so that the differences between the counties under this heading were mainly due to local variations. The demands on heads were least, by about one half, in County B and only average for the deputies. This would suggest that fewer demands were received by heads in County B than those in the other counties, but that suggestion would be greeted with pure disbelief by the heads and deputies themselves. Heads in County C were the hardest hit but the deputies the least affected, possibly because those heads who have only one deputy felt obliged to handle most demands of this sort themselves. The most severe sufferers amongst the deputies were in County A. They accumulated over 50% more ticks for this heading than their counterparts in County B and twice as many as in County C. The heads in County A also collected appreciably more than the average for the three counties. Taking the heads and deputies together, those in County A made 70% more responses to administrative demands from outside than did those in County B, which must be an indication of the different requirements of their LEAs. Thus the management styles and practices of LEAs as well as the size and complexity of schools are factors which significantly affect the daily tasks undertaken by heads and deputies.

Local custom as well as LEA practice also appears to affect the things that heads and deputies spend their time doing. An example is "moving around the school". This item ranked a surprising second for the heads and fourth for the deputies in County B, significantly higher than for either heads or deputies in the other two counties. It could be said that this happened because of the larger and more spread out buildings in County B, but as County A also has many large school buildings this would be an unlikely explanation. It is more probably a result of local practice and perpetuated by custom especially when deputies are promoted to headships within the county. Whatever the reason there is a lot to be said for top managers regularly taking planned walks around the school to see for themselves what is going on, and in order to exercise a presence.

The pattern of the working week

The distribution of activities over the working week of five days turned out to be as one might have predicted for both the heads and the deputies. In both cases Monday had the highest number of ticks, 24% of the whole week for the heads and 22.5% for the deputies, and Friday, with 18.5% for the heads and 18% for the deputies having the lowest. There were no significant differences between the counties. Any head or deputy could give good reasons why Mondays are always hectic, especially in the early part of the morning, but the relative slackness of Fridays is less easily explained. It might be that there are fewer things to do and problems to solve on Fridays because many of them have been dealt with earlier in the week, or because other members of staff are feeling too jaded by Friday to bother to raise issues with top management, or because the heads and deputies themselves are by then feeling the strain and are understandably less enthusiastic about initiating action. Most likely it is a combination of all these reasons which, in any case, interact the one upon the other.

It may also be that Monday is a particularly busy day partly because Friday is relatively slack. At the end of a hectic week it is very easy to say "Oh, leave that till Monday" so making Friday easier but at the same time making Monday worse. Knowing that Monday is always a busy day and that the temptation to pass things on from Friday is a very strong one, it would pay heads and deputies to look at their Monday activities to find those things that do not necessarily have to be done right at the start of the week and which could be moved to another day in order to spread the load more evenly. It could be illuminating for heads and deputies to look closely at what they do each day, not only on Mondays, to see which activities are specifically related to a particular day and cannot be moved and which others could be moved to a known slacker time. It is always necessary to schedule diaries weeks in advance for meetings and other school calendar events, but in order to spread the load it is important also to schedule fixed times which are to be available for less firmly planned activities, eg for a talk with a particular pupil, or a discussion with the caretaker, or a visit to a particular area of the school to look at the displays. To further reduce the number of occasions when everything is happening at once, and to reduce the stress this causes, it is essential to schedule blank spaces in the diary to allow for the unexpected, which we all know will happen even if we do not know what it will be.

Also, why not schedule spaces for thinking time? If we are too busy to find time to think it is probably because we are chasing around crisis-managing problems which, by spending a little time thinking and planning ahead, we could have avoided. There is a vicious circle here in which it is only too easy to become trapped. It needs a strong nerve to insist on thinking time. The trouble is that when we are sitting quietly thinking we do not appear to be working, but when we are rushing around in too much of a hurry to do anything properly we believe that our colleagues will feel we are doing a good job and getting things done. Far too often, these things we are getting done we need not be doing at all. Many of them could be done by somebody else instead who may well profit professionally from the experience and, having more time, might even do them better than we could. This is an argument for planned delegation, not ad-hoc off-loading, and it has implications for the management structure and accountability patterns of the school.

The pattern of the working day

The way in which the activities clustered around particular times of day showed little variation in pattern during the week. Whilst the total of activities on Monday was greatest and on Friday least, the general pattern of these two days was the same as that of the other three. There were, however, significant differences between heads and deputies and between the three counties, but the one common feature was the half-hour period from 8.30 a.m. to 9.00 a.m. which was by far the busiest of each day for both heads and deputies regardless of county, and on Monday was the busiest half-hour of all.

The pre-8.30 a.m. period over the whole week for all the deputies averaged out at 5.1% of each day's total ticks, and the post 5.30 p.m. period averaged out at 5.2%. Early in the morning the activities are each likely to have been of short duration but in the evening they would undoubtedly be much longer, for example marking or preparing lessons. Thus whilst the total of "out of school hours" activities ticks amounted to 10.3% of the day's total, the percentage of actual time spent on school work out of school hours was certainly very much greater, probably around 20% to 25%.

For the heads the story was much the same, the pre-8.30 a.m. period averaging 4.4% of the day's activities and the post-5.30 p.m. period 3%, giving a total of 7.4% of the recorded activities occurring outside school hours. The argument about the lengths of time taken by early morning and evening activities applies in much the same way to heads as to deputies, but some of the heads' evening activities are likely to be even more time-consuming. It is highly likely that, from the evidence of this investigation, heads and deputies spend approximately the same number of hours on school work in their "private" time.

For both the heads and the deputies the second largest number of activities after the 8.30 a.m.-9.00 a.m. rush was recorded in the half-hour immediately following, namely 9.00 a.m.-9.30 a.m. This suggests that heads and deputies arrange to have non-teaching periods at that time because experience tells them that there will be plenty of non-teaching jobs to do. An alternative argument is that the timetable compilers gave them non-teaching time then which they promptly filled with activity. The next busiest time for deputies was from 10.30 a.m.-11.00 a.m., the morning coffee break when staff and pupils are available for discussions. Not surprisingly, the final really frantic period for deputies was the lunch break. This is also a time when staff and pupils are available for discussions, and even formal meetings.

From the evidence of the completed schedules, heads appear to have much more peaceful morning coffee and lunch breaks than deputies do, but they become busy once more between 2.30 p.m. and 3.00 p.m. and again around the end of afternoon school. It is easy to understand why heads should find themselves well occupied when both pupils and staff are finally freed from their classrooms, but not so easy to understand why the half-hour starting at 2.30 p.m. should be a peak period, especially as few schools now have a mid-afternoon break. A likely explanation which emerged in the group discussions is that the middle of the afternoon is generally a peaceful time when heads can get on with the activities that they had planned to undertake and that with only a relatively slight risk of interruption they get a lot done.

This analysis showed very clearly that deputies, and to a lesser extent heads, are very lucky indeed if morning and lunch breaks are breaks for them at all. Deputies in particular recognise that these breaks are times when they can find people - staff and pupils - that they want or need to talk to. They can often be seen chasing round the school with lists of people they are seeking, or waiting near the door of the staff-room to catch them as they come in for their well-earned breather. So the deputies do not get a break, which they must need as much as their victims, but also their victims lose at least part of theirs too. Classroom teaching nowadays is a tough and stressful occupation and teachers, including deputies, do need a chance to relax, if only for a quarter of an hour, but school staff-rooms are rarely relaxing places during breaks. More often they are places where plans are laid or changed, instant decisions are made, extra jobs are acquired and cups of tea left only half drunk as their occupants scramble to grab piles of exercise books from overloaded tables en route to their next classes. What would professional people working in industry and commerce make of business conducted in this sort of way? Certainly, they would not expect senior managers to be going into the staff rest-room to do business during meal breaks. Instead they would have scheduled meetings in working hours with their line managers or task group leaders and it would be these middle managers who would then make arrangements to meet the people they need to see. Thus the necessary day-to-day contacts are the responsibility of the line managers or task group leaders. In school terms this means heads of departments and year or house heads with whom and through whom the deputies should work, instead of taking over part of their responsibilities from them and so diminishing them professionally and restricting their professional development.

Some management issues arising from the analyses

There is no doubt that a time-task analysis followed by a time-management analysis can be a valuable aid to self management. How often do we hear people saying, at the end of a busy day, "I don't know where the time has gone"? Well, to be blunt, a manager ought to know where his or her time has gone, and the emphasis should be on "know". Too often impressions and the facts about how time has been spent are not well-matched. Without hard facts carefully recorded there is no sure basis for a necessary re-think about how time is being used, let along managed, and the balance of time spent on different activities cannot be compared with the priorities placed upon them.

More often than not the "action" component of the well-known cycle "assessing - processing - action" is disproportionately large compared with "assessing"; and the "process" part almost becomes lost altogether. This is a recipe for crisis management and a manager on the edge of a nervous breakdown. Time must be gained from somewhere for critical reflection following the assessment of situations and for both short and long term planning. If it is not, action will be little more than reaction to situations that have arisen because they were not foreseen. The problem is how to make time available for the things that are known to be important. No-one can manufacture time, but almost everyone can use better the time that they have.

Were the heads and deputies using time well? Did they get the balance of time right? Only they could answer such questions because only they knew the particular circumstances under which they worked. The important thing is that they should ask themselves these questions and, preferably, also ask them of a "critical friend", a colleague whom they trust who could help them in their search for improvement.

The tables in figures (4) and (5) provoke questions of this sort and so do the data about times of the day and days of the week. For example, figure (4) shows that for the heads as few as 6 of the 35 items on the schedule accounted for over half of their total recorded activities for the week. The top quartile of the items accounted for very nearly two-thirds of the week's activities, the other three-quarters effectively being of little importance in terms of the time spent on them. Figure (5) shows that for the deputies, excluding teaching (which is not a management activity in this context), rather less than one quarter of the items on the schedule accounted for just over half the recorded tasks. Comparison of the tables for the heads and deputies shows that 5 of the heads' top 6 activities also appear in the top 7 of the deputies' list.

The tables show that there is a very small number of activities which dominate the working hours of heads and deputies and occupy an overwhelming proportion of the time available. This being so it appears to be crucial that these are the right activities to take up so much time and energy.

But are they indeed the 'right' activities? Perhaps, but the following questions which were put to the heads and deputies at the end of the presentations of the results of the surveys as useful initial steps towards an appraisal of the way they spend their time, provoked a lot of discussion and raised some doubts. They also helped identify crucial issues.

- Are all these activities things you feel you must do yourself or could some of them, or parts of some of them, be done by someone less senior? If so, what would you do instead?

- If someone less senior did some of the things you do would it
  a be helpful to their professional development?
  b encourage them towards feeling themselves to be a more valued part of the school's life?
  c use their talents more widely or develop talents that they did not think they had?
  d be a threat to you if, perish the thought, they were to do them better than you do?

- When you delegate do you define the task, responsibility, authority and accountability clearly, or just off-load work? Having delegated a task to someone properly, do you then let him or her get on with the job without interfering?

- Do you choose to do these things to the extent shown? If so, why? If you believe that some are forced upon you, what do you do to resist the pressure?

- Do you hang on to some tasks because you enjoy using your now redundant skills on which your reputation used to be based? Are you simply being self-indulgent?

- Do you take work home because you find it interesting and enjoyable or because you think you must in order to keep on top of the job, or perhaps, to impress your colleagues with your industry and give your self-esteem a boost?

- Could you rearrange some of your work in order to spread the load more evenly through the day, week, term, year?

- Given a free choice how would you change the order of time priorities shown in the analyses?

- How could you improve your managerial skills in order to make more time available for the important things that tend to be pushed aside by pressure of work?

- What are you really trying to do? Does the way you use your time match with your intentions?

Post-analysis discussions with heads and deputies

In the working groups which then followed, a number of issues were explored by the course members, working from their own experiences. Inevitably, the question of whether heads should undertake regular teaching commitments quickly arose. The heads who were fairly new in post argued that they wanted to teach in order to show their staffs that they could do it well, to set an example and to get to know the pupils. They mostly argued in favour of teaching their own specialist subjects and defended themselves strongly (perhaps too strongly) against accusations of self-indulgence and the retention of redundant skills in order to give themselves a feeling of security in a new situation. They did, however, admit that the number of pupils they came to know through their teaching was necessarily only a small proportion of the school and that they were too often unable to take their classes because of other, usually inescapable, demands on their time. The more experienced heads accepted that it is often useful in the early days of headship to demonstrate that one is a good teacher but doubted that any example that might be set was ever really taken up by colleagues, few of whom could have any personal knowledge of the head's performance in the classroom. Most of this second group either taught non-examination subjects such as sixth form minority time or took a full part in the substitution system, or sometimes both. The obvious danger in teaching non-examination subjects is that these subjects, often considered by pupils to be of little importance anyway, are further diminished if the head is frequently unable to take the classes.

Generally it was agreed that experienced heads could most usefully contribute to the teaching in the school by taking a full part in covering for absent teachers. By so doing they will meet a wide variety of pupils, demonstrate to their colleagues that they can cope with them and show that they are willing to take on an always unpopular task. Also, and very importantly, by taking a wide range of classes in a large number of different classrooms they will be able to make assessments and form judgements about a lot of things that are happening in the school. The deputies, in their groups, expressed a strong preference for heads who did not have regular teaching commitments but instead were available for substitutions. They did, of course, accept that in small schools it is usually necessary for heads to teach main-stream classes in order to make a timetable that would work.

The notion of "the accessible head" (or deputy) also caused a good deal of argument, but there was confusion between accessibility and availability. The manager who says "my door is always open" may be speaking the literal truth, but what really matters is that his mind should always be open. Accessibility is an attitude of mind, a willingness to give time to people, to listen to them, to enable them to feel that the listener does care about them and has really taken notice of what they have to say. It is about what his colleagues think of the manager rather than about whether they can see him at any time to suit themselves. To be always available is, anyway, impossible, and to be too readily available can actually make one less accessible. If an interruption on the "open door" principle is allowed whilst having a discussion with a pupil or teacher then availability is granted to the interrupter but accessibility is instantly withdrawn from the other person and he feels thereby diminished. It was felt to be more useful for heads to have set times when appointments could be made for colleagues and pupils to see them and during which they could be truly accessible to the person who wants to talk with them. On this question of availability the heads felt that it is sometimes difficult to persuade others, especially visitors such as parents and LEA officers, that they do not always need to see the head and that a deputy or head of year, for example, would often be a more appropriate person to see and would probably have more ready access to any information they might want.

A very high proportion of the week's recorded activity for both heads and deputies was spent on discussions with individuals and this was explored at length in the working groups. It was clear that everyone rated talking with pupils and staff, both teaching and ancillary, as a most crucial part of their work in team maintenance. Staff and pupils like to feel that the top managers are interested in them, that they care for them as individuals, are willing to listen to them and willing and able to help them. But there is a risk here if top managers not only listen and talk but also take impulsive action themselves when the right person to take the action is somebody else. By maintaining team confidence with one individual or group they could destroy it with another by doing their jobs for them. For example, a deputy who resolves a form tutor's problem himself might improve his relationship with that tutor but will damage both the self-esteem of the year head and the whole principle of year group cohesion. This is part of the confusion between accessibility and availability again, but in a different form. It also may be another case of an unwillingness to give up things one used to enjoy doing in the past.

Much of the time spent on discussions was thought to be not truly on discussion at all, but rather on the passing on of information in one direction or the other. Receiving information is unquestionably an essential part of the heads' and deputies' roles in assessing what is going on in the school, but care is needed in the collection of this sort of information. A large amount of the information received will be "filtered" - people tend to tell their superiors what they want them to know and to keep quiet about other things. It is therefore necessary to talk with a variety of people with different levels of responsibility and areas of interest in order to get a balanced picture, and this needs some careful planning because it is easy to spend too much time with some groups and too little with others. Not only might this give rise to a reflection in a distorting mirror but it could also cause some groups to be perceived as favoured and others to feel neglected. When heads and, more frequently, deputies find themselves seeking out colleagues just to pass on a piece of information, they really ought to ask themselves if it would be more efficient and effective to write a brief note and put it in a pigeon-hole and so avoid interrupting both their own flow of work and that of their colleagues. Of course there are occasions when information has to be passed on quickly, but these are emergency situations which are, or should be, rare. Usually the need to pass on information in person arises because somebody has not looked ahead in order to allow time for a written message to reach its destination, probably because they have not allowed themselves time to think and plan. They are then not in control, but are themselves controlled by situations that should not arise.

Issues

INSET aimed at heads and deputies tends to concentrate on the strategic aspects of educational management like relationships with parents and governors, the management of change, developing community links, planning staff development, curriculum innovation, staff appraisal and, inevitably, falling rolls. Only rarely is support and advice given about the tactics of handling those day-to-day organisational and administrative tasks which so often take up time and energy which should be devoted to thinking about principles and strategies for long-term planning. The heads and deputies in the working groups made it clear that they would welcome help to improve their use of time spent on "shop-floor" managerial tasks and to make it more effective. More efficient tactical operations would, they believed, release more time for thinking about strategies.

Few managers in schools acquire the experience of working with secretarial staff that is normal for managers in industry and commerce, and even fewer receive any training in this direction apart from that which a good secretary herself can give. Just like managers, secretaries can be more efficient and effective if they can plan their day's work in advance. They, too, dislike interruptions and work handed to them at the last minute, and they strongly dislike being called away from their current tasks to take frequent short dictations which break the flow of their work. The dictating machine is a great help to both the manager and the secretary. It can be used for dictation at a moment's notice anywhere and it allows the secretary the same sort of flexibility in her work. Instead of passing out work to secretaries as it becomes ready, it is surely better to collect together all that they need to do, including dictation tapes, and see them just once each day, preferably in the late afternoon, to allow them to see in advance what the next day's tasks will be. Each piece of work should be marked with a "wanted by" date rather than "urgent" or "as soon as possible", phrases which leave the secretary asking herself "When does he really want it?". In a few of the schools represented in the groups the principal secretaries attend the weekly meetings of top management teams and so are aware of plans made and decisions taken which will affect their work and can give advice about what will need to be done in the office and how long it will take. The more efficiently secretaries are allowed to use their time, the better can they help their managers to use theirs effectively.

Paper work is increasing and sometimes seems already to have reached unmanageable proportions, and this is so not only for heads but increasingly also for middle managers. This is partly because it is inefficiently handled, in particular because it is not well categorised. There are really only three categories that matter. Firstly there is the "Action" category of things that must be dealt with by somebody in the school, secondly the category of "Information" which is needed by somebody in the school and thirdly the "Reading" category consisting of things of interest but on which no immediate action is needed. Everything else can go straight into the waste paper basket. After putting all the paper into three folders, one for each category, all that is then necessary is to mark it to indicate who should receive it and pass it out to the office for distribution. This process should take very little time providing the manager concentrates on the job and does not allow himself to be diverted into starting work on his "action" file before the task is completed.

Other ways of saving time suggested in the groups included scheduling time each day for paper work, fixing finishing times as well as starting times for meetings together with timed agenda items, and then keeping strictly to them, and allowing fewer interruptions to one's scheduled work. Another useful strategy is to insist that any written proposals for initial consideration should be confined to one side of A4 paper at the most. This makes the writer focus his mind on the really important things he wants to say and saves the reader time which would otherwise be spent ploughing through masses of detail not needed at that stage.

The exercise described in this chapter was not designed as a piece of academic research. It was a "snapshot in time" devised to sensitise heads and deputies attending the management courses to the way they spend their time as part of a consideration of self-management. The responses of the course members and the reports of the DES evaluators indicate that it was successful in achieving its aims. In particular it helped the heads and deputies to ask themselves "What am I trying to do? What am I actually doing? could I find a better match between the answers to these questions by using my time differently? How can I find time to think?" In a time of continually increasing pressures, which are too often allowed to force conscientious managers into doing more and more, it is important that the issues raised here are examined closely in order that the stress suffered by heads and deputies, some of it self-inflicted by poor time management, can be reduced. Up to a point increased challenge can produce improved performance, but beyond that point additional stress can, and often does, seriously impair the effectiveness of those responsible for running schools. The danger is that whilst working harder they may be accomplishing less, and be unaware of it. It is only too easy to confuse activity with efficiency and both of these with effectiveness. In the final analysis and after the dust of all the hectic activity has settled, effectiveness is the only thing that matters.

References

Buckley J (1985) The Training of Secondary School Heads in Western Europe NFER/Nelson ISBN 07005 0691 8

Morgan C and Hall V (1982) What is the Job of the Secondary School Head - A summary of the POST project Education, 18 June

Chapter 5

SUBJECT HEADS IN SECONDARY SCHOOLS: CONCEPTS AND CONTEXTS

Peter Ribbins

This chapter argues that while much has been written already on the role of subject heads, there is still room for a more detailed approach because in reality we still know very little about what middle managers actually do. Having first established the curricular context, notably the nature, justification and status differentiation of school subjects, Peter Ribbins then goes on to examine some of the key issues in the running of a department by detailed reference to an actual case study. In particular, much emphasis is made of the head of department's task of monitoring the work of the department, a task which is neither easily achieved nor, apparently, necessarily accepted as appropriate.

Introduction

The idea that secondary schools need managers, and in great numbers, is a comparatively recent one. Its widespread institutionalization can be traced back to the Burnham pay settlements of the early and middle 1950s, which enabled extra payments to be made to teachers designated as carrying 'additional responsibilities'. What, exactly, was meant by 'additional responsibilities' was not made clear then, was still uncertain at the time of the Houghton Report of 1974 (see Siddle 1978 p3), and remains a matter of doubt and uncertainty to this day. At a time when radical re-structuring of the teaching profession is in the air (see Sutton 1984 p5), it is necessary now, more than at any time over the last thirty years, to develop as clear an understanding as we can of what is and what ought to be expected not only of heads and deputies, but also of heads of departments.

For anyone who wishes to tackle this task, there is a substantial literature on the notion of the school subject, the subject department and the role of the subject head of department. There is a good deal that can be learnt from that part of the literature which considers the role of the subject head but it is also limited in at least four main ways. First, much of it assumes the kind of functionalist perspective which has been very much the dominating paradigm within the study of educational management for the last thirty years (see Hughes 1985, Ribbins 1985a). Second, its published research base is very thin. Third, much of what has been written, decontextualizes such roles from the actual organizational and institutional settings in which they are located. Finally, it tends to take the meaning of such problematic terms as 'subject', 'department' and the like for granted. With these criticisms in mind I have argued elsewhere for more studies of the role of middle managers of all kinds in secondary schools which adopt an in-depth, case-study approach based upon an interactionist perspective:

> What we still know very little about, is what middle managers actually do, how they account for their actions, and how they interact with 'relevant others' within particular schools. To explore these kinds of issues a quite different approach is necessary: one which adopts an interactionist conception of role and a broadly ethnographic methodology. (Ribbins 1985b p 363)

As far as I know, no such studies which focus specifically on the role of the head of subject have as yet been published although the accounts of 'Bishop McGregor' (Burgess 1983), 'Rivendell' (Best et al 1983), 'Beachside' (Ball 1981) and the earlier studies of 'Lumley' (Hargreaves 1967), 'Hightown' (Lacey 1970) and 'Nailsea' (Richardson 1973) have all got a good deal to tell us about the kind of contexts in which staff operate.

In this chapter, I shall attempt to contribute to our understanding of the role of subject heads by examining the managerial, professional and social structures, which are the settings in which they have emerged and evolved within the contemporary secondary school. Since I have criticized much of what has been written for its tendency to decontextualize, I shall draw heavily in my analysis upon an in-depth case research study of 'Revelstone' where, for a number of years, I have been engaged in an examination of the subject department and the role of the subject head using the kind of modified interactionist approach which was developed in a study of 'Revendell' (Ribbins et al 1981, Best et al 1983).

Secondary schools can seem places of labrynthine complexity for those who do not work in them. At Rivendell, with its system of faculties, subject departments, houses, years, schools-within-schools, it was so for many of the staff, several of whom described it as a "bureaucratic nightmare". Revelstone, a co-educational, comprehensive with some 1,200 pupils and 75 teachers, taking pupils from 11-18 and located in the Midlands had institutionalized a rather more conventional and certainly a simpler system. This was based upon a 'dual-system' of subject departments (each with its head of department) and 'houses' (each with a head and assistant head of house). Much of this chapter will be especially concerned with its curricular structure.

Curricular structures

Very few teachers at any of the schools in which I have researched have ever questioned the need for some kind of structure to support their curricular activities, although I have come across some very different ideas as to what such structures should look like. When asked to account for such structures teachers offer a wide range of quite different explanations, some of which exhibit a degree of scepticism of conventional functionalist answers. There is a hint of this in the reply of the Head of Revelstone:

> It is historical, there is an awful lot of inertia in schools. Schools could probably get away without subject departmental structures but I am not sure it is worth the bother. Most people who come into schools, come in with the background of a particular discipline behind them ... A particular thing which they are interested in. However, the days in which you could come into schools and spend the rest of your life studying and teaching something you particularly liked have passed ... Even so it is useful to have people in those sort of groupings ... Also, if we are talking about academic excellence, it is better to have people who specialise in those sorts of areas. I realize the difficulties and the extent to which this can cut across the idea of joint studies of one kind or another and that it may involve artificial boundaries from time to time. But I am not sure that anyone else has come up with anything better.

In other conversations he dismissed the idea of a faculty organization on the grounds that it made for "artificial marriages" between subjects and took the view that many attempts at integration were "misguided". I have quoted these remarks at some length because they are so rich in the different kinds of meanings that might be given to the concepts of the 'subject' and the 'subject department' and also of the sorts of justifications which are offered for their existence. With some slight appearance of reluctance and for want of a realistic alternative, the head seems here to be accepting what Warnock has questioned - the necessity of the 'Tyranny of Subjects'! Perhaps, what is even more interesting is that what he has to say entails a recognition that subjects and subject departments in schools may be justified on social and managerial as well as epistemological and pedagogic grounds. What else does he and other staff have to say about the subject and the subject department at Revelstone?

I was told many things relevant to this issue and have space, here, only to consider a few. Firstly, many staff spoke of the 'academic philosophy' of the school as a legacy of its grammar school origins:

> The ethos of this school is most certainly on the academic side and I wonder if this is a hang up from when it was a grammar school ... This is not necessarily a criticism ... in general terms it can be no bad thing, in that the school has some ambitions in terms of standards of achievement. But although the emphasis is here on academic achievement it doesn't always work out that way. If you look at our department's results in terms of external exams it has probably got the best record in the school. Which is ironic since the emphasis of the school is towards achievement in the academic subjects.

Others, whilst acknowledging that the school had an essentially 'academic philosophy', interpreted the term rather differently. Thus the Head of Art, having agreed that the school had such a philosophy went on to remark:

> ... and it's very much geared to the vocational end ... for example, if there were a choice between my subjects and Physics they will say "What can I do with Art?" I would question this ... Because of the area we are in, the head does tend to support the vocational view in that he feels that we owe it to the parents around here to be seen to be preparing their children for jobs ...

Yet other staff argued that the school's 'academic philosophy' was not the only legacy of its grammar school past. So, also was the existing pattern of the subject department structure only slightly modified by its 10 years and more as a comprehensive school. As the Director of Studies put it:

> Really, it was much the same then as it is now ... One new department has emerged and this is Commerce ... There has also been some increase in the significance of some departments ... for example, of Craft and Home Economics, both of which have experienced some internal sub-division ... other things have declined or disappeared ... the school had quite an active tradition in Classics ... But as the transition was gradual, it was not too painful ... the only things, really, which have disappeared are Greek and Russian ... Also there were two Classics teachers, but they have now both gone.

The ideas that differences exist in the significance of departments but that these differences are not immutable are worth considering further. The Director of Studies was by no means the only member of staff to believe that significant differences existed in the perceived status of different departments and that these differences were related to essentially 'academic' criteria but that, more recently, 'vocational' criteria had gained in significance:

> Do you feel that there are some areas that are given higher status than other areas in the school?
> Yes I do. For example the Sciences, and in many ways this is understandable given the pressures from outside, from society. But I still think the Science department is held in greater esteem than it ought to be ... Another area is Technical Studies, because of the nature of the kids we get ... This is an area where a lot of children choose to go to Technical Studies ... because they think it will help them to get a job in that kind of work when they leave ... They are surely sometimes correct. And to be fair to the school I do think that all departments are pretty fairly treated ... although I do still think that the Science department is given undue preference.
> (a head of department)

The two subjects most often regarded as especially "important" were English and Maths, in that order, and, whilst many staff felt that Science had also been accorded that status within society, the educational system as a whole and by the school, they also questioned whether this was really justified:

> I think probably there ought to be a hierarchy (of subjects) ... In this school, being in the Arts, I feel very much a pull between the Arts and the Sciences ... Obviously English and Maths are very important, but beyond those I don't think that I could rank the subjects ...
>
> Only a fool would say "Maths isn't important, take Art" ... One has to be sensible, there are certain subjects which are more important than Art ... I wouldn't like to say that the Sciences are more important, perhaps more relevant to certain pupils ... Certainly English and Maths, but not just any aspect of Maths ... I doubt, for example, if Computer Studies is more important. It is being pushed very hard ... sometimes novelties do get pushed very hard ...

Towards the end of our discussions, the teacher quoted immediately above, offered one of the most economic and elegant summaries of the issues involved in the character and processes of status differentiation between school subjects which I have heard in a decade of research. I had asked him how Art was regarded at Revelstone and mentioned that I had recently heard somebody say that Art wasn't always regarded as a particularly important subject in schools. His response is worth quoting at some length:

> I totally agree. But this school tends to have a very good approach to the Arts in general. They haven't, perhaps, been so caught up in the euphoria of Technical Studies and Science for Sciences sake ... You can't always blame the school. In some areas education is very much seen as just a preparatory stage before work and so poetry and painting does not carry very much weight. Now that may be very short sighted of people in general and schools are just people ... when the pressure is on worthwhile bits of the curriculum can get squeezed out. And Art is one of those bits, and even when it does not get squeezed out it becomes a 'dustbin' subject where you put your remedial and awkward kids, those that aren't regarded as 'good enough' to do German or a third Science ... Art is seen as a form of oocupational therapy rather than as a really educational experience ... Even here, certain subject areas have to fight for their survival, and they do it very well. We are lucky to have a sympathetic 'Hierarchy' to the Arts, they see the

> quality of the work produced ... and our head of department fights very hard for our place on a balanced curriculum.

In one respect, at least, this teacher may be wrong. In the late 1970s and early 1980s no subject area had made such advances as did Design Studies, and although this advance may not have amounted to the school being caught up in "the euphoria for Technical Studies" it must also be said that this department experienced a spectacular renaissance in its fortunes. In no small part, as we shall see shortly, this was due to the activities of a head of department appointed in the late 1970s. To some extent, he was undoubtedly helped in his efforts by the greater significance that began to be accorded to the vocational dimension of schooling at about that time and which was later to be expressed in such initiatives as TVEI. Furthermore, as one of the members of the Design Department commented, in the many general curriculum documents produced by the DES, HMI, the Schools Council and the like during these years, considerable attention was devoted to 'design'. Whilst such factors may have favourably disposed some of the senior staff at Revelstone towards Design Studies, the head of department made little attempt to play the vocational card. Rather, he sought to improve the image of the subject within the school by stressing what he saw as its 'educational' value:

> This department has seen a great deal of change, due in part to some massive national changes. We have always taught and been reputed to have taught manual skills ... where kids have been taught to do things like knock nails in. In my opinion, this has no educational value at all ... Really what we are trying to do can be summed up in the idea of 'Design Education'. Instead of simply teaching to take a drawing of some object and then to make it, which I would describe as no more than 'vocational training', we try to make the kids resolve problems.
>
> We have always suffered from the idea the "Oh, he is not very good at Maths or English, take him down to the Craft department, they will do something with him". It is an absolute fallacy. Our work involves real intellectual activity. An able child in Maths and French is an able child with me ... The less able tend to be as ham-fisted with their hands as they are with their minds.

> In 1979 we implemented a Design based approach ... we changed the name of the department for that reason ... to reflect the fact that we weren't simply teaching little engineers and little craftsmen. But that we were educating kids and we were doing the same job as everybody else ...

Perhaps the clearest statement of the image of its work which the department was trying to present is to be found in the Design Departmental Staff Booklet. This contains a detailed statement of aims 'Intrinsically Related to Craft and Design'. At its most general level, the aim of this aspect of the work of the school is said to be "To develop cognitive and affective abilities and skills, and psychomotor skills that may be applied in a variety of situations in the making of sensitive, rational judgments and decisions in the solving of problems". This overall aim is then sub-divided into seven more specific aims such as "To develop an ability to engage in acts of creativity". Each of these sub-aims has attached to it 'Terminal Objectives' (21 in all) such as "Development of the 'Creativity Factor' in thinking, or 'divergency'; the ability to use the imagination, 'flashes of insight', the production of innovatory (for the pupil) ideas".

The comments of many other staff attested to the success of this effort to lift the image of Craft related work within the school, for example "they have worked very hard and pretty successfully to remove the old 'Craft' image and to instil a new 'Design' image". However, a few staff continued to call them and to think of them as the 'Craft Department', some who recognized that changes had taken place continued to think of them as the 'Craft Department', yet others used the term 'Technical Studies' and finally, a head of another department dryly commented that "the Craft Department are a very efficient department ... also its now turning into something else. It is not the Woodwork Department any more or even the Technical Studies Department ... Do you know its new name? I hear they are after something like the Department of Higher Technological Studies!".

In my experience teachers are much more likely to be surprised if they are asked why secondary schools need subject departments than if they are asked to explain the need for pastoral divisions. I can only conclude from these reactions that, whereas 'pastoral care' remains a problematic activity for teachers, the need for some kind of subject based curriculum structure does not. Schools, it seems, need subject departments because they need subjects just as universities need discipline based departments because they need disciplines. Such a view is largely taken for granted amongst the great majority of teachers I have spoken to, but it has been challenged in various ways. For example, writing of higher education in the United States, Falk (1980) stands the theory presented above on its head. He argues that as higher education has grown, the importance of the academic department has increased:

> This is believed to be so because the increased specialization of knowledge has made it imperative that faculty members identify with that unit of university life from whence their discipline derives all its resources, that is, the department. (But) it can be argued that specialization of knowledge is not the cause of departmentalism but the effect. Thus, some say that 'departmentalism erodes the unity of knowledge' and that, in addition, departments actually prevent the growth of new areas of endeavour because 'established' faculty fear that new ideas could threaten their control over funds and students (p79).

Some may dismiss this as the struggle for place in an educational sector and in a culture so different from secondary schooling in this country that we have little to learn from it. This is a comforting view but could it be that the pattern of 'subjects' found in the contemporary secondary school is more the consequence than the cause of existing patterns of subject departments? There are hints from some of the things we have already heard from the teachers at Revelstone that this may not be an entirely fanciful speculation. What can we learn from the literature of the origins, evolution and nature of the subject?

For heuristic purposes, I find it helpful to identify three main kinds of explanations of subjects classified according to the extent to which they emphasise philosophical or sociological criteria on the one hand and theoretical or empirical criteria on the other. In this chapter, it will not be possible to do more than offer the briefest sketch of some of the ideas and issues involved. The first, and probably most influential set of explanations, I shall term the Philosophico-Theoretical Approach. What the set of often quite different theories which share this approach have in common is a concern to examine and if possible to identify significant logical and other divisions in the nature and the structure of knowledge and to explore the educational implications of their analysis. Some of the issues involved can be illustrated by focussing on the work of Paul Hirst. Goodson (1981), a persuasive critic of the 'philosophico-theoretical approach', offers the following brief summary:

> Hirst and Peters argue that "the central objectives of education are developments of mind" and that such objectives are best pursued by the development of 'forms of knowledge' (a definition later broadened to include 'fields of knowledge'). From these forms and fields of knowledge so defined, school subjects are themselves derived and organized. Hence what is implied is that the intellectual discipline is created and systematically defined by a community of scholars, normally working in a university department, and is then 'translated' for use as a school subject (p166)

Goodson acknowledges that this is not the interpretation which Hirst makes of his own ideas, a necessary qualification since it bears only a quite superficial resemblance to what Hirst has actually written, rather it is the interpretation which others have commonly made and is the form in which it has been influential in shaping thinking about the origin, evolution and justification of subject based structuring of the secondary curriculum amongst educationalist and laymen alike. This essentially philosophical view of the school subject has been criticised by Young (1971) on the grounds that it is based on

> an absolutist conception of a set of distinct forms of knowledge which correspond closely to the traditional areas of the academic curriculum and thus justify, rather than examine, what are no more than the socio-historical constructs of a particular time (p23)

What of sociological approaches to the study of school subjects? Musgrove (1968) suggests that these should

> Examine subjects both within the school and the nation at large as social systems sustained by communication networks, material endowments and ideologies. Within a school and within a wider society subjects as communities of people competing and collaborating with one another, defining and defending their boundaries, demanding allegiance from their members and conferring a sense of identity upon them. They are bureaucracies, hierarchically organized, determining conditions of membership, establishing criteria for recruitment to different levels ... even innovation which appears to be essentially intellectual in character can usefully be examined as outcome of social interaction ... (p101).

I shall say something about two sociological approaches distinguished essentially according to the nature and depth of their interest in the socio-history of school subjects.

The first of these might be labelled the Socio-Theoretical Approach. The classic statement of this approach is contained in the series of papers published in the influential book on the sociology of knowledge, Knowledge and Control, edited by Michael Young (1971). As we have seen, Young rejected the kind of philosophical view of the school subject in part at least, because of its supposed historical character. But there seems some doubt as to how 'historical' are some of the key contributions to Knowledge and Control. Young (1971), for example, asserts that:

> Academic curricula in this country involve assumptions that some kinds and areas of knowledge are much more 'worthwhile' than others: that as soon as possible all knowledge should become specialized and with minimum explicit emphasis on the relations between subjects specialized in and between specialist teachers involved. It may be useful therefore, to view curricular changes as involving changing definitions of knowledge along one or more dimensions towards a less or more stratified specialized and open organization of knowledge. Further, that as we assume some patterns of social relations associated with any curriculum, these changes will be resisted in so far as they are perceived to undermine the values, relative power and privileges of the dominant groups involved (p34).

This seems plausible, but what is the evidence for it? As Goodson (1981) points out; "the most underdeveloped aspect of Knowledge and Control in respect to school subjects is the scrutiny of the process whereby unspecified dominant groups exercise control over presumably subordinate groups in the definition of school knowledge" (p 165). In a later paper he sharpens his attack:

> much of the work of these sociologists ... can be characterized in two ways: (a) either history is not used, or alternatively (b) history is misused, or to use Silver's (1977) elegant phrase 'raided'. Much of the work actually ignores historical background and no evolutionary historical process is provided. Studies develop ... horizontally, working out from theories of social structure and the social order (p391)

The second set of sociologically orientated studies of school subjects share what might be termed a Socio-Empirical Approach. 'Empirical', not because they eschew the development of theories which describe and explain the origins, evolution land character of school subjects but because they wish to do so on the basis of evidence gained from rigorous socio-historical and ethnographic research. There are now a number of such studies available to teachers and others interested in, for example, Biology (Goodson 1983), English (Ball 1982, Ball and Lacey 1980), Environmental Studies (Goodson 1982, 1983), Mathematics (Cooper 1983), Geography (Goodson 1981, 1982, 1983), and Science (Cooper 1983, Layton 1972, 1973). For a collection of such studies, the reader might turn to Defining the Curriculum: Histories and Ethnographies of School Subjects edited by Goodson and Ball (1984). To read these studies is to be emancipated from the idea that school subjects are simply the way in which the educational community translates university disciplines into school subjects in the interests of children. It is also to be released from the theory that existing patterns of school knowledge can be accounted for as just another expression of the values, relative power and privileges of the dominant groups involved. Whilst we need to take great care in the use we make of such 'socio-empirical' studies, Goodson (1983), for example comments that: "Of course the specificity of curriculum histories often acts against their capacity for generalization", there are some generalizations that can be made with some confidence: "Curriculum histories point to the evolutionary nature of subjects as coalitions 'more or less delicately held together under a common name at particular periods'. The nature of these coalitions responds both to the structuring of material interests and to the 'changing climates' for action. Because of the manner in which resources (and associated career prospects) are distributed and status attributed, 'academic' subject groups normally develop as 'dominant coalitions'" (p406).

Many of the studies listed above focus on the 'subject', in Musgrove's (1968) agenda, at the level of the nation at large. At the time, he identified the need for such studies at the level of the individual school and remarked that "studies of subjects in these terms have scarcely begun at least at school level". We are still not particularly richly endowed with such studies although a few have been reported which focus on a variety of subject departments within a number of secondary schools including a study of a 'Newsome' Department (Burgess 1983), a Humanities Faculty (Best et al 1983) and of a Maths Department (Cooper 1983). Finally, Ball and Lacey (1980) suggest how we might view the subject department sociologically:

The subject department provides a set of constraints that should not be confused with subject disciplines (as epestimic communities). In the secondary school ... the department ... provides the basis for political action and as such demands allegiance from its members. The rewards of cohesion are tangible and immediate in such fields as the timetable, teaching of desirable or undesirable pupils, accommodation ... and secure academic status. Cohesion, therefore, demands strategic compliance from actors on a whole range of issues that contain within them differences of importance when viewed from the perspective of the subject discipline. In other words, differentiation of the epestimic community is normally suppressed in favour of organizational and status gain" (p150).

The notion of the subject department and its head

With these remarks in mind, how might we view the subject department as a managerial unit and the role of the head of department as a manager? In attempting to offer some answers to this question, I shall turn again to Revelstone and, in particular, to the case of its Design Department and the activities of its head of department. Before attempting this, it seems worth saying something more about what is logically involved in the notion of a department and of a head of department.

Bailey (1981), has attempted to do this:

"In principle, a department begins to exist (1) when two or more teachers begin to teach a subject formerly taught by one; (2) when those teachers begin to co-ordinate their work so that together they can perform tasks which no one of them could perform singly; and (3) when, however informally, one teacher begins to lead and another begins to follow" (p106)

By such criteria, the 'departments' and 'heads of department' of the pre comprehensive era hardly qualify as such. As Bayne-Jardine and Hannam (1972) point out, the cirumstances of those schools differed greatly from the modern comprehensive school and in the subject groupings that developed within them there was little notion of working as a team under a head of department whose responsibilities are both professional and managerial. Various attempts have been made to determine what should be expected of heads of department as managers. In one early account, HMI listed five sets of tasks under the following headings: curriculum, supervision, organization, communications and finance. In a much more recent analysis focusing on the role of the Head of Science, Siddle (1978) concludes that: "Although written for the guidance of HMIs during the 1960s, the general job specifications provided under the five headings appear ... to be relevant today" (p6). Much the same lists of duties and tasks are to be found in the many other studies which have been concerned with the role of the head of department (see Bailey 1973, Hall and Thomas 1977, Ogilvie and Bartlett 1979). No other writer has been so influential in shaping thinking about the managerial role of pastoral leaders and subject heads than Michael Marland and he lists the following ten tasks for the latter whom he sees very much as the leader of a team of subject teachers:

> ... to create a cogent internal structure ... Take a major part in appointing teachers ... Deploy teachers ... Monitor teachers' work ... Assist the development of teachers' professional skills ... Contribute to the initial training of student teachers ... Take a part in the planning of the school's overall curriculum, and lead the planning of the curriculum of the department ... oversee the work of pupils ... Manage the finances, physical resources and learning methods efficiently ... Assist the overall leadership of the school (Marland and Hill 1981 p2)

Whatever the merits of this account, there is a good deal of empirical evidence that by no means all heads of department accept or practice anything like this conception of their role.

The key issue seems to be the extent to which heads of department should be responsible for monitoring the work of their departmental staff (Bailey 1973, Marland 1981). This view was particularly forcefully expressed in the Cockcroft Report on the teaching of Maths in 1982:

> We regard it as an essential part of the work of the head of department to be aware of the quality of teaching which is going on within the department ... In our view it should be normal practice for the head of department to visit lessons given by other members of department.

However, for every writer who emphasises this aspect of the responsibilities of the head of department there is another to stress that this aspect of their tasks is, in practice, the one such heads are most likely to find most difficult or even to reject (Hall and Thomas 1977, Siddle 1978, Howson and Woolnough 1982 and especially Lambert 1975).

'Official' descriptions of the role of the heads of department at Revelstone can be found in the comments of senior staff and from a 13 point list of the 'Duties of Heads of Department' drawn up by the head in 1973. This list contained references to kind of curricular, administrative and other duties commonplace in the literature. It also stressed in its opening statement ("A Head of Department is responsible to the Headmaster for:") and in three of its items the extent to which the head saw his departmental heads as his managers in the departments. It also stressed in another three items, the responsibility placed upon the head of department to monitor the work of his departmental colleagues. However, taken out of context, this may give a rather misleading impression of the expectations which this head had of his heads of department. Thus although the head was sure that he had given a copy of the document to all his heads of department, I found few of them could remember much from it and the only one who did described it as "very superficial ... full of gaping holes". Furthermore, it was widely accepted by staff at all levels that the regime at Revelstone was based on the idea that departments should be given a good deal of autonomy to manage their own affairs:

> It has always been my policy to allow departments to be as autonomous as possible ... Given the fact that promotion is going to be rather more difficult to achieve ... that many people are already in the position they are going to be for the rest of their teaching lives ... I think that you have to allow them as much independence as possible ... now in order to allow that you have to accept that certain mismatches will exist between the quality of what is done in different departments. In the end you may have to step in and say where things are going wrong and that if departments are to be more autonomous then they need to be more self critical as well (the head)

Most staff, particularly departmental heads , acknowledged and welcomed this high level of autonomy. As one remarked: "I think we are quite fortunate in this school to the point where some heads of department would like more direction from the top ... here as long as you are producing the goods they are quite willing to let you get on in the way you want to ... the head of department here is quite free to run the department". However, during the time I was at the school there was a growing feeling at all levels of staff that as many as three heads of department were not "producing the goods" and that something needed to be done. This view was particularly forcefully expressed by one head of department:

> The head's a trusting man. A smashing man. But he has tended to leave the departments alone and to assume that "I have appointed a head of department and he must know what he is doing. I will let him get on with it". In too many cases that has fallen down because, although that head of department has been appointed, he has not been capable of taking on the work he should do ... I would back all the way the head taking a more monitoring approach with the heads of department and expecting them to do the same with their staff as well ... otherwise the kids are suffering and really that is the main issue ...

If, as some staff argued, the price of departmental autonomy was that some departments did not perform as well as they ought, its benefit was that it enabled others to work superbly well. In this, a very great deal depended on the quality of the leadership given by the head of department. This can be illustrated from the case of the recent history of the Design Department. The extent of the contribution of a new head of department appointed in the late 1970s is assessed by a member of the department:

> I think that when 'David' arrived here ... the department, which wasn't a Design Department then but more of a Craft Department, wasn't very high on the list in the pecking order within the school and as far as the head was concerned ... it tended to get the left over kids ... David has shaken it up since he has been here ... We are now a much more efficient department ... and I think we are fairly highly regarded by the staff ... We get more than our fair share of the able kids now ... On the pecking order we are fairly near the top. We have an image of a successful department ... Kids want to do the subject, they are opting for it.

How and why was he able to achieve such a dramatic change? In this chapter, I can only offer a few hints and, in doing so, will rely on what he, and others, told me.

The most significant change, we have probably already identified. In redefining the work of the Department from its original 'Craft' conception ("producing little engineers and craftsmen") to that of a 'Design' orientation was important in itself but to do so by stressing the 'educational' justification for such a change at a time when it might have been tempting to play the 'vocational' card was surely a master stroke within the context of the kind of school that Revelstone was. But, as 'David Potts' quickly recognized, it would not be enough to change the Department's subject image, it would also be necessary to improve the status of its staff within the school and amongst other teachers. To achieve this, it was necessary for members of the department to lose their image as the:

> woodwork teacher who pours his team from the glue kettle, hides away most of the time and has always got a workshop coat on and mends chairs for people. We are members of staff in this school. For example when I came I told the staff that "I don't want you to go up to the staffroom or to mark your register in your overall. Please take it off and put your jacket on ... You will be regarded as a member of staff if you are professional enough". Do you know, it really worked.

Such manipulations of the subject and staff image of the department were clearly important variables in improving its status within the school. But on their own, they would never have been enough if they had not been accompanied by changing perceptions as to the quality of the work done within Design Studies. Since the role of the new head of department is seen by his own and staff generally as crucial in achieving this, how did he go about it?

To begin with you need, it seems, time and a plan:

> If a department needs reorganization, it's got to be a 3 year plan, minimum ... If you try to do it all in one year, I think you will make a right 'pig's ear' of it. I don't think that any head of department ought to take this job on and not see it through for at least 3 and probably 4 years. The big problem can be getting the staff right and the pupils right. I was very lucky in having co-operative staff who worked, not only at school but outside as well. Without the backing of the staff I would have had no chance at all.

The plan had a number of aspects including getting the syllabus right, translating this into effective practice by getting the staff right, and fighting for the interests of the department within the context of the school as a whole. On syllabus construction, Potts remarked that:

> My own view is that it has got to be done by consultation and discussion within the department. My own syllabus was arrived at by my putting out a discussion document ... We then went through this

> at a meeting. From that we arrived at a general agreement about what we ought to be doing and decided that we ought then to go on to the question of how to do it. We had a series of meetings. At the same time, I had not got a head of Metalwork, we had appointed a man who was still serving his notice, so we had meetings after school and he came over. Obviously, he wanted to be in on what was going to happen ... From our discussions, I drew up a rough working document on method, content and so on ... which we then worked on ... At the end we produced a very full and detailed syllabus ... which had all come from discussions which we had all played a part in ... at the end I wrote it all up as a rough draft ... Most of my summer holiday that year was spent doing this ... We all agreed to the final document before I put it to type. If you do this, I think that you have picked everybodies brains ... and secondly, nobody has the right to deviate ... (since) we had all agreed to it.

Getting the staff of the department 'right' involved a number of things:

> The staff in the department enjoy their jobs ... Nobody is disillusioned and nobody is a weak and ineffective teacher ... I can always get my staff to do what I want them to do ... I have had to lean on certain members of staff ... and I feel that a department is only as strong as its weakest link ... as a head of department, on a professional basis, you sometimes have to take people to task if you feel they are not performing as they should ... But, if you do, you must be sure that they know what they should be doing ... All my staff have specific job specifications which we have discussed before I have them typed out ... We have therefore agreed what the job should entail, and that that is the minimum which I will expect from them ... The problem is being able to give someone the 'rocket' they need, get them back into functioning efficiently, without losing the social friendliness ... When I took the job on, I felt that it was terribly important to get the department operating well on a social plain and right from the beginning we have had social evenings which have often turned into professional meetings in which things can be thrashed out in a relaxed situation ...

The idea that heads of department have a responsibility to be involved in the close monitoring of the work of departmental staff and for taking action where their performance was perceived to be in some way inadequate was not one which was universally shared by other departmental heads at Revelstone. But, although Potts described this aspect of his work as "unpleasant" and that "it gets your blood pressure up a bit to do it", he also felt that it was necessary. He also felt that if such monitoring was to be "real" then it was necessary for the head of department to observe his staff at work but that this should be part of a two way process. As such, it could make a major contribution to staff development:

> We are lucky in this department because we are able to wander around and see each other teach and I think that this is a major point on staff development. I can pick up hints, even from students let alone other teachers ... I encourage people when they are free to walk into somebody else's lesson and see what they are doing ... I rarely go a week without seeing at least three lessons ... 10 or 15 minutes, not the whole lesson ... the members of my department do all go and see each other teach and they watch and they listen ... they come and see me teach ... I think that is very important.
>
> At a recent heads of department meeting we were discussing evaluation (of the work of probationers) and of the need to look at teachers teach. They chewed all over the problem and some argued that it was not necessary to go and see staff teach all the time ... at the end, when I was asked by the head, I said that I thought it was very important for probationers to be watched monitored and checked on by their head of department ... but that we should not only be concerned with watching probationers but others as well ... they also may have faults.

Similar views about the department were expressed by its other members. The newly appointed Head of Metalwork recalled his initial impressions of the department as being:

> That it was very busy ... and it is, it's very busy. The work rate, my own personal work rate has trebled as compared with my last school ... I have found the department a pretty 'tight ship' so far, which is good because this is entirely the opposite to what I had grown used to. But there

is a lot of pressure ... Pressure to make sure that I have got the work marked on time, syllabuses and schemes of work adequately prepared, work sheets prepared ... you may have noticed that the Metalwork work bank was nowhere near as well organized as the Woodwork bank at the moment. Come again at Christmas and it should be. I believe that if the children's work is to be good the teacher's work has to be good.

Another member of the department expressed much the same view, emphasised the role of the head of department in the success of the department and hints at the hostility which their improved fortunes seems to have evoked amongst some other staff:

> I think that we are a successful department ... at the social level, we get on well, and on the academic level, the work side ... David is a very efficient head of department, he is a very hard worker and he has some good ideas ... He also keeps a fairly tight rein on things. You have got to be up to date with what you are doing and ... on top of what you are doing ... and that is good. We have a reputation in the school for being hard working ... I have mixed views on that because a lot of staff on the academic side seem to resent us. Not openly, there is bound to be something between departments depending upon how successful you are within the school ... I don't mind people regarding (us) as hard working members of staff ... but I recently heard another member of staff liken us to mini-robots ... It happens, I think, because we are efficiently run. A lot of other departments are not as efficient ...

There certainly were some criticisms of the Design Department but before I turn to consider these it is worth getting these criticisms in perspective. In analysing my field notes and transcripts of interviews with over 60 of the staff at Revelstone I found that only one other department, Geography, was as often identified as outstandingly efficient, effective and innovative as was Design Studies. The criticisms that I did hear of the Design Department were of two main kinds. Firstly, that they tended to try too hard and secondly, and more seriously, that they were given to 'empire building' and that they were not always as scrupulous as they might be in the game of interdepartmental politics:

... the Craft and Domestic Science Departments are always very much on their metal with us ... because they feel for their own status and I think that is very sad. The Craft Department is very, very efficient ... it runs very well ... almost to the point of being officious because they seem afraid of making mistakes ... I think there is an element of their trying to defend themselves because of what they see as the low academic status of their subject.

I think Design is a very tightly knit department where the head of department rules the roost, but it is well run and he rules it well. They run their own detention system and keep any problems they have within the department .... This is the impression I get ... They work very hard to remove the old 'Craft' image and to instil a new 'Design' image ... They have a very high opinion of themselves ... their head of department is a very strong and forceful speaker at heads of department meetings and elsewhere. He is very forceful and works out carefully what he is going to say and how he is going to act and says what he wants with great gusto ... I do think they are a very well run department although I also think they are a bit underhand sometimes ... they have certainly trodden across our path several times.

The Craft Department is full of heads of department. Head of this, head of that and head of the other and that's the way they play the game when it comes to membership of the heads of department meetings ...

To an extent, members of the department did know of the existence of such criticism. As one put it: "I have noticed whispers in certain meetings to the effect 'Ah, they are at it again'". And another remarked that: "In some quarters, there has been some resentment (of our success). I think this has been so because we have been held up by the head as an example of how things ought to be, "Why can't you do it?" ... Another critic, who admits that things have greatly improved, has said that "It's still the case that they are only interested in the boys!". How did the head of department see his extra departmental role and how did he 'play' it?

Potts saw himself as very much the department's principal representative within the school at large and to the senior staff in particular and to influence both in the interests of the department. With regard to the latter:

> I think the key thing there is to get your superiors to respect your abilities and to respect you as a person. And to make sure that you know what you are talking about. I don't like to go and see the head about something unless I have had time to think it over very carefully ... He is a quicker thinking man than I am so that when I go in I like to have done my homework thoroughly.

He expressed the need for similar care and attention to detail in trying to use the heads of departments meeting for departmental or other ends. Other heads of department were sometimes less wary:

> I don't talk as much in the heads of department meetings as some of the others. To be quite honest I have seen too many of them talk themselves into a hole... 'Johnston', for example, a fabulous bloke who runs his department outstandingly, so many times seems to tie himself up by what he says in that meeting ... I think the meeting can be useful to air views or as a sounding board.

He went on to make it clear that if he wanted to have an idea considered he was more likely to take it to the head or one of the deputies, 'depending on what the matter is', but only after having taken a number of careful soundings with other staff: "I would go and see the head of English, the head of Maths and others and say 'I am concerned about this. Does it affect you?' ... If the major support was not there then I might not raise the issue ... I tend to sound people out first if I have a problem".

With whatever reservations and for a variety of sometimes quite incompatible reasons, many of the staff at Revelstone identified Design Studies as a worthwhile subject, as a 'good' department and as being led by an effective head of department. What do staff look for as the characteristic features of a 'good' head of department and what do they see as the marks of a 'poor' department and an inadequate head of department?

One senior member of staff offered the following answer to the question, "What do you look for in a good head of department?", which may be taken as representative of the views of many other teachers. Primarily, this had to do with making the work of the department a genuine "educational experience for its pupils". Beyond this:

> First of all ... he must be a good teacher. One who can not only tell others what to do but to actually show them how to do it. He should set an example in every possible way including on punctuality, attention to marking and lesson preparation and in every other thing he would like his department to do ... Also a really good head of department should be able to pick up the threads of any lesson taught within his department ... If a member of staff is absent ... he should have no worries about going into a class and finding out what they are doing and to do something positive with the children ... He should have total command of his subject, over its teaching area and, preferably, beyond that area as well. He should be someone who really can inspire and lead what are sometimes quite large numbers of teachers. He should encourage his staff to attend courses and other professional meetings, to innovate and experiment and more generally to keep abreast of all major developments within the subject ... To encourage staff to discuss problems ... I think that the actual role of a head of department is to a certain extent dictated by the staff he has. In a very small department ... with experienced and competent staff then the role of the head of department is much easier than in a larger department where the head of department may have to lay down quite closely what he expects of his staff and what they should do. He may need to guide some staff, even academically in what they are doing ... To a certain extent, the head of the school bears a certain responsibility to see that the heads of department work in the way that he wishes them to do. I am sure that every school issues guidelines ... and this school is no exception. Thus each head of department here has a list of responsibilities produced by the head and I am sure that most discharge these ...

Few staff would disagree with this, but it must also be said that many teachers at all levels, some within the departments concerned, identified three departments as giving some cause for unease. In each case the relevant head of department was held to some extent responsible. Before considering this further, let us consider what staff felt to be the marks of the 'poor' department:

> I suppose, firstly attendance. If a department is functioning badly a member of the department who is not feeling 100% is much more likely to say

> something like "I'll have a day off, I can't face it today" ... Secondly, punctuality and thirdly, feedback from senior House staff. If a department is functioning badly then I believe that its members will be functioning badly not just in the classroom but outside it as well. Fourthly, we get quite a lot of feedback from the children and fifthly, from their parents as well at parent evenings and at other times and in other ways. Sixthly, when if there is any 'Option Scheme', children are given a choice, they will quickly sort out which subjects are worth doing ... it is very difficult but over a number of years you can also build up a pattern of exam results and say that these results are not up to standard. But I think that the other signs are more evident ... I think a lot of the evidence is subjective. I suppose other things you look for have to do with the general organization of the department. Little things like the way in which internal exam papers are prepared ... Lots of little pointers.

Whilst such general statements have their place, more often when staff talked about specific cases they were likely to distinguish different levels and dimensions of inadequacy in their analysis of those departments and heads of department which they designated as such. In one case, for example, it was widely felt that whilst a great deal of good teaching went on within the department, it lacked a coherent overall purpose or philosophy which informed the approach taken to its subject. To an extent the explanations offered suggest that the department concerned reflects the strengths and limitations of its head of department in so far as he is regarded as a fine teacher but does not really see his role in any significant sense as managerial. Such a view of the role of the head of department may be taken to have much in common with what might be dubbed as a 'grammar school' conception. As Bayne-Jardine and Hannam (1972) have pointed out, the circumstances of such a school differ greatly from that of the contemporary comprehensive school and in the subject departments which first started to develop in them there was little emphasis on the notion of a team approach and heads of department tended to be appointed for their skills as subject teachers and not for any perceived aptitudes or appetites for management. Holt (1981) makes the point exactly: "(it is) still possible for the insular-minded departmental head to follow historical precedent, to run his own show, and leave the members of his department to run theirs".

This was not the only department of its kind at Revelstone. Another was described in similar terms by many of the staff as containing a number of good teachers and a concerned head of department but which lacked a coherent overall approach and was short on effective leadership. Some things were different. Firstly, there had been a good deal of illness amongst members of the department. A point emphasised by the junior member of another department: "It is not generally their fault. They do have valid health reasons. But they do have a lot of absences. It is generally felt in the school that two out of every three covers you get are over there. I am sure that does not help their image". She also felt that the department was widely felt to be rather poorly run. Much the same view was expressed by a much more senior member of staff: "The difficulty there is getting cohesive leadership. One of the difficulties in achieving this, is that he himself (the head of department) feels that he is giving it cohesive leadership. How do you get around that?". The case of the third department was much more straightforward. It was very poorly run. One of the milder expressions of this 'theory' was expressed by a junior member of staff who, having identified the department as one of the weakest in the school, tried to assess what was wrong with it: "Basically, it is the head of department. Obviously, you have got to lead from the top. You can't lead from the bottom of a department ... this department just has a very weak head of department".

Conclusions

My task in this chapter has been to say something about the role of the head of the subject department. In tackling this, I have questioned the kind of structural/functionalist conception of role which very much constitutes the dominating paradigm within the literature of educational management dealing with this theme. I have done so for a number of reasons. Firstly, because I think that it tends to take for granted the meaning and justification of many of the key concepts involved such as the notion of the 'subject' and that of the 'department' (see Ribbins 1985b); secondly, because I think that such an approach tends to ignore, or at least to undervalue, the dynamic aspect of role play. Social actors do not simply take roles, they make them as well (Turner 1969); thirdly, because such an approach tends to confuse prescription and description in the analysis of such roles. As we concluded from our study of pastoral care at Rivendell: "the structure of officially designated roles is one thing, but the reality in practice may be another" (Best et al 1983 p54); fourthly, because I think that conventional studies tend to decontextualize such roles in various ways; and finally, because I feel that studies of the role of the head of department as they have been conventionally organized have taken us about as far as they are likely for the time being using such an approach.

For all these reasons and others I have taken an essentially interactionist approach and have focussed much of what I have had to say upon the particular case of one school and even upon one department within that school. I recognize the dangers of attempting to generalize from particular cases. Perhaps I have said enough to suggest that no two departments at Revelstone are alike nor do I think that any two schools exist in exactly similar contexts or face precisely the same problems. This does not mean that we cannot learn from each other's experience. It is for the reader to judge what, if anything, within the account I have given of Revelstone is of relevance to his or her needs. If the purpose of educational research is in some way to assist in the process of the improvement of educational practice, then Bassey (1981) is surely right when he argues that:

> an important criterion for judging the merit of a case study is the extent to which the details are sufficient and appropriate for a teacher working in a similar situation to relate his decision making to that described in the case-study. The relatability of a case-study is more important than its generalizability (p85)

Do schools need subject heads? I hope I have said enough to make it clear that this question raises complex issues and may have no final answer. Equally clearly, this question is being asked elsewhere. It is being asked with even more point about the pastoral head (Best and Ribbins 1983). Some of the signs are discouraging. A recent HMI (1984) report suggested that "The status of heads of department in Welsh secondary schools has diminished in recent years at the same time as their responsibilities have increased". There seems little reason to believe that what is true of Wales is not true of England as well. The report also concludes that: "Whether a pupil achieves or underachieves is largely dependent on the quality of planning, execution, and evaluation that takes place in individual departments". Over the last decade I have undertaken research in-depth in four schools and if I am reasonably sure of any generalization it is that good departments have effective heads of department. On this issue, perhaps I should let one of the Deputies at Revelstone have the final word. I asked him if you could have a good department without a good head of department:

I cannot envisage that really because I think that the very nature of large schools requires a certain amount of direction from the top within a department ... If it is weakly led, then it is very difficult ... It is a very important role indeed ... and if a department is made up of disparate personalities and is geographically dispersed, then I think a weak head of department spells disaster for the department and for the subject ... I also think that if you have a good head of department he will have the qualities to not allow a weak department to exist around him. He may have weak members of department but he will know the strengths and weaknesses of his department and will overcome these by giving its weak members a lot of help ... You can't achieve change overnight, especially if you inherit a department which has become accustomed to working in a certain slipshod manner and contains members who are likely to resist change if they feel it is going to make their life more uncomfortable, if it is going to mean extra work ... But a good head of department will achieve a change.

References

Bailey, P (1973) 'The functions of heads of departments in comprehensive schools' in Journal of Educational Administration, V(1)

Bailey, P (1981) 'Appraising the performance of departments in maintained secondary schools' in Ribbins, P and Thomas, H (eds) Research in Educational Management and Administration, Coombe Lodge: BEMAS

Ball, S (1981) Beachside Comprehensive, Cambridge: Cambridge University Press

Ball, S (1982) 'Competition and conflict in the teaching of English: a socio-historical analysis' in Journal of Curriculum Studies, 14

Ball, S and Lacey, C (1980) 'Subject disciplines as the opportunity for group action' in Woods, P (ed) Teacher Strategies, London: Croom Helm

Bassey, M (1981) 'Pedagogic research: on the relative merits of search for generalizations and study of single order events' in Oxford Review of Education, 7(1)

Bayne-Jardine, C and Hannam, C (1972) 'Heads of Department' in Forum, 15(1)

Best, R and Ribbins, P (1983) 'Rethinking the pastoral-academic split' in Pastoral Care in Education, 1(1)

Best, R, Ribbins, P, Jarvis, C and Oddy, D (1983) Education and Care, London: Heinemann

Burgess, R (1983) Experiencing Comprehensive Education, London: Methuen

Cooper, B (1983) 'On exploring change in school subjects' in British Journal of Sociology of Education, 4(3)

Falk, G (1980) 'The academic department and role conflict' in Improving College and University Teaching, 27(2)

Goodson, I (1983) 'Subjects for study: aspects of a social history of curriculum' in Journal of Curriculum Studies, 15(4)

Goodson (1981) 'Becoming an academic subject: patterns of explanation and evolution' in British Journal of Sociology of Education, 2(2)

Goodson, I and Ball, S (1984) (eds) Defining the Curriculum: Histories and Ethnographies of School Subjects, Sussex, Falmer

Hall, J and Thomas, J (1977) 'Research report: mathematics departmental headship in secondary schools' in Educational Administration, 5(2)

Hargreaves, D (1967) Social Relations in a Secondary School, London: RKP

Hirst, P (1965) 'Liberal education and the nature of knowledge' in Archambault, R (ed) Philosophical Analysis and Education, London: RKP

HMI (Wales) (1984) Departmental Organization in Secondary Schools, Welsh Office: HMSO

Holt, J (1981) 'The head of department and the whole curriculum' in Marland and Hill (eds) op cit

Howson J and Woolnough B (1982) 'Head of department: dictator or democrat' in Educational Management and Administration, 10(1)

Hughes M (1985) 'Theory and practice in educational management' in Hughes et al (eds) op cit

Hughes, M, Ribbins, P and Thomas, H (1985) (eds) Managing Education: The System and the Institution, London, Holt Rinehart and Winston

Lacey, C (1970) Hightown Grammar, Manchester: Manchester University Press

Lambert, K (1975) 'Research report: the role of the head of department in schools" in Educational Administration, 6(1)

Layton, D (1972) 'Science as general education' in Trends in Education

Layton, D (1973) Science for the People, London: Allen & Unwin

Marland, M (1971) Head of Department, London: Heinemann

Marland, M and Hill, S (1981) (eds) Departmental Management, London: Heinemann

Musgrove, F (1968) 'The contribution of sociology to the study of the curriculum' in Kerr, J (ed) Changing the Curriculum, London: London University Press

Ogilvie, D and Bartlett, V (1979) 'Departmental Heads in England and Australia' in <u>Studies in Educational Administration</u>, 15

Ribbins, P (1985a) 'Organization theory and the study of educational institutions' in Hughes et al (eds) <u>op cit</u>

Ribbins, P (1985b) 'The role of the middle manager in the secondary school' in Hughes et al (eds) <u>op cit</u>

Ribbins, P et al (1981) 'Meanings and contexts: the problem of interpretation in the study of a school' in Ribbins and Thomas (eds) <u>op cit</u>

Richardson, E (1973) <u>The Teacher, the School and the Task of Management</u>, London: Heinemann

Siddle, J (1978) <u>The Head of Science and the Task of Management</u>, Herts: Association for Science Education

Sutton, J (1984) 'Burnham restructuring 1. Report by the Burnham representative' <u>SHA Headlines</u>, June

Turner, R (1969) 'Role-taking: process versus conformity' in Lindsmith, A and Strauss, A (eds) <u>Readings in Social Psychology</u>, New York: Holt Rinehart and Winston

Young, M (1971) (ed) <u>Knowledge and Control</u>, London: Collier Macmillan

SECTION 3: APPROACHES TO STAFF APPRAISAL

Chapter 6

COUNSELLING AND PERFORMANCE APPRAISAL: AN LEA PERSPECTIVE

John Berridge

This chapter gives an indication of a particular LEA's attempt to develop a system of performance appraisal which has the stated intention of upholding the rights of teachers to be provided with the support necessary to ensure effective teaching and learning in the classroom. Examples of the instruments used are presented in some detail, and the process of teacher appraisal, written from the perspective of a local authority inspector, is described. Even more important than these operational details is the context in which they are placed. Appraisal is not seen as being punitive, but as an essential part of professional and curriculum development. The author emphasizes that the person conducting the appraisal is equally in need of feedback on performance, so that appraisal becomes a two-way process.

1 Introduction

Almost all teachers share a general intention to improve their performance and thereby to facilitate the learning and development of their students. It is with this intention in mind that Nottinghamshire has embarked on the development of a series of processes designed to enable teachers to discover an answer to the question 'How am I doing?', to reflect on that which they discover, and, in the light of this, to consider appropriate strategies for professional development.

It is recognised that the teaching profession has always been concerned with the effectiveness of its work but it seems that until the last few years it has been reluctant to get to grips with the complexities of performance appraisal and the related evaluation procedures.

Only three years ago I was a classroom teacher. I knew that someone somewhere had a view of my performance, and since I was a deputy headteacher I assumed that, in general, my performance in the past must have met with approval. I knew that my headteacher considered me a 'good' teacher, since he frequently discussed both my performance and my career prospects with me, and although in general terms we shared a well understood philosophical approach to education, we had no agreed, explicit list of the criteria on which such judgements were based. How my headteacher's view of my performance was transmitted to the gnomes in County Hall I had neither asked nor discovered, although I had of course made the usual assumptions relating to 'secret' files. While I have understated the mechanisms, including departmental feedback, by which I had become aware of my own performance, I am aware that for many teachers the process is shrouded in mystery and that they are extremely suspicious about the motivation and purposes of the appraisors.

Now that I am a Local Authority Inspector I am in a position to negotiate with teachers about the criteria upon which any judgement relating to their performance might be based, and to discuss with them the ways in which such findings might inform decisions about their professional development. I am able to illuminate the process for teachers by virtue of recent developments in Nottinghamshire which I will describe in this chapter.

Throughout the chapter I will use the term 'student' to refer to any learner, of whatever age, and the term 'teacher' to refer to the person enabling that process of learning to take place. In general the term 'school' should be taken to include both schools and colleges although there is no intention to suggest that either teachers or schools have any monopoly of the learning process.

Finally, I would wish to make it clear that the construction of the professional development model in Nottinghamshire is the work of a number of colleagues in the Advisory and Inspection Service and is subject to continual modification resulting from teacher generated feedback. In no way would I wish to claim personal ownership, as such a system takes on corporate identity. This chapter records my views of the development and should not be taken necessarily to express the policy of Nottinghamshire LEA.

2 Context

Neither performance appraisal nor professional development occur in a vacuum. There are contexts relating to curriculum and climate which need to be taken into consideration in any attempt to understand such developments.

Education in Great Britain is undergoing a number of radical changes. Although the initiatives, to which the changes are linked, are in some cases in their pilot stages and therefore not universally accepted, there are trends which it is quite possible to identify.

In order to decide where education might be going in the future, and therefore to decide against which criteria it will be appropriate to measure the performance of teachers, it is necessary to consider what education has been like in the past. Figure 1 describes a knowledge based model of British education which has been more or less predominant during this century. This model has influenced the experience of students, for many of whom, self evidently, it has not been suitable. Fundamentally the system has recognised only a limited range of objectives related to cognitive ability. Such a narrow perception of the process has conditioned the teaching methodology which has been necessarily didactic, assuming activity only on the part of the teacher, who has monopolised wisdom and dispensed knowledge. The learner has played the part of passive recipient and memory has been misunderstood as understanding. The system has been evaluated by the results of factual recall examinations and this has necessitated individual and competitive working. The goals of the system have been devised and dominated by the examination boards. The examination boards have in turn been dominated by the persuasive influence of the nation's universities, and although the universities provide entrance for a very small proportion of the population, they have determined the framework and purposes for all.

One of the most significant contributions to a changed view of the ways in which we might meet the needs of all students in today's rapidly changing circumstances, has been provided by the six year action research programme of the Curriculum 11-16 Project. Figure 2 recognises that young people in statutory education have a common entitlement and presents a model of a wider curriculum. The model represents what could be the future, and in that sense it describes what I see to be a series of imperatives. It also represents the present, since many of the individual initiatives are currently being developed. Evaluation of the developments and of construction of a system which can serve the needs of all students will present a major challenge but could make a positive contribution to the nature of society and the quality of life.

The model recognises that experiencing success is a major motivational force and that the narrow range of objectives of the past have reinforced a pass/fail mentality which has failed to recognise and value the majority of pupils. Accordingly the affective and the psycho-motor have been included and objectives are expressed in terms of skills, attitudes and concepts, an appropriate body of knowledge being chosen as a vehicle for the achievement of the learning objectives. Necessarily, a range of teaching strategies needs to be deployed. The role of the teacher changes, becoming a facilitator and an enabler, and much of

Fig 1: Knowledge Based Curriculum Model

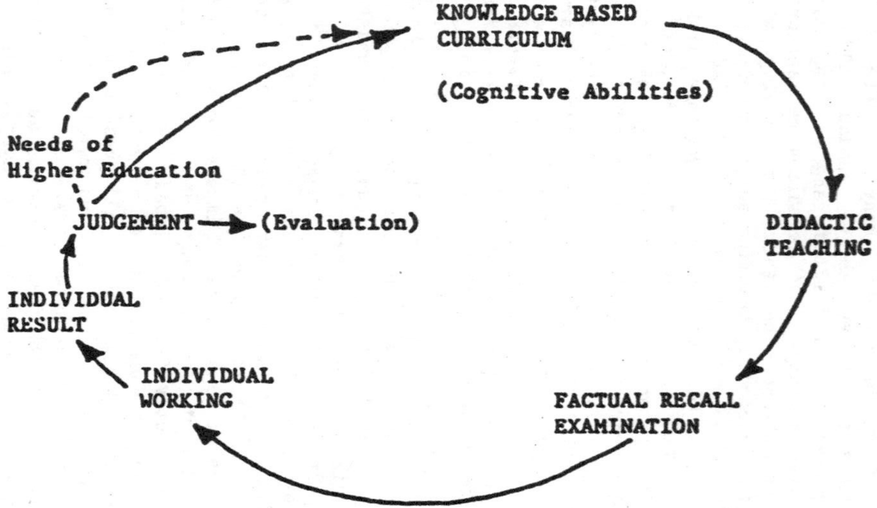

Fig 2: A Wider Curriculum Model

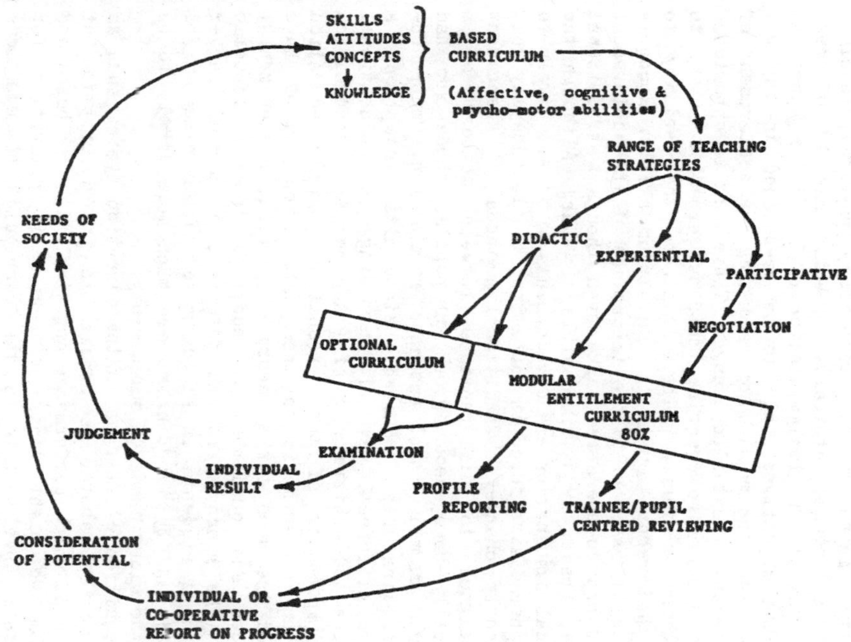

the learning is achieved through activities that groups of students co-operatively engage in, and could conceivably negotiate and plan for themselves. The curriculum framework within which this learning takes place may also change. The notion of common entitlement suggests that there will be fewer opportunities for choice if choice implies the possibility of opting out of the eight areas of experience (linguistic, mathematical, scientific, physical, social, creative, spiritual, ethical). Choice may be offered, however, through the implementation of a modular approach. If learning objectives are to be re-defined in the way suggested, then the methods of recording the achievement of those objectives must also change. There must be opportunities for students to describe their own experiences and to review their progress. There must be the facility to identify and record across-the-curriculum skills. Recognition needs to be given to the importance of the achievement of shared and co-operative tasks even though a traditional individual grade may be impossible to award. Although the traditional examination and developments of it are likely to remain a persuasive force in education, the balance may well significantly change. Traditional methods of assessment were designed to differentiate between members of a theoretically homogeneous group of pupils, those who had passed the grammar school entrance examination. Comprehensive schooling has required, since its inception, a radically different way of recording the educational experiences and achievements of young people. Recognition of the importance of the personal and social education process and an emphasis on the pastoral curriculum have identified the need for a record of personal achievements, experiences and qualities in addition to any academic record. The human worth and potential of a much larger proportion of students in statutory education needs to be recognised; and by so doing we are much more likely to be meeting the wider needs of our society.

Recognition of changes in the education system such as those described above, is crucial to the description of criteria upon which performance appraisal might be based and upon which we might design a series of priorities for professional development. As the curriculum becomes less knowledge-based and the philosophy less authoritarian, as the individual becomes more important than conformity, as creativity becomes more important than work and learning more important than teaching, then the necessity to define and develop the skills to implement the changes becomes paramount.

There is much evidence at present which suggests that the development of performance appraisal is being considered in the context of remuneration rather than professional development. Such a climate is unhelpful since it proposes a judgemental management system in which teachers will make decisions based on the prejudices and predispositions of their line manager and in which the system of appraisal will be seen to be a punitive instrument of accountability. Such a system will focus on the negative by making judgements about past performance rather than setting past performance against a series of positive, task-related goals for the future, in a continuous spiral of appraisal and development.

3 Parallels

It may be useful to view the developments currently being made against the backdrop of education as a whole. The work of a local authority inspector, while narrowed by its confinement to one LEA, is at the same time given a much wider perspective than colleagues in schools, by virtue of policy development work and its dissemination and implementation over a large number of schools.

This wider perspective has led me to the conclusion that a number of parallels exist between the work of professional development of teachers and curriculum development designed to improve the quality of learning. The school based curriculum and professional development movement exemplifies the trend and can be paralleled with the work done to develop student autonomous learning. Both are enabling the subject of the development to take control of their learning and therefore their development. Both are recognising that commitment to, and therefore investment in, any human activity is much more likely to result in a higher level of motivation. The growth of teacher teamwork enabling a higher level of personal support is paralleled by a recognition that co-operative learning within the pastoral curriculum, or indeed anywhere else in the curriculum, will similarly provide support for students. If such support and reflection on practice improves the performance of teachers why should the same not be true for students?

The closest parallel of all is between performance appraisal itself, designed to enable teachers to review their progress and to negotiate goals for the future, and records of achievement, the formative part of which has precisely the same objective for students.

These parallels add up to an acceptance of the fact that education is about personal growth and that although we artificially restrict the formal education process to a limited number of years, education does not cease when a student leaves school and neither does the process of personal growth. This holds true as much for teachers as it does for any other people. It is possible that a conscious understanding of the similarity of the experience between teacher and student might bring about a reduction of the tension in the pedagogic relationship.

4 **Performance appraisal in Nottinghamshire**

In order to consider recent developments in performance appraisal in Nottinghamshire it is necessary to be aware of the underlying assumptions. The following list is reproduced from the document '<u>Teacher Professional Appraisal as part of a Development Programme</u>' which has formed the basis of discussions about performance appraisal in Nottinghamshire.

1 That the employer has a right to know about performance in schools.

2 That teachers have a right to know what is written about them.

3 That teachers have a right to expect a programme of professional development.

4 That employers have a right to expect teachers to improve their skills.

5 That teachers should be involved in negotiating the criteria by which their performance might be judged.

6 That teachers generally wish to improve.

7 That the local authority should enable teachers to take part in the appraisal system.

8 That teachers have the right of access to skilled, informed and sensitive professional guidance and counselling.

9 That students have a right to well qualified and skilled teachers.

10 That teachers have a right to expect feedback on observed performance.

11 That teachers have a right of appeal.

12 That performance appraisal should eventually be managed in schools by school staff.

The development of this set of assumptions has taken place at the same time as the teachers' professional associations have been negotiating the terms of access to teachers' confidential files, which should be regarded as complementary to the process of climate building necessary to any such development.

The assumptions encapsulate the purposes of professional development which, in the last analysis, is about improving the quality of learning. Teachers can only improve their practice and therefore the quality of learning if they are aware of the level and consistency of their performance. The performance appraisal section of the professional development model is dependant upon guidance and counselling in order to lead to appropriate professional development activities designed to achieve the goals negotiated as a result of the appraisal. This process is illustrated in figure 3, the Professional Development Model (a conceptual map).

This spiral of activity and development may continue in one job within one institution for some time, until such time as the teacher may wish to seek significant change. In the model this significant change is called the nodal point and may lead to a number of alternatives. Amongst the alternatives are the self explanatory secondment, task specific secondment, retraining, retirement and other activities outside the teaching profession. In addition job change is an option and could include any of the following;

1 Lateral transfer.
2 Teacher exchange.
3 Redeployment.
4 Changed post or role in the same institution.
5 Additional post or role in the same institution
6 Changed post or role in a different institution
7 Same post or role in a different institution
8 Changed post or role in a different branch.

The assumption is often made that the purpose of professional development activity is promotion. In the days of an expanding education service and teaching profession, when funding was more generous and the profession more mobile, the chances of promotion were much greater. In the current circumstances the reversal of fortunes means that any explicit, or indeed implicit, promise of promotion is to offer what will be for many very conmpetent teachers a false promise. It is with these facts in mind that we must continue to offer opportunities for development, refreshment and support which will maximise job satisfaction without necessarily leading to enhanced status or higher remuneration.

No matter how restricted the opportunities become we will always have a proportion of teachers seeking a change in their circumstances through secondment, retraining or job change. It is important for teachers to approach such challenges in as professional a manner as possible in order

Fig 3: The Professional Development Model: A Conceptual Map

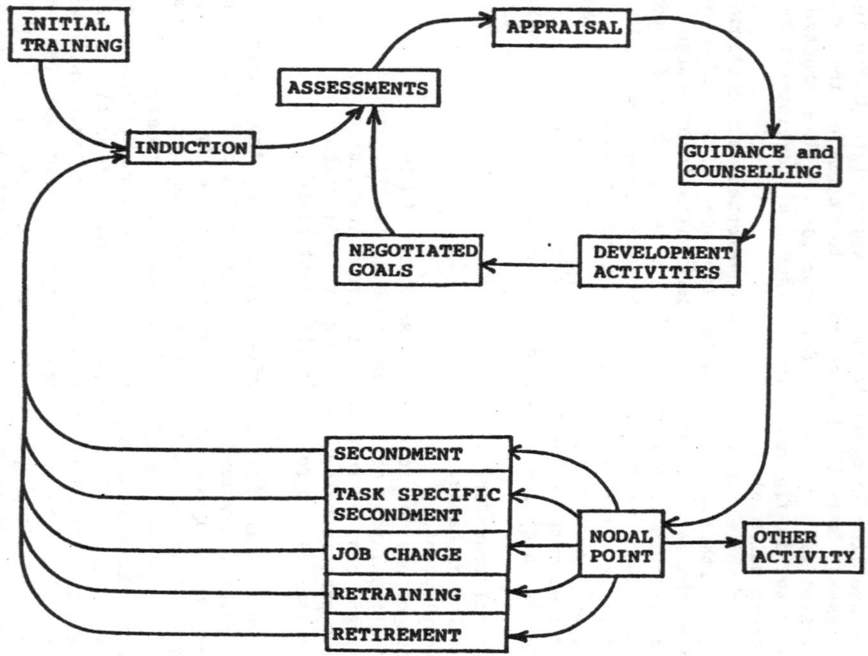

to maximise effective matching of candidate to post, and to improve the level of reality upon which applications are based.

It is possible that teachers will have a longer term view about their career. If this is the case it is desirable for them actively to prepare for developments by identifying new work and seeking opportunities to develop appropriate skills. From time to time prospective applicants will need to seek information about specific new posts in order to achieve an accurate idea of the nature of the post and the skills and attributes required. The prospective applicants will also need to have an accurate view of their own skills and to set about the process of matching as objectively as possible. It is possible that candidates may not achieve an absolute match to a job description, but may have other attributes or skills to offer. It is my view that in such circumstances the applicant should make such matters clear in the application, since there may be an opportunity for negotiation. If candidates are to have an accurate view of their own performance and general competence, there will need to be a well established system of continual performance appraisal, as represented by the upper cycle of the professional development model conceptual map.

Clearly if the business of performance appraisal is to become an established and continuous process in schools, there will need to be a series of training and introductory procedures both for the appraisors and appraisees. Theoretically, all teachers in Nottinghamshire will eventually have their performance regularly appraised and will have developed the skills to appraise their colleagues. A series of courses have begun at which the theoretical rationale is examined and the necessary skills are developed. It will take a great deal of time to develop the systems to a level of operational consistency satisfactory to the profession. As an external agency the Advisory and Inspection Service have a responsibility to model the procedures in their work. Indeed for many teachers, working with an inspector on a teacher assessment profile (REP 3 Form; Figure 4) is the first occasion on which they will have encountered the process of performance appraisal. The teacher assessment profile is an instrument which can be used in the process of working with an outside observer in order to begin to answer the question, 'How am I doing?'. The procedure may often initiate an institution-based and regular process. The example given is purely fictional and does not represent any single teacher. The comments are, however, typical of the style of remark which I make.

It is necessary for the reader to bear in mind that the use of such a document relies on human interaction, and although a degree of conformity is guaranteed by both the

Fig 4: REP 3 Form

Nottinghamshire County Council — EDUCATION DEPARTMENT — INSPECTION AND ADVISORY SERVICE

REP 3.

TEACHER/LECTURER ASSESSMENT PROFILE

Name of Teacher/Lecturer	Post Held & Subject(s) Taught	Scale	Age Range
Y	Head of P.S.E. Lifeskills, Sociology Social Studies	4	11 – 18

School/College	District	Name of Inspector	Date(s) of Assessment
X	Z	John Berridge	15.3.85. 1.4.85. 15.4.85. 25.4.85.

A: PRESENT POST & RESPONSIBILITIES

Mr. Y. is designated Head of Personal and Social Education. His functions as a Head of Department include the administration, management and organisation of the following areas of the curriculum.

1. The common core lifeskills course.
2. Careers Education including vocational guidance, work experience and a summative records system.
3. Examination courses at CSE and 'O' level in Social Studies and Sociology.
4. Liaison with Heads of Year in order to co-ordinate the ATW programme.

B: PREVIOUS EXPERIENCE

Mr. Y began his teaching career as a biologist in 1968. His probationary year was completed at school a. where he was subsequently promoted to Sc. 2 in 1973 with responsibility for devising and teaching a Mode 3 social studies course. In 1976 Mr. Y moved to a Sc. 3 post at school x where he was responsible for Lifeskills, Social Studies and careers education. In 1980 he was promoted to Sc. 4 with an additional responsibility for co-ordinating the pastoral curriculum.

Fig 4 (Continued)

C: CLASSROOM WORK Mr. Y's great strength is in the classroom. He is both liked and respected by most pupils with whom he enjoys a positive and friendly relationship. He is familiar with a wide range of teaching techniques and endeavours to plan his lessons in order to offer a number of varied tasks to stimulate and motivate his pupils. Many materials are school produced and some attempt has been made to differentiate worksheets with mixed ability classes in mind. Like many classrooms in secondary schools attention to display could improve the learning environment.
D: CURRICULUM DEVELOPMENT WORK Mr. Y takes an active part in the school curriculum and professional development committee where he is considered to be an innovative and persuasive force. He has also been involved in a number of county wide curriculum development initiatives including Health Education and Careers Education. Mr. Y has published a book on political education and he is justifiably proud of his curriculum development work in the field of education for political literacy.
E. MANAGEMENT & ORGANISATIONAL SKILLS Mr. Y operates a well organised department which is functioning positively and developing continually. The management of a department largely comprising of staff who also have other subject responsibilities is not an easy task, but Mr. Y has skillfully enabled a departmental identity to develop which has enhanced the motivation and job satisfaction of his colleagues.
F. LEADERSHIP QUALITIES Mr. Y is acknowledged as an 'expert' in his field and as such is exercising a very necessary leadership function both for the members of his department and other staff. His position and influence are widely recognised although some colleagues regard him as too innovatory and are anxious about some of his ideas.

Fig 4 (Continued)
REP 3. cont.

Name of Teacher/Lecturer________________

TEACHER/LECTURER ASSESSMENT PROFILE

G: PROFESSIONAL RELATIONSHIPS

Although Mr. Y has a pleasant personality and in general relates well to his colleagues, he readily admits that his ability to forcefully defend his views has not always resulted in the kind of compromises which are sometimes necessary. This has occasionally resulted in tension between himself and other Heads of Department. Mr. Y asked me to discuss his work with members of his own department and they loyally describe him in glowing terms.

H: PROFESSIONAL DEVELOPMENT

Mr. Y has been very willing to take part in in-service courses throughout his career, including those activities which have contributed to his general professional development. Of particular relevance is a middle management course and a course concerned with pre-vocational education. MR. Y is currently studying for an O.U. degree but is concerned about the time entailed. He is a part of the LEA A.T.W. team and has contributed to a number of courses and in-service events.

I: OTHER SKILLS & INTERESTS

Mr. Y is a keen form tutor, committed to the development of A.T.W. which he sees to be linked to the P.S.E. process. He has contributed to outdoor pursuits and is keenly interested in residential visits which he sees as exercising a powerful influence on the development of pupils. Mr. Y is an active member of the P.T.A. and is well known and highly regarded in the community. He drives the school minibus and takes part in orienteering and canoeing.

Fig 4 (Continued)

SUMMARY

Mr. Y is a committed and enthusiastic teacher who carries out his duties as a Head of Department in an exemplary fashion. His positive contributions to professional and curriculum development have enabled both the P.S.E. department and the school to make significant progress. His sensitive approach to children has not always been matched by a similar relationship with colleagues, which indicates a need to consider the relationship skills necessary for senior management.

HAVE THE CONTENTS OF THIS ASSESSMENT BEEN FULLY DISCUSSED WITH THE TEACHER/LECTURER?

TEACHER/LECTURER COMMENTS:

I am satisfied with this very fair assessment of my work. Having been in my present post for 5 years, I have been actively considering the next stage in my career. This appraisal has given me an opportunity to discuss the matter. I recognise that my failure to fully develop A.T.W. might in part be a consequence of an overbearing entusiasm and I am keen to improve my practise. I would welcome an opportunity to discuss the matter further.

Report also discussed with ______________ Post held Head Teacher

Signature ______________ (Inspector)

Date 25.4.85.

NOT VALID AFTER 2 YEARS i.e.

REP. 3 2

NCC EDU 1506 7 83

established orthodoxy and the instruments themselves, there will be significant differences in the application of the system according to the individual inspector involved. The following is an account of the modus operandi which I have evolved and which is subject to continual change as a result of experience.

I preface any performance appraisal work with teachers by a negotiation session at which the performance appraisal process and the purposes and uses of the documentation are explained. It is also agreed how the assessment procedures shall be carried out and where we shall seek evidence. Generally there are a number of sources of both factual information and judgements about the work of the appraisee. First of all the appraisee themselves will have a clearer idea than anyone else about their career development so far, and I always invite them to supply a written account, which is called a 'milestones' document, describing their view of the key developments which their career has undergone. They may also include a personal judgemental view of their performance in any of the areas indicated by the REP 3 form. Such a perspective is very useful when it comes to a consideration of the view of colleagues about their performance and may illuminate the reality of the appraisees' judgement.

I also invite the appraisee to nominate colleagues from whom I will be able to gain informed judgements about agreed aspects of the performance of the appraisee. I usually consult with at least two or more normally three such people. Experience reveals that a line manager and the headteacher should be amongst those consulted. As a result of such discussions it may be revealed that there are other people who have a key opinion or information, and after discussion with the appraisee they too will be consulted. It is possible that the appraisee may not enjoy a positive relationship with, for example, the headteacher, and may not be happy about such a consultation. Clearly if such an occasion arises then a series of questions will be raised. It is possible for a negative relationship to be a reflection on the performance of the headteacher and it may be the headteacher's judgement which is irrational. It is my judgement, however, that on balance it is better to include the headteacher in the appraisal process and I would so advise the appraisee. Arrangements are made, over a period of time, to visit the school and speak with the colleagues concerned. The results of such interviews are recorded carefully and during the interview statements are summarised, clarified and a form of words agreed.

One of the sections of the REP 3 form refers to classroom practice, and in addition to the views of colleagues it is appropriate to observe a number of lessons which represent the variety of work undertaken by the appraisee. Once again a discussion with the appraisee leads to an agreement about which work will be observed. A REP 2 form is used for this purpose and a copy completed about a fictional teacher is included below (Figure 5). The REP 2 form illustrated is currently under review and as a result of the experience gained from two years use. It is likely that the criteria, which may be amended, will be much more loosely tied to the comments made and will serve as an aide-memoire only. At the end of each observation, or where one observation follows another closely, at the end of the session, I give the document to the teacher to read. At this stage the prose and syntax may not be in a finished form but the main observations and conclusions should be clear. A discussion follows and the teacher's comments are recorded on the form. There may be a need for incorrect facts to be corrected or there may be a disagreement about value judgements which may need discussion in order to reach an agreed form of wording. It is possible that, at the end of the ensuing discussion, my professional judgement is unchanged and the teacher disagrees with my observations. In such an eventuality the disagreement would be recorded, if necessary, on a continuation sheet (REP 5). The reader should note that it is possible for the REP 2 form to be used for routine classroom observation purposes and not in conjunction with a REP 3. In any event, a copy of the document, which is self carboning in triplicate, remains with the writer, another is sent to the divisional inspector and yet a third goes into the personal file of the appraisee. I also photocopy the original and give this fourth copy to the appraisee to keep. It will be noted that the document is valid for two years only and theoretically therefore should be updated after two years have elapsed.

To summmarise then, the following evidence will have been accumulated as a result of the procedures described above.

1 Written evidence from the appraisee in the form of a milestones document

2 Evidence from the discussions with colleagues of the appraisee.

3 Evidence from the REP 2 classroom observation document.

4 Evidence from discussions with the appraisee him/herself.

It is at this stage that I assemble the information I have into a first draft of a final form of words on the REP 3 document. I also begin to think about the implications for the future development and performance of the appraisee. At a final meeting with the appraisee, which

Fig 5: REP 2 Form

Nottinghamshire
County Council

REP.2.

EDUCATION DEPARTMENT

REPORT ON A CLASSROOM VISIT

INSPECTION AND ADVISORY SERVICE

DISTRICT	SCHOOL/COLLEGE	NAME OF TEACHER/LECTURER	POST HELD
Z	X	Y	Head of P.S.E. Sc. 4
CLASS/GROUP	**AGE OF PUPILS/STUDENTS**	**NUMBER OF PUPILS/STUDENTS**	**SUBJECT TAUGHT**
3a	15/16 yrs.	25	Lifeskills
DATE OF VISIT	**DURATION OF VISIT**	**NAME OF INSPECTOR**	
1.4.85.	60 mins.	John Berridge	

REASON FOR VISIT:

Lesson observation related to REP 3.

LESSON CONTENT

1. Activities to explore feelings and understandings about trust.
2. Discussion in small groups. 3. Role play.

	CLASSROOM PRACTICE	COMMENT/OBSERVATION
1	Preparation	Thorough preparation and appropriate lesson notes indicating activities and timing.
2	Knowledge of Content	N/A.Processes fully understood.
3	Use of Resources	Information and worksheets school produced-Graphics professionally finished.
4	Organisation of Work	Equipment and resources fully organised in a filing system which facilitates easy retrieval for members of the dept.
5	Classroom Management and Environment	Classroom furniture arranged in an appropriate manner for the tasks. -
6	Relationships with pupils/students	Positive and friendly relationships with most pupils.
7	Pupil Participation	All tasks involve participation of all pupils. Not all the pupils chose to be fully involved in all activities.

Fig 5 (Continued)

8	Questioning Techniques	Occasional use of closed questions.
9	Control/Discipline	No problems observed.
10	Assessment of pupils' work	No individual pupil marks awarded. Lesson evaluated by discussion with pupils.
11	Lesson content and task match	The process and activities provided the content.

GENERAL REMARKS & ADVICE GIVEN:

1. The practical trust exercises may well be taken more seriously if an appropriate climate is created. Perhaps the blind walk could be a role play for example.
2. The warming up and relaxing exercises worked well. The teacher receiving the pupils from you should be getting them 'in a reasonable frame of mind'.

HAVE THE CONTENTS OF THIS REPORT BEEN FULLY DISCUSSED WITH THE TEACHER/LECTURER? Yes

TEACHER/LECTURER COMMENTS: Not enough time left for small group discussion. Timings need to be adjusted.

Report also discussed with – Post Held

Signature: John Berridge (Inspector)

Date. 1.4.85. NOT VALID AFTER 2 YEARS i.e. ....

NCC EDU 1138 7 83

might be as long as three months after the first negotiating meeting, a copy of this first draft is revealed to the appraisee and a discussion follows about its factual accuracy, my interpretation and value judgements, and its implications. The process, although usually more thorough, is much the same as that of the REP 2 form. In addition to the document itself, agreement is reached about an appropriate set of objectives for the next year or so and a matching set of tasks defined in order to achieve those objectives. As with the REP 2 form, final draft copies are kept by myself and distributed to the divisional inspector and the personal file of the appraisee. Disagreements are resolved by discussion and negotiation or remain unresolved and are thus recorded. It is usual to discuss the final report and objectives document with the headteacher for whom there may be some responsibility to provide the necessary support to achieve the objectives.

It is possible that there are implications for the work of a number of colleagues within a department and the performance appraisal of one member of the department may lead to activities which are shared by all in order to achieve a general professional development. Where a department is engaged in professional development activities of this nature it is possible that school-based action research may be instituted which will enable members of the department to reflect individually or as a group on the achievement of operational goals. In this way shared performance appraisal and therefore professional development may be established. A common model for school based action research is reproduced in Figure 6, and although it is not the purpose of this chapter to dwell on these matters it is worth recognising that they may have an important part to play in institutional performance appraisal.

Teachers seeking to change their circumstances by application for secondment or retraining or job change are likely to undergo an interview if the initial application procedure is successful. Although it is not the purpose of this chapter to deal in detail with interview technique, interview debriefing does have an important part to play in the guidance and counselling a teacher has a right to expect. I, myself, am unhappy about the function of the interview as a performance art and I feel that there is much that local authorities might do to improve the effectiveness of the techniques they employ to identify the right person for the right job. Notwithstanding the selection techniques, an interview debriefing is a useful feedback for both successful and unsuccessful candidates. I always offer feedback and am surprised that not all candidates take up the offer. When candidates are from Nottinghamshire it is possible for the interview debrief to lead to a fuller performance appraisal procedure.

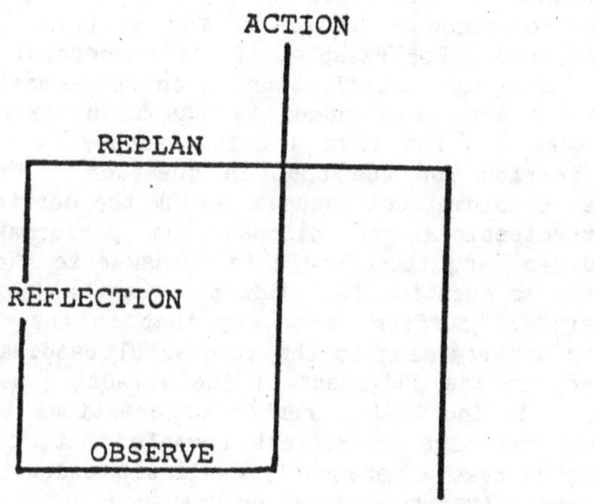

Fig 6: The Action-Research Spiral

Interview debriefs may raise a number of problems, especially in the case of the unsuccessful candidate. I usually ask candidates to spend at least 24 hours reflecting on the interview before meeting them to discuss the matter. I will have taken quite full notes during the interview which will describe the interview performance and the impressions it has given, the level of understanding of the issues raised, and other pertinent factors. It is my view that if a candidate is shortlisted and interviewed for a post then the candidate should be able to presume that the factual evidence revealed in the written application is satisfactory. For example, if the successful candidate has higher academic qualifications than unsuccessful candidates it should not be presumed by the unsuccessful candidates that they did not have a satsisfactory level of academic qualification for the post in question. This raises a further problematical issue. During the debrief I regard it as unprofessional to discuss the performance of other candidates, and therefore a full answer to the unsuccessful candidate's question 'Why didn't I get the job?' might prove impossible. Suffice it to say that on the day there were factors appertaining to the successful candidate which made him/her, in the judgement of the selection panel, a better choice. I find that a number of questions to a candidate who has had time to reflect reveals that, in most cases, candidates have a reasonably realistic understanding of why they were either successful or unsuccessful.

The most important part of the debriefing tends to be concerned with the longer term and may therefore consider assessment and appraisal as well as professional development opportunities and experience gaining strategies. In short the debriefing often develops into a vocational counselling session and it is possible that a plan of action may be agreed in which there will be a clearly communicated programme of development. After interviewing, a REP 4 report on an interview is completed and an example containing fictional candidates is reproduced in Figure 7. A copy of this form is kept by the writer, a copy goes to the divisional inspector and copies are placed in the candidate's files.

At the end of a performance appraisal cycle with a teacher I invite the teacher to inform my practice. Although at present there is no appropriate report form it is envisaged that one will be developed. I base this procedure on the assumption that teachers have a right of access to skilled, informed and sensitive professional guidance and counselling. Unless I receive feedback on my performance in this matter it will be very difficult for me to improve my practice. If performance appraisal systems are to be institutionalised it is important that the two way dialogue is modelled by those who seek to disseminate the practice.

Otherwise I feel that it is likely that a hierarchical judgemental system will develop in schools which will be threatening, unpopular and in the long term counter productive.

5 <u>The helping relationship</u>

The operation of the system places the appraisor in a potentially difficult relationship with the appraisee and it is most important to preserve the integrity of that relationship if the system is not to be thrown into disrepute. In this final section of the chapter I will consider the nature of the relationship, identifying appropriate skills and examining potential problems.

Based on the assumption that teachers have a right of access to skilled, informed and sensitive professional guidance and counselling, it is necessary to examine the nature of this counselling relationship. In this context I am using it to describe a helping relationship in consultation with a teacher and it should not be taken to imply the kind of complex psycho-therapeutic work undertaken by fully trained professional counsellors. There are many parallels between the kind of helping relationship which teachers might find themselves involved in with students and the relationship between two adults in a performance appraisal situation. Douglas Hamblin (1974) maintains that learning and learning processes are at the heart of counselling and that counselling is therefore a proper activity for teachers, provided they allow the client to learn rather than instructing them rigidly. Clearly such a view suggests that the skills associated with counselling might have a place in an activity which is participatory and developmental. Leona Tyler (1961) sees the purpose of counselling as facilitating wise choices, of the sort on which a person's later development depends, and Blocher (1966) maintains that the counselling task must ensure that each individual has an opportunity to master the tasks that will equip him with the coping behaviours necessary for handling those roles and relationships that are involved in his next stage of development.

The relationship between the counsellor and the client is seen to be of fundamental importance and it is generally agreed that the goals for the client are those of;

self understanding
self awareness
self acceptance and
self determination

Fig 7: REP 4 Form

REP.4

REPORT ON AN INTERVIEW

DISTRICT	SCHOOL/COLLEGE	ADVERTISED POST (incl. Scale)
Z	X	2nd in P.S.E. Dept. responsible for vocational guidance Sc. 3.
DATE OF INTERVIEW	**NAME OF INSPECTOR**	**SUCCESSFUL CANDIDATE**
1.4.85.	John Berridge	Mrs. D.

NAME: Ms. A. **DISTRICT:** **SCHOOL/COLLEGE:** W **SCALE:** 1

Ms. A has relatively little experience in personal and social education. She failed to persuade the panel that the expectations raised by her letter of application would be realised. Ms. A did not take advantage of the opportunity and her very relaxed interview technique conveyed the impression that her application was not serious.

Have the interview and report been discussed with the candidate?
Comments: A debrief has been offered but not yet accepted.

NAME: Mr. B **DISTRICT:** **SCHOOL/COLLEGE:** Y **SCALE:** 2

Mr. B withdrew before the formal interviews. He indicated that the school did not match his expectations.

Have the interview and report been discussed with the candidate?
Comments: A debrief discussion has been arranged.

Fig 7 (Continued)

NAME: Mr. C **DISTRICT:** **SCHOOL/COLLEGE:** X **SCALE:** 2

Mr. C's graphic descriptions of his industrial experience and his obvious commitment and enthusiasm for careers education made him a potentially successful candidate for this post. However, Mr. C. failed to convince the panel that he had a wider understanding of the work of a P.S.E. department or that he had much experience of individual guidance work.

Have the interview and report been discussed with the candidate? Yes

Comments: An immediate debriefing was requested. Mr. C understood the reasons for his failure on this occasion and was not surprised. He has requested a further discussion about opportunities to gain experience. A REP 3 might be appropriate.

NAME: Mrs D **DISTRICT:** **SCHOOL/COLLEGE:** Z **SCALE:** 2

Mrs. D. has a persuasive understanding of the Personal and Social Education process. Her lively but sensitive approach to vocational counselling and her well sustained view about education for unemployment convinced the panel that she could effectively manage even the most controversial aspects of her work. A pleasant personality, confident and telling questions and an enthusiastic head of department enabled this candidate to be offered the post.

Have the interview and report been discussed with the candidate?

Comments: A debrief discussion has been arranged in order to offer support.

Signature .... *Inspector*

Date: ....

NOT VALID AFTER 2 YEARS

i.e. ....

The counsellor and counselling do not monopolise positive developments. Many other relationships may well enable development to take place. The fact that many relationships do not contain the following elements may account for their negative nature or brevity.

a Respect or acceptance of the client is important. The client should be accepted as a unique individual. There should be an understanding that individuals may differ from one another without derogatory value judgements. Respect may also be demonstrated by punctuality, unwillingness to be distracted, familiarity with the client as a person and with his or her case.

b Empathy or sincerity is communicated by the counsellor who 'feels' the situation for the client and feeds back a valid and reliable picture of what he or she is thinking and feeling. Empathy needs to be distinguished from sympathy and pity, which is a self-centred and often rather negative emotion. The counsellor should try to understand how the client feels and communicate that understanding without subjective qualifications.

c Genuineness is communicated by the counsellor who manages to remain himself. If the teacher has chosen a particular colleague to undertake a performance appraisal, then this has been done knowingly and that teacher does not expect the colleague to adopt a new and different personality because of the changed circumstances of the relationship.

d Warmth is communicated by the counsellor who genuinely cares and believes in the ability of the client to be able to manage the results of the performance appraisal.

e Confidentiality is an important element in the system. Under normal circumstances the teacher seeking performance appraisal has a right to expect that information will only be communicated to those colleagues whom the teacher nominates, and those within the agreed system. (In the case of Nottinghamshire the Divisional Inspector.) There may be rare occasions when performance appraisal reveals a situation which is prejudicial to the health, safety, well being or education of students, in which case a higher loyalty will prevail, and after consultation, appropriate officers informed.

f Trust is clearly linked with the notion of confidentiality and a counsellor who is not trustworthy will soon have a bad reputation amongst colleagues who will consequently cease to refer themselves for performance appraisal.

In addition to the counselling skills which it is appropriate for the appraisor to deploy during consultations with the appraisee, the appraisor will also need the following skills:

a Research skills in order to make available the most comprehensive description possible.

b Reporting skills in order to describe the situation accurately and effectively

c Contracting skills in order to negotiate with the appraisee with regard to the conduct of the performance appraisal.

d Data handling skills in order to analyse and interpret the information collected and observed.

e Self monitoring skills in order to recognise bias and prejudice both in oneself and others making contributions to the evidence.

There is a need for an understanding of the influence of bias and prejudice within the system. Making assessments or judgements about people, systems or situations is a natural and continual human activity. Such judgements pre-suppose a position from which those judgements are being made and such a personal position may be described as a values construct. The values concerned are the criteria by which we make judgements and each value is a complex concept about worthwhileness and as such, functions as a standard.

THE NATURE OF THE JUDGEMENTAL SYSTEM

JUDGEMENTS	A JUDGEMENT
<--------------------	------------------->
Opinion or attitude modification	Opinion or attitude reinforcement
¦	¦
Appraisal and appraisal with the appraisee	Patronage or discrimination for/against
¦	¦
Obective evidence and information	Pre-judgement (prejudice)

I see the judgemental system to be a continuum at one end of which is a firmly held judgement reinforced by preconceived opinions or attitudes giving rise to patronage and discrimination based on prejudice borne of ignorance. At the other end of the continuum are a series of judgements open to modification, used to inform and based on objective evidence.

Clearly if a performance appraisal system is to work effectively then the appraisor has a duty to inform his judgements to the extent that they are open to modification and not prejudiced by pre-conceived notions.

Although performance appraisal may well be challenging for the appraisee it is important that the appraisor provides the support necessary to maintain a progressive and positive relationship as is illustrated by the diagram below.

Although both positions on the high support side of the model are valid, most is gained by a level of support which is matched by a high level of challenge. The positions on the low support side of the model are never acceptable in my opinion, but the construct may go some way to describe the reasons for the current state of the profession. In general terms it is the person who should be supported but the issue which should be challenged.

SUPPORT AND CHALLENGE MODEL

HIGH CHALLENGE

HIGH SUPPORT	LOW SUPPORT
Aim for here	Hostile and aggressive, feels threatened
Contact making point but little achieved	Apathy, low

LOW CHALLENGE

I am indebted to Chris Saville, formerly Principal Inspector of Nottinghamshire, for access to the following model which describes the process of appraisal on a framework which recognises the background against which the process can take place. In this context the word APPRAISAL, meaning 'to inform', will be more appropriate. Clearly it is the intention of the policy in Nottinghamshire to operate an enabling process which is positively diagnostic and which allows for consultation and negotiation to take place. It is, however, recognised that many teachers will see the process as one of control and it is to be hoped that an appropriate programme of sensitively handled in-service education can inform and alleviate fears.

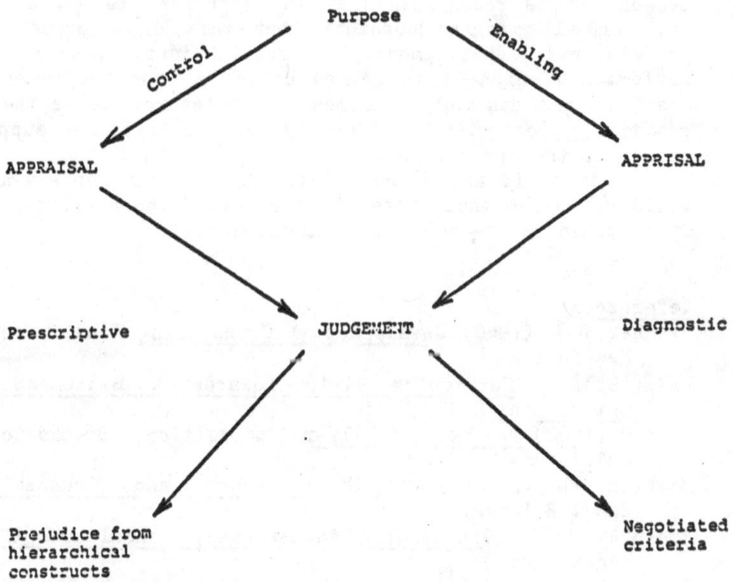

6 Conclusion

There is no doubt in my mind that both the systems and the instruments in Nottinghamshire will continue to respond to changing circumstances and changing needs. No pretence is being made that the state of the art of performance appraisal is at a high level yet. I feel we can be justifiably proud of the fact that we have begun to consider the issues and have responded to the challenges presented in recent years by successive calls for accountability and evaluation.

The systems which have been introduced do not bypass teachers, they recognise that teachers have both rights and responsibilities and the assumptions take account of those factors. Criticisms of more open styles of appraisal have suggested that such systems lack rigour and that judgements are blunted by the fear that the appraisee may have recourse to action should s/he disagree with the appraisal. It seems to me that the consultancy model adopted to manage the appraisal system could theoretically provide opportunities for difficult or critical issues to be discussed openly because it is recognised that the appraisal is not a once and for all single judgement, but part of a process of professional development. Thus, identification of performance which it is agreed could be improved is not a negative and damning indictment of a teacher but rather a positive opportunity to identify and receive the support necessary to improve.

I doubt if any teacher, adviser or inspector anywhere would not agree that there are aspects of their performance which could not be subject to improvement.

References

Blocher D H (1966) *Developmental Counselling* Ronald Press, New York

DES (1983) *Curriculum 11-16 Towards a Statement of Entitlement* HMSO, London

Egan G (1982) *The Skilled Helper* (2nd edition), Brooks/Cole, California

Hamblin D H (1974) *The Teacher and Counselling* Basil Blackwell

Jones A (1977) *Counselling Adolescents, School and After* Kogan Page

Nottinghamshire County Council Education Department (1984) *Teacher Professional Appraisal as part of a Development Programme* Advisory and Inspection Service, Nottingham

Tyler L (1961) *The Work of the Counsellor* Appleton Century Crofts

Chapter 7

TARGET SETTING AND APPRAISAL AT WARDEN PARK SCHOOL

David M Trethowan

Any plan for promoting staff development must contain a system for the appraisal of need so that any setting of targets may be based on sets of agreed personal, departmental and institutional priorities. In this chapter the author describes in depth his own experiences over a number of years in introducing and managing a system of target setting and appraisal which is based on the key principles of respect for the individual and participative management described in previous chapters. The author pays tribute to the help received from industry, and the chapter provides those who are seeking to set up systems of appraisal and target setting within their staff development policies with much practical help and detailed advice.

How the system began

We did not set out in 1973 to build a school management system at Warden Park. We developed those activities which were helpful and effective, and dropped those which were not. The result is a system called Target Setting and Appraisal.

The origins of Warden Park's target setting system may be represented as three strands of a common root. Firstly, there was the need to provide guidance to the middle management of the newly created school. Secondly the need to allow every member of staff to make a contribution to the school's development and to give feedback on our progress, and thirdly, my own personal commitment to a participative style of management in the long term.

Warden Park School is an 11-16 comprehensive school of 1450 pupils at Cuckfield in Sussex which became comprehensive from a 700 pupil secondary modern school twelve years ago. On taking up the Headship in April, 1973, in a document presented to the local education authority, I wrote "The greatest need at this school is for a pastoral care system, for even at present it has grown too large to leave to chance the exercising of the care and concern for the whole child". Consequently, by September, 1973 we had appointed pastoral care heads and set up a pastoral care system where none had existed previously.

In the academic field, new heads of department were appointed to the Art, English, History, Languages, Mathematics, Music, Boys Physical Education, Remedial, Religious Education and Science departments. Of all these new departmental heads, only four had previous experience as head of department. The average age of the remainder was 27, with their average experience on appointment being less than five years.

As a new head, therefore, in the academic and pastoral fields, I was faced with an inexperienced, if capable, group of middle management. The disadvantage of inexperience in both these fields, however, could, I felt, be offset by constant encouragement, support and guidance from me. That "middle management guidance system" was one root of the present target setting system used at Warden Park School.

The second root springs from my early discussion with staff. Although I wanted rapid change in the school in April, 1973, with a comprehensive intake due in September, 1974, the first step was to talk in a personal, private interview to every member of staff - what were their hopes, fears and frustrations; what was good about the school of which I had so recently become head, and equally important, what was wrong with it. Once I had been personally and professionally accepted by the staff, the practice of personal, private interview became one of the most fruitful sources of feedback and suggestion in the development of Warden Park as a comprehensive school. This, then, formed the second part of the root of our target setting system at Warden Park School.

The third and final root of the origin of the Warden Park target setting system comes from the need to manage a school in a participative style rather than a "tell" style. As I wrote in a recent *Times Educational Supplement* article, on arrival at the school:

> I felt that I knew what I was doing in every facet of comprehensive re-organisation: with hindsight I see this as the confidence of inexperience. I personally checked all record books, dictated how the timetable was to be written, watched every teacher in the school in action as often as possible, usually daily. In every aspect of school life I was willing to take my decision, back it with action and make it work. I felt that I could raise, single-handed if necessary, the tone and discipline of the school with the staff being invited to help if they felt they wanted.

But this is not the way to run a school in the long term. It was clearly going to be necessary to coach and develop staff to be able to manage whole aspects of the school. It was never my intention to advocate dictatorship.

> An insensitive, inflexible, mechanical style of management which persistently leads to teaching staff being told what to do and how to do it alienates the best and diminishes the stature of all.
>
> Participating, sharing, discussing, delegating, are pursuits which lead to personal and professional growth.

Clearly to achieve this style of leadership required frequent interviews with teachers, a record of what we had agreed to undertake and a review to assess our achievements.

The early development of the original Warden Park target setting system

The basis of the Warden Park target setting system has always been a one-to-one meeting for the purpose of task guidance and of staff development. The meetings have always been pre-planned, personal, private and are conducted in a non-threatening atmosphere, though that is not to say that the meetings cannot be a rigorous examination of past performance. They began as annual meetings when I met each member of staff, developing techniques and styles of discussion which suited each of the staff and encouraged them to relax and speak frankly about their work. There was no fixed interview format. Some teachers seemed happiest with a formal interview as we sat opposite each other with a desk between; others appeared to prefer us to be seated at a coffee table, on low armchairs. I usually offered people the choice as they entered my room.

Interviews were timetabled by my secretary and could take place in "free" periods, or after school, or during pupil holiday periods such as the half-term break. The interview almost invariably fitted the time of the 40 minute teaching period used at Warden Park, though it was by no means rare for a continuation period to be arranged to complete the interview. Such "two-stage" interviews most often grew out of the need for the teacher to prepare further material, to investigate a matter raised, or to consider a point at length. The least satisfactory interview timings were those which ideally would have lasted for 50 minutes and not the scheduled 40 minutes. What does the interviewer do? Rush the last 20 minutes into ten? Close the interview with obviously only a few minutes and meet again next week? My advice to anyone planning these interviews is to be generous with the time allocated to the original interview. Allow ample time to research performance evidence in the weeks before the interview. Allow 20 minutes beforehand to focus one's thoughts, allow about 40 minutes for the interview and allow about 30 minutes for follow-up or making notes while the detail of the interview remains fresh. This will form the basis of an agreed written record of the interview. Time may still be needed to take follow-up action.

Staff preparation document

Within a year of the foundation of the practice of interviewing every member of the academic staff, I had found it useful to design a staff preparation document. Impressive as it may sound it really is nothing more than a series of questions relating to personal, departmental, pastoral and school performance to which staff are invited to reply. The questions formed the basis of the first part of the interview, and the teacher either had no comment to make or wrote in a brief reply and then discussed the matter at interview if he or she so wished. Initiative was not entirely with the teacher. The interviewer too, could direct discussion to one of the topics or to its written reply. Modesty, forgetfulness or merely wishful thinking might lead to a teacher overlooking a topic which really should be talked through. It is up to the Head to see that such matter is raised.

ORIGINAL FORM OF THE WARDEN PARK 'STAFF PREPARATION DOCUMENT'

Name ....

Review of the past year

The positive aspects of the past 12 months:

1 What kind of work experiences have given you the greatest satisfaction over the past year?

---

2 Have any classes or pupils been particularly rewarding?

---

3 Has anyone in particular on the staff been of special help this year?

---

4 Which forms of training or courses or further education have you undertaken this year? (Remember to consider departmental training within your department or house as well as external courses.)

The negative aspects of the past 12 months:

1 What do you dislike doing that you must do in your present job?

---

2 Have any tasks been especially difficult this year?

---

3 Have any classes or pupils not been satisfactorily dealt with

---

4 Which of your skills and talents are most under-used?

---

5 What aspects need strengthening of your technical competence, managerial competence, personal relationships, etc

---

6 Would you wish to attend courses on these? Or how else do you propose to gain the necessary experience and improvement.

The School

1 Do you have any positive comments to make about the School?

---

2 Do you have any suggestions for improving the School?

Any other points you wish to discuss:

That document has changed little over the years. I believe it is well that it should not, for it is the constancy of certain replies which causes more concern, most especially those which indicate stagnating, personal development.

Sharing the responsibility with middle managers in school

For seven years between 1973-1980, in a growing school in which staff numbers doubled, I personally conducted all the interviewing of staff. This was clearly the greatest weakness, having the scheme depend upon one person, and yet in some ways that was its greatest strength as well. One person set the tone for the scheme, one person developed its practices and one person co-ordinated the individual and team targets which resulted from the interviews. This latter function, the co-ordination of targets, became increasingly complex as the school grew in staff numbers. In theory it was easy to design a sequence of interviews in which one level of target setting flowed from another: school targets first, then departmental and pastoral targets, then individual targets. But target setting is a dynamic process: the departmental target set in one month may have required modification by the time I met a particular member of that department two months later. Should I re-interview the Head of Department or should I allow his or her departmental colleague to set a target which appeared not to be in accordance with where the department was heading. If I accepted the targets, might that cause conflict with the teacher's head of department? The minimum number of interviews required of me was, therefore, eighty per year: with re-interviews, checks, clarification, interim-feedback etc this could almost double in number. Four interviews a week for a 40 week school year may seem quite a task, but it could never be planned in that way. The whole range of targets, school, team or individual, needed to take place at one planning period, with preferably the whole of an academic year to run in which to achieve those targets. The target setting season clearly had to be at the tail end of one academic year, ready for the next. It was this gradual condensing of the period in which targets were set which finally decided me to have heads of department interviewing and setting targets with their own team.

Industrial influence on the system

The best form of learning is Action Learning: learning by seeing and doing. The Target Setting system at Warden Park has greatly benefited from contact with firms which I believe to be outstanding in their staff management practices. I found help to be unstintingly given by all of the firms I chose, but clearly, since their organisational styles were different, the contribution requested from each was not the same. The most positive, practical, professional help came from IBM, both from its Management Development team in Sussex and from managers at the sharper end of the business in sales. The contribution to the professional development of myself and my school which I owe to IBM is enormous. The hallmark of quality was on all they undertook with Warden Park.

Other outstanding firms made their contribution mainly through helping us to acquire the skills associated with Target Setting and Appraisal. Marks & Spencer and Shell proved especially useful in this field. Individual colleagues at American Express and Visionhire added further skills.

These firms allowed my staff and I to join their courses, discussed issues with my staff, and designed special training days for us all. Finally, they led units on my courses for other heads, helping me to acquire and develop the essential training skills needed before a practice such as Target Setting and Appraisal could be successfully introduced. Indirectly, through the courses I led, many other heads and deputies have reaped the benefit of this industrial contribution to educational philosophy and training. The only, if modest, way in which I have been able to repay the firms to whom I owe so much is to teach on some of their own experienced manager courses.

Industrial techniques had to be adapted to school ethos and practice. The annual financial incentive given to a Grade A performer in a firm was not available as an incentive to my staff. Also, setting criteria for the successful completion of a target is not easy in education. Finding a line of accountability in schools presents another problem. But with help, advice, and discussion these problems have been resolved.

I must pay particular tribute to Education for Industrial Society which has been a constant source of encouragement, from outside the school system. Warden Park now tries to live out in practice what is preached and taught by the Society.

Developing and controlling the internal school organisation

The years of target setting interviews had built up amongst heads of department and their staffs a depth of expertise and common expectation and so the switch to departmental target setting was not as traumatic as I had expected. Many departmental heads welcomed the opportunity to conduct these sessions. It strengthened the team.

To ensure parity of standards between heads of department a "Basic Task Checklist" was prepared. Its purpose was to remind the departmental head and the teacher of areas which the teacher might need to be encouraged or developed or in which the teacher should be assured that he or she was performing well. A three week tour of U.S. schools in 1978 helped me to avoid some of the dangers of "checklist" appraisal as practised in many schools on the U.S. Eastern seaboard. That checklist in outline is given to all heads of department for all their staff. The agreement between Head of Department and teacher to discuss targets is confirmation that the checklist items are being covered well. If, for example, classroom management or marking were below an acceptable standard, then these areas would immediately become targets without any others being added. Any such cases would be discussed by the teacher and head of department with me only if there were any doubts, objections or even reservations from either party, thus reducing the headteacher involvement at the initial target setting stage to a minimum number of referred cases.

The greatest advantage, from my point of view, was having targets set by those with greater expertise in what the department needed, who could guide and direct more closely the targets of the staff and who by their daily contact could encourage, counsel and help. The worst instance I can recall of a failure in the early target setting system, where I had acquiesced in the resurrection of a target which the departmental head had spent the previous term trying to bury without trace, was now never to be repeated. Departmental heads were now to agree the targets of their own staffs themselves.

How was the school co-ordination to be maintained? That task fell and still falls to me as head. I set annual targets with departmental heads, review the previous year's performance, discuss their identified problems in staffing, syllabus design, accommodation and finance. I undertake to help to remove as many as possible of the identified problems and to meet as many as possible of the identified needs.

One other task I reserve to myself, although the system does not require it as an essential feature. I continue to meet annually at a personal, private interview, every member of staff. It forms a type of "leap-frog" or "grandfather" interview, which checks on targets and progress towards targets, and forms an early-in-the-year check that targets have been fairly set, that they still seem achievable, and that reasonable progress is being made towards them. It is suited best to an October to November period and at present I have found few disadvantages in that as the ideal period.

Senior staff

Throughout the whole period of headship one of the most personally and professionally rewarding practices has been the target setting practice with my own "top-management" team. Each deputy head - I have three - has a day of the summer break devoted to his or her performance over the previous year and the targets for the forthcoming one. These "reviews of progress" are supported by mid-year reviews at least once, during the year.

At these sessions arrangements are made for any task rotation among the Deputies which has been earlier proposed and agreed. It has always seemed to me foolish to make a wholesale switch of jobs between deputies in a job-rotation scheme. It makes much more sense to be rotating certain tasks only, leaving each deputy with a minimum of new experience to acquire in the forthcoming year. But task rotation does increase the "depth" expertise amongst the deputies, which not only brings a greater appreciation and understanding of each other's task, but leaves the school stronger in emergency situations or on occasions of senior staff absence.

Roles in the present system

Headmaster

Directs the system.
Guides heads of departments/heads of house on counselling and target setting.
Operates the system for the deputy headteachers, appraising their performance and agreeing their targets.
Provides and updates checklist.
Runs "leap frog" meeting with each teacher once a year.
Operates the system for heads of department, appraising their performance and agreeing their personal targets.

Holds annual review meetings with each head of department to agree Departmental targets, assess their achievement, together with a mid year review of progress.
Agrees individual targets set by every teacher with the Head of Department.
Personally reviews progress of every teacher towards the agreed targets.

Head of Department
Reviews performance of each teacher twice a year.
Agrees development needs, using checklist.
Identifies and agrees targets for coming year.
Monitors performance, takes action to resolve problems.
Provides input to Head on each teacher before annual "leapfrog" meeting.
Prepares for own annual review with head on progress of all his staff.

Subject Teacher
Uses preparation document once a year to provide a self-assessment of performance.
Meets with the head of department and agrees target and possibly a development plan for the coming year.
Review performance at least twice a year with head of department.
Meets with the head once a year to discuss performance and to agree targets and development plan.

Head of House/Year
If necessary, provides input on pastoral/tutor group targets and performance to head of department or pastoral deputy.
Monitors performance, takes action to resolve problems with tutors.
Reviews performance of each tutor within limits of authority.
Agrees targets, takes action to resolve problems.

Deputy Head (Pastoral)
Runs the system for heads of house.
Provides input on teachers as appropriate especially in Induction programme, pastoral administration, etc to departmental heads.

Deputy Head (Internal Organisation)
Provides input on teachers as appropriate especially on clubs, societies, extra curricular activities, contributions to school administration, timetabling etc to departmental heads or pastoral deputy.

Deputy Head (Academic Organisation)
Runs the system for ancillary, clerical, caretaking and technician staff.

Benefits and problems
The first great benefit of the Warden Park target setting system is the depth of skill it has built up over the years in setting, directing, interviewing and appraising. No course, no background reading, no televised simulation could have given us the real-life day-to-day skill my staff have acquired in operating the system, and I in directing it. This successful experience has strengthened my belief in the need for appraisals. I believe this so ardently that I teach appraisal skills on every course I am invited to lead, and support every effort made by leaders of other educational management courses nationally to encourage its development. The key appraisal skills are:

Questioning
Reflecting
Summarising
Disciplining
Praising
Asserting
Listening
Negotiating
Counselling

Nevertheless, there are problems to be faced. The chief of these are time, skills, an effective system, and expectations.

Firstly, it is a time consuming practice. Every interview undertaken requires three times as long spent in researching performance evidence and other general preparation and an equivalent time spent on follow-up. Secondly, the shortest and the most skilful part of the whole process is the setting of performance targets and their appraisal. These skills require training and practice. Badly set targets are meaningless. A badly conducted interview leaves both parties disillusioned and demotivated.

Thirdly, schools at present are designing their own appraisal systems. Many of these are not appraisals at all but friendly chats with a self-selected consenting colleague, who is not at all accountable for that teacher's performance. This is often too cosy to be effective with the very teachers who most need an honest appraisal. On the other hand, those who know least about successful professional staff appraisal seem most opposed to it, whilst the majority of teachers having no experience of it at all are torn between extreme positions on the issue.

Fourthly, we must beware of expecting too much of target setting and appraisal. It does not in itself solve any organisational problems. Given the appropriate trusting ethos it can help to identify the issues, it can make clear how these issues can be resolved and those whose responsibility they are. But we are left with the same heads and staff to solve the problems: don't expect the system to be "magic dust". Much depends, as it did before target setting, on the quality of head and staff.

Organization and personal gains from the target setting and appraisal process

What is the organisational and personal case for target setting? The case on behalf of the organisation - be it school or college, can be made in several ways.

Firstly, there is the argument based upon the obligation for the school to use its resources effectively. In a typical comprehensive school the community has invested the value of the land, the buildings, the equipment, the cost of heat, lighting and power, the salaries of professional staff and their ancillary workers. To what purpose? A school has an obligation to know what it is doing and where it is going. No-one has any business leading a school staff who does not know what the organisation is doing and how he or she will know when it is done. A plan is essential. A plan allows us to monitor our performance, to identify our priorities, to assess whether we are 'on course' to achieve our plan, to assess the risks involved in change, and make the appropriate adjustments to achieve that change. If you don't know where you're going how will you know when you've got there? More seriously, how can we not accept the need for and the value of objectives, aims or targets in schools?

What else does the school gain from target setting and appraisal? It is certainly helped, through the process of target setting, to distinguish between essential and non essential activities. At times of stress and overload, or in times of crisis or when Unions want to "withdraw goodwill", it will be very desirable to be able to encourage or to direct staff effort towards essential activities. How important is a school drama production, or a residential fieldwork exercise, or the accurate marking by staff of pupils' work, or the activities within tutor groups or communication through pupil reports with parents? Which of them can be temporarily shelved with least harm to the main purposes of the school?

A related aspect of this same point is that teachers themselves represent a scarce resource. They represent staff time, staff salaries and staff goodwill, all of which have to be used in the most effective way. Even goodwill is not in unlimited supply. Ask teachers at the end of a term to produce a play, plan a carol service, mark examination papers, and run pupil discos and parties, and then see how much goodwill remains to meet and discuss reports with parents.

If we accept the need, let us ask by what managed process are the targets, objectives and aims of a school not only identified and agreed, but delegated and achieved? What happens if corrective action is needed? We need to plan to be able to identify what is wrong, to identify the degree of deviation. How else do you know where you are, where you are going or where you need to change?

The target setting process assists not only with identification of purpose but with control of the tasks teachers undertake. I have quoted this example many times, but it well illustrates the need for management control:

> In 1980 there was a head of house who in addition to his teaching (which he may call task A) accepted for his pastoral role four major tasks which could be identified as tasks B, C, D and E. He was keen to accept responsibility for two other tasks which interested him greatly, the clerical work for the School Combined Cadet Force Unit (which we may call task F) and responsibility for all transport hired by the school (task G). Tasks F and G were low priority because they could have been delegated to clerical staff and were only delegated to the head of house because of his interest and at his special request. The headmistress was delighted with the arrangement. By 1981 however, pressure of work in Tasks F and G was lowering the house head's standard of performance in tasks A and B. This situation intensified in 1982 and by 1983 task A (teaching) was being badly prepared and marked, task B (knowing well the pupils and parents of the House) was scarcely done at all, but all other tasks, including tasks F and G were being performed well and taking all of the time the house head could reasonably be expected to devote to school-related work. He felt he was a committed member of staff, performing well for the school, and was amazed to learn that the head felt dissatisfied with his performance.

The moral of course, is that with an effective target and appraisal system this situation would have been corrected in 1981 or 1982. The targets set for that house head would have re-directed his effort into the two areas of tasks A and B where good performance was essential and would have reduced the input to the level warranted in those areas which were optional extras as far as the school was concerned. Target setting in such cases allows the school to control the input of staff effort to areas which have been agreed as priorities.

Probably the most important reason for target setting with each teacher arises from respect for the individual. The most soul destroying employment is employment without aim and purpose. Every teacher ought to be able to say "I know what we are trying to achieve in this school and I am happy to help. I know what is expected of me: I know that my contribution matters to the department and to the school and because of this, I know that I matter". Every teacher has the right to target setting.

Imagine the demotivated reaction of the teacher who, for example, prepared worksheets for her mixed ability group last week only to find the policy changed a month ago to ability sets! Valuable teacher effort can also be wasted on activities which the school did not require at that particular time with that particular group and no matter how worthwhile these activities appear in themselves, they do not significantly contribute to what the department or year group or school is trying to achieve at the present time. How many overworked teachers are taking on tasks which add a disproportionately small contribution to the success of the school? How many tasks in the school are being undertaken by teachers without the knowledge of their head of department, deputy head, or head, and which, given that knowledge, they would not require or expect the teacher to undertake? How many teachers are unaware of what their own school or even their own department is trying to achieve, who if their target were made more clear to them would willingly contribute to its successful achievement? Contributing to a plan can in itself become a great motivator.

Target setting therefore ensures that the teacher's effort contributes effectively to the targets of the department and of the school. Teachers willingly accept the need for a syllabus, a school timetable, a duty rota and other such plans to ensure co-ordinated staff activity. In all aspects of school life, teachers are entitled to find their work is not unnecessarily duplicated and that their efforts are not wasted because they are not part of a plan.

Yet another reason for using target setting and appraisal is that it facilitates staff development. How many teachers should be undertaking personal or career development tasks but have not had the opportunity to be advised of the wisdom of these? Pressure of time or lack of professional advice have prevented many teachers from preparing for the next stage of their career. Target setting meetings help resolve these problems.

The school, and the local education service in general also gain from an analysis of certain aspects of the appraisal returns. These aspects are those concerned with identifying existing weaknesses. These can indicate training needs, either school-based or LEA-based or drawing upon a wide market, depending upon demand. Such training requirements may become apparent through individual target setting and appraisal or through the assessment of the performance of an academic or pastoral unit within the school. Recent departmental reviews, for example, with the approach of GCSE may indicate the need for INSET for staff in new forms of pupil assessment or reveal the need for further training and education in new "teaching styles" such as the conducting by pupils of "investigations" in Mathematics. An effective analysis of training needs would be far more satisfying both to the providing establishments and to their consumers, than provision based on the providers' knowledge, skills and hunches.

This same analysis will also reveal underused skills in the staff. Such skills may be useful in any situation but in the present secondary climate of falling rolls and rationalisation, versatility amongst staff is at a premium for schools to maintain their performance. An LEA will want its teachers trained and developed to their full potential to enable it to discharge its obligations to the community. (For detailed consideration of this, see Joan Dean's chapter.)

A final point about target setting and appraisal. The system used at Warden Park allows every teacher to contribute to the setting of targets: not only to the personal targets which are related to that teacher's personal and professional development, but to those targets related to the improvement of the department, the pastoral unit, or of the school itself. It allows for these proposals and comments to be presented in writing or orally, and allows time for discussion of them with the head of department and the head of school. Target Setting is a democratic system of proposing targets, combined with a hierarchical system for ensuring that those targets which are agreed are carried out effectively. Below is a description of target setting through negotiation:

TOM BRAGSBY

Tom Bragsby is a Scale 1 BEd Mathematician, newly married, aged 24, with one year's teaching experience. He passed his probationary year very successfully. He found teaching suited him admirably. His discipline is sound, his relationships with pupils are good, though staff find him a little conceited and irritating. All his work in the Mathematics Department is prepared and marked well. He teaches effectively, and it is clear from all his internal and external examination results, that he has the ability to teach well. His administration is first class in all aspects of school life. He has one weakness with pupils, which is a tendency to become too informal, and then to over-react if pupils are informal in return. During one incident he over-reacted and struck a boy on the nose. He bitterly regretted the incident, though still tends to flare up from time to time. A further weakness is pointed out by his head of house who fears that his tutor group, unlike his mathematics class, is often in disorder and while he is perfectly willing to involve himself with small groups of pupils the remainder of the tutor group give the impression of chaos. He hopes to gain promotion in the academic field, and attaches minimal importance to pastoral tutoring.

Tom is keen to accept responsibility for training, running and arranging fixtures for a school rugby team and take them to matches and on a tour of South Wales. He has also offered to lead a school trip to California where he has recently been undertaking summer holiday work in a youth holiday camp. He is now at the mid-point of his second year teaching.

Negotiating his targets his head of department convinced Tom that he lacked the experience to lead a school visit and that a target of assisting an experienced leader was a more suitable challenge. Tom also accepted responsibility for a school rugby team under the guidance of the head of Physical Education, with a view to planning and leading a rugby tour when he had more certainly acquired the appropriate skills and experience.

Two other targets took much more discussion. Firstly, a programme of improvement of pastoral care practice. A County course, a series of visits to other tutorial groups, some planned reading of "Active Tutorial" books and more active coaching from his head of house all formed part of this target.

The final target took all the interpersonal skills of the head of department to convey. Tom was made aware of his image with his colleagues. He felt that he was good and wanted to be sure others knew it. He accepted a personal target of improving relationships with his colleagues, although the feedback on their attitude towards him and the confidence that he was already seen as very promising, made that target much easier for him to achieve.

The needs of the individual and the needs of the school

Occasionally conflicts do occur between the needs of the school and those of the individual teacher. One example of such a conflict is when the teacher wants to prepare for and develop mixed ability teaching in his or her subject, but the school policy is one of sets based on ability and does not want the extra effort applied in the way the teacher suggests. These should be talked through at target setting meetings. Few general guidelines can be given here. Usually it will amply repay a teacher to meet the needs of a school, even in an area which does not appear to have particular career prospects. However, schools seldom get the best from teachers who feel the school is thwarting their career development. Examples of this conflict are when the school is asking a teacher to accept a target of responsibility for its Duke of Edinburgh Award Scheme arrangements, but the teacher prefers to devote the extra time involved to developing counselling skills and would like the school's help towards that target. Is there a way of reconciling these targets? If there is, then there is much personal security and confidence to be gained from knowing that a particular target is not only providing a teacher with professional development but is a vital contribution towards the achievement of a school target.

Finally, the target setting system is not merely a management technique. It is a school management philosophy and as such it is based on certain assumptions about human nature. Firstly, it assumes that teachers will commit themselves more strongly to targets which they helped to suggest, to define and to set. Inexperienced teachers may need targets set for them, the unwilling or lazy may need their targets imposed or may need help in raising them to higher standards, but in general increasing professional maturity brings the willingness and ability to set high but achievable targets . This latter group particularly value mutual agreement on what has to be done, but appreciate effective delegation. In particular, once targets have been agreed, they do not expect to be told in detail how to do the job. They expect as able, qualified, experienced professionals to use their professional knowledge, skills and judgements to achieve the agreed result. A final aspect of this first assumption is that everyone feels more secure and works better when they feel they have some control over what happens to them.

The second assumption of the target setting system is that teachers like an answer to the question "How am I doing?". Teachers like to measure their progress. Measures of progress may be difficult to find but the target setting system requires us to spend time on the search for performance criteria and for standard of performance. Subjective and professional criteria may be used alongside objective and lay criteria, but in some way or other it has to be possible to find indicators that a teacher's performance is developing.

The third assumption is that teachers like to feel they belong to an effective pastoral unit, departmental unit and school. Pride in team performance matters as much to teachers as to any other group in society and the feeling that we are making an important contribution to some or all of those units matters to all.

Simple as they seem, I have acted upon these assumptions and found them to be effective, ample motivators in building a target setting and appraisal system. The benefits are here at Warden Park for anyone to see in the high calibre of staff performance, in the level of personal pride and of morale. I believe that no other system I could have introduced could bring such positive benefits to a school.

SECTION 4: STRATEGIES FOR STAFF DEVELOPMENT

Chapter 8

STAFF DEVELOPMENT: SOME PROBLEMS IN PROMOTING PROFESSIONAL LEARNING AND CHANGE

Christopher Day

This chapter discusses constraints upon the management of staff development in the contexts of the twin external pressures for control of the curriculum and demands for contractual accountability, socialisation and psychological factors, and leadership roles played by senior management itself. The author argues that the current rhetoric promoting more school-centred professional development, may simply be substituting one cluster of superordinate decision makers (the LEA and school senior management teams) for another (the DES and institutions of higher education) and that individual teachers perceive their needs to be increasingly subordinate to those collective needs of the institution perceived by its managers. He argues that there is an increasing need for participative management of staff development in which staff feel they have a stake and to which they can feel a commitment; and that managers need to have the necessary and appropriate skills to enable success to be achieved.

> In-service training should begin in the schools. It is here that learning and teaching take place, curriculum and techniques are developed and needs and deficiencies revealed. Every school should regard the continued training of its teachers as an essential part of its task, for which all members of staff share responsibility. An active school is constantly reviewing and reassessing its effectiveness and is ready to consider new methods, new forms of organization and new ways of dealing with the problems that arise. (D.E.S., 1972)

While this quotation from the James Report emphasizes potential benefits to be gained from professional and curriculum development work in schools, at the same time it fails to highlight some significant problems for those concerned with its management. No account seems to be taken, for example, of external political and economic forces or social and psychological factors which may act as restraints. A cynic might say that the authors' assumption that 'curricula and techniques are developed' and that 'needs and deficiencies are revealed' is an assertion of belief rather than fact. Similarly, it might be said the statement that 'all members of staff share responsibility' for the continued training of themselves and colleagues is an aspiration rather than a present reality. The further statement that 'an active school is constantly reviewing and reassessing its effectiveness' etc might be said by the headteacher who has problems in keeping up to date with and responding to legislation and the plethora of reports, recommendations, new curricula via MSC, CPVE, TVEI and TRIST and demands for accountability of one kind or another, to be naive in the extreme. Life in schools these days, claimed a headteacher attending a recent management course, is principally concerned with 'crisis management'. Another, on being asked to undertake a time-task analysis as part of his pre-course work, claimed that he did not have the time! Whilst it may be unreasonable to claim that all or even most schools (and LEAs) are largely reactive rather than pro-active in their responses to staff development demands, and that few schools have staff development policies, there can be little doubt that managing staff development does have its problems. It is the purpose of this chapter to highlight some of these; and in doing this, to provide some principles for managing professional development in schools which may be applied to the opportunities for staff development described by Ben Kerwood and Simon Clements in the next chapter.

The chapter will consider staff development in the context of innovation and change and makes three assumptions: 1) most teachers do not regularly participate in formally organized staff development activities, 2) most schools do not have a staff development policy, 3) increasingly, staff development is initiated from above rather than from below.

'School-centred' in-service has been described as embracing:

> both 'school-based' activity, a mode of in-service education which takes place on the school premises, and 'school-focused' activity, a mode which accepts that the professional requirements of the school and the staff as a whole provide a focal point around which a whole programme of in-service work is planned. (Ruddock, 1981)

Staff development, then, is seen to embrace work that is primarily intended to complement a combination of needs - those of the individual, the department and the institution. The emphasis on the requirements of the school and staff as a whole as well as the individual teacher has been reinforced in recent years by, for example, the DES. In 'Making INSET Work' (1978) it was stated that:

> too often in the past INSET has been thought of only in terms of individual teachers attending courses which are designed and provided by outside agencies ... The basic INSET needs are also to do with a) the teacher and his immediate needs, b) the needs of functional groups within a school and c) the needs of the school as a whole. (D.E.S., 1978)

Economics was cited as one of the disadvantages of the traditional 'off-site' course. The expense of travel and subsistence, in addition to the fee for attendance at a course out of which the department or school may derive little or no direct benefit was given as a reason for changing the locus of the course. In addition, it had become recognised that no one interest group should have a monopoly on the relatively few available resources which are made available for professional development work. It is not only the individual who may identify a need, but collective needs of department and school may also be identified and claims may be made upon resources in order to meet these needs also.

There were other equally important reasons for a move towards school-centred professional development, however. It had become increasingly apparent that the top-down approach to the management and provision of in-service work, which was largely designed and tutored by people who were from outside the school and classroom and had appeared to be well-suited to meeting the personal and career needs of individual teachers, had now come to be judged as irrelevant by many teachers, and, 'by no means well suited to meeting the needs of the education system at its various levels since it ignores the problems faced by teachers when they return to school and seek to implement their new ideas ... The actual diffusion of real change was very limited and regression towards former practices seemed to be rather rapid, even where INSET seemed to have led to an initial disposition towards organizational or curricular change' (Henderson and Perry, 1981). There were problems, then, in terms of 1) matching the 'needs' of teachers with the content of courses, 2) transfer of knowledge to classroom and school contexts and 3) dissemination of knowledge, either because of lack of status, support, resources or feedback mechanisms.

Further problems (which in this writer's experience continue to exist) concerned a lack of understanding of the ways in which teachers learn, the roles of the interventionist(s) in this process (on the assumption that learning by teachers does not begin and end with a planned course or learning event), and why teachers change (or fail to change).

The chapter will argue, with Rogers and Shoemaker (1971), that there are in practice two distinctive groups of decision-makers - the superordinate group and the subordinate group - which can be identified at every level of the education system, and that it is the degree of control exercised by one group over the other which will affect the extent to which policies and activities associated with policies are adopted or adapted. The degree of control may be identified both by the use of authority and the model of dissemination used:

> In a high-control condition, we would say that administrators rely on their formal authority to try to get things done the way they want them to be done, by exerting influence over people, processes and the use of resources. In a low control situation, power is 'equalized' ie distributed among the involved parties so as to reduce the assymmetry of one group's influence over another. (Marsh, 1984)

External and internal constraints on staff development will be related in part to this notion and in part to psychological and socialisation factors.

Three kinds of constraints for those who as part of their designated role are expected to engage in leadership of staff development within their institutions, will therefore be explored. The first major constraint concerns a combination of intended and unintended external factors which in one way or another adversely affect the climate in which professional development may flourish. The second is to do with socialisation and psychological factors which may affect the responses of colleagues who are invited to participate in professional development which takes time and energy and which may result in change which is not always entirely welcome; and the third constraint is the kinds of leadership roles and strategies used by the leader him(her)self. The final section of the chapter will suggest principles for learning, leadership and change.

External constraints on staff development

In 1980, the DES spelt out very clearly, not only that in-service provision would be governed by the level of resources available, but also on whose shoulders the onus for its future management would fall:

> Developments in in-service provision in the years to come will be influenced by many factors, and chief among these is likely to be the level of available expenditure ... The resources available in higher education for this purpose need to be flexibly deployed if they are to be used to the best advantage, and this implies freedom of movement. In-service training, whatever its form, depends for the impetus it receives and for its success upon heads and senior staff. (DES, 1981)

This addition of another 'provider' and identifier of in-service need signalled a significant shift in the purposes of provision for the professional development of teachers. In effect an institutional layer was added. Teachers were now to be increasingly accountable for their professional learning - where this was funded by DES and LEA - to the department and institution in which they worked, as well as to themselves and their profession at large. Headteachers and senior staff were in their turn to be more directly accountable to their LEAs for ensuring that staff development activities of all kinds were relevant and appropriate to the needs of the institution as well as to those expressed by the individual.

The recognition of the importance of school-centred INSET, not only as a cost saving exercise but also as a means of ensuring greater participation by teachers in planning of the work related to their own and their institution's needs, to some extent reflected various models of in-service which had been developing throughout the 1970s both independently in certain LEAs and nationally through DES funded projects which relied on the active commitment and collaboration of LEAs. The DES Survey of Induction and In-service Training of Teachers (INIST, 1979) found that 'it was the policy of nearly all the responding authorities to develop programmes of in-service training based on individual schools or groups of schools and to provide support for the programmes from the authorities' advisory service. In sixty six authorities, support was also provided by the staff of local teacher centres and over half the responding authorities drew support from the staff of teacher training institutions' (in Bolam, 1982).

It is perhaps paradoxical that the development of more effective models of professional learning should be accompanied by a radical change in the political and economic climate of education so that, far from democratizing the system or enhancing the professionalism of teachers, the increasing emphasis upon a school-centred approach to professional development may have the effect of simply shifting the locus for decision-making and change from one superordinate group (off-site) to another (on-site). It is against this background that all those involved in promoting and managing the professional development of teachers must work.

While it is not the function of this chapter to present a detailed historical account, there can be little doubt that the business of working in schools has become more complex over the last thirty years. A relatively superficial examination shows that with the introduction of comprehensive schooling (a political decision) schools became bigger, the mix of pupils and staff became broader, and so the management and organisation of the 'plant' became more difficult. Heads were forced to delegate to survive. Academic and pastoral care systems, setting, banding, and mixed ability groupings were established to cater for staff and pupils who did not necessarily share the same philosophies of education. In the 1960s innovation was the bandwagon upon which many schools jumped. New 'relevant' syllabi were devised either centrally through Foundations (eg Nuffield Science), the (now defunct) Schools Council (eg Geography for the Young School Leaver), or locally with like minded colleagues meeting in Teachers Centres. The fact that many of these centre-periphery models for curriculum development were not adopted in classrooms should not detract attention from the point that they took time, effort and resources. New CSE Mode 3 examinations were devised which increased teachers' (rather than universities') control of content and standards. At the same time, the school leaving age was raised (ROSLA) creating new problems for heads and staff, and there was a growth in the LEA inspection and advisory services which in its turn led, with the accompanying growth in the numbers of Teachers Centres, to more in-service provision much of which was in reaction to current immediate organisational needs of schools and classrooms. Work experience schemes, integrated studies, and personal and social education became curriculum growth areas. 'Deschooling Society' (Illich, 1972) and 'The Underachieving School' (Holt, 1971) became fashionable phrases, although there are few examples of either, and some LEAs flirted with new modes of secondary school organization (eg Countesthorpe in Leicestershire, Abraham Moss Centre in Manchester and Stantonbury Campus in Milton Keynes).

Then the progressive expansionist bubble of the ideals and ideas of the 1960s burst. In 1967 Risinghill (Berg, 1968) and its head, Michael Duane, had become a 'cause celebre', and this was followed by William Tyndale (Auld,

1976). Both were important in 'establishing that there were limits to teachers' freedom in deciding on the curriculum' (Lawton, 1981). It may be argued that this interest was related to broader economic factors. However, the fact is that throughout the 1970s politicians, local and national were beginning to take a more active interest in the curriculum, pedagogy and evaluation of schools. The Taylor Report (1977) sought to strengthen the influence of the consumer on the curriculum. Earlier (1974) the DES had established the Assessment of Performance Unit in an attempt to provide national criteria through the development (albeit partial) of a system of monitoring standards.

Essentially, the consensus which had allowed schools to operate with relative autonomy had broken down. Now not only were teachers accountable to themselves and their pupils and parents for the education that they provided, but politicians, responsible ultimately for public expenditure in a declining economy in which unemployment was rising, wanted to see 'value for money'. Callaghan's speech at Ruskin College in 1976 launched the so-called Great Education Debate, which was essentially an attempt by Government to exert direct influence on the selection of curriculum content through the manipulation of resource provision to LEAs and schools.

The consequences of this have been, over the years, a plethora of DES and HMI discussion papers and reports on aspects of school and the curriculum which have become more and more demanding in their prescriptions for more efficient and effective curriculum content, transmission and methods of assessment. In addition, there have been reports and legislation affecting all schools and teachers across the curriculum, with the publication of 'Aspects of Secondary Education' (DES, 1979), 'A Language for Life' (DES, 1975), 'Mathematics Counts (DES, 1978), 'Warnock' (DES, 1982) and the Swann Report (DES, 1985). All this, together with demands for curriculum guidelines and the reform of the public examinations system has caused unprecedented pressure to be placed on heads and teachers.

The new word introduced to everybody's vocabulary in the 1970s was <u>ACCOUNTABILITY</u>. Although there are different kinds of accountability - moral, professional and contractual (East Sussex Accountability Project, 1979) - it is the latter which has been, and continues to be, emphasised at Government and Local Government level in the perception of teachers.

The DES document, 'The School Curriculum' (DES, 1981), was the first climax to the discussions which had begun with the Great Debate of 1976, and represented 'the first explicit and definitive attempt by Central Government for over half a century to steer curricula in a particular direction' (White, 1981). Later in the same year, the Government followed it up by issuing a circular to all LEAs:

> Circular No 6/81
> 1 October, 1981
>
> DEPARTMENT OF EDUCATION AND SCIENCE, ELIZABETH HOUSE, YORK ROAD, LONDON, SE1 7PH
>
> THE SCHOOL CURRICULUM
>
> 1 'The School Curriculum' was published by the Secretaries of State for Education and Science and for Wales on 25 March, 1981: copies were sent to every local education authority with a request to distribute them among the schools maintained by the authority. This circular should be read in conjunction with 'The School Curriculum' ...
>
> 2 The Secretary of State considers that each local education authority should, in the light of what is said in 'The School Curriculum':
>
> a review its policy for the school curriculum in its area, and its arrangements for making that policy known to all concerned;
>
> b review the extent to which current provision in the schools is consistent with that policy; and
>
> c plan future developments accordingly, within the resources available ...
>
> 6 The Secretary of State looks to governors to encourage their schools, within the resources available, to develop their curricula in the light of what is said in 'The School Curriculum' ...
>
> 7 The Secretary of State also draws the attention of authorities and governors of schools to his view that schools should set out in writing the aims which they pursue through the organisation of the curriculum and in teaching programmes; and should assess regularly how far the curriculum - in the schools as a whole and for individual pupils - matches the stated aims ...
>
> 8 The Secretary of State proposes, after consultation with the local authority associations and the voluntary bodies, to review the steps which have been taken in response to this Circular. He envisages that this will be done in about two years from now.

This caused LEAs to consult with schools who were required to provide written statements on curricula where they did not already exist. At about the same time other developments were occurring:

1 The declining birthrate and an accompanying fall in resource provision was affecting curricula and morale of schools.

2 The opportunities for individual teachers to gain promotion either within their own school or by moving to another were diminishing.

3 HMI were making suggestions for changes in the management structures of schools in order to assist in decision-making processes (DES, 1977).

4 The Government disbanded the Schools Council, setting in its place two bodies - a Schools Examination Council and a Schools Curriculum Development Committee (the use of 'Council' and 'Committee' possibly indicating the relative importance attached to each body by the Secretary of State).

5 The increasing dissatisfaction with the content of the curriculum by a significant majority of pupils, coupled with the rise in youth unemployment particularly led to increasing external intervention in the curriculum of the 14-18 year old by agencies such as the Manpower Services Commission through pre-vocational and other schemes of work.

6 The Taylor Report (1977) set the seal on a process which is still occurring in which parents and others were to have increased power to influence the curriculum.

7 The Warnock Report (DES, 1978) and the resulting legislation has meant that schools have had to plan a curriculum to fit a broader ability range than previously.

8 The Secretary of State for Education and Science, in a speech at the North of England Education Conference in January, 1984, called for a nationally defined curriculum for pupils aged 5-16. This was followed by 'A Note by the Department of Education and Science and Welsh office' entitled 'The Organisation and Content of the 5-16 Curriculum'. Essentially, this was a follow up to Circulars 6/81 (above) and 8/83. The purpose of the paper was 'to raise questions and invite comments on them, with a view to establishing as wide a measure of agreement as possible', on a) the objectives of learning at school,

b) the contribution of each main subject area or element, c) the content of the 5-16 curriculum as a whole, and d) objectives for attainment at the end of the primary phase and for the secondary (11-16) phase. Since then, there have been more DES and HMI Discussion Papers offering more 'guidelines' for curriculum.

The consequences of these and other factors have been a perceived if not actual deterioration in the conditions of service for headteachers. There has been more paperwork, more meetings both in and out of the school have had to be held. More people from within and outside education have articulated their opinions , beliefs, wishes, concerning the planning, teaching and assessment of the curriculum, and these have had to be processed, weighed and taken into account. Some have perceived this as an exciting opportunity for a new form of partnership between schools and their local and broader community. Others have been less enthusiastic, and have felt the need for further training in management in order to cope with the increasing complexities of headship. Others have found themselves increasingly having to deal with teachers who, themselves feeling the pressures of extra workloads and diminishing resources, have begun to withdraw the goodwill upon which much of the quality of school life depends. One year of discontent has stretched into another and, resentment has grown, as more demands have been made for more work and more accountability.

At a local level, growth in political desire to ensure that school standards were maintained has resulted in an increasing politicisation (and, paradoxically, a decline) of some advisory services. 'Advisers' have become 'Inspectors' and while many have retained their brief to promote curriculum development in particular subject areas and phases of education, they now have to spend more time monitoring and inspecting schools (through observation, appraisal interviews, and reports to Education Committee). Pressure has been put upon heads of schools to make available job descriptions for each member of staff, and to ensure that regular staff reviews take place and are documented. Legislation has now made it mandatory for each school to provide a school policy document for parents.

The increasing intervention in schools by the 'employers', whether as DES, LEAs or other agencies, in the areas of testing (CPVE, 16+ etc), visitations (through HMI inspections and the published results of these), specification (DES, HMI reports on curriculum matters) and staffing (performance and appraisal reviews) may be related to the model of dissemination of innovation which was devised by Rogers and Shoemaker (1971). Here, members of the superordinate group (eg DES, LEA, MSC) are primarily concerned with 'Knowledge, Persuasion and Decision', whereas the prime function of members of the subordinate group (eg head-teachers) is to implement. This group is, therefore, concerned with 'Communication and Action'.

Figure 1 An authority model of change based on pseudo-participation with clients

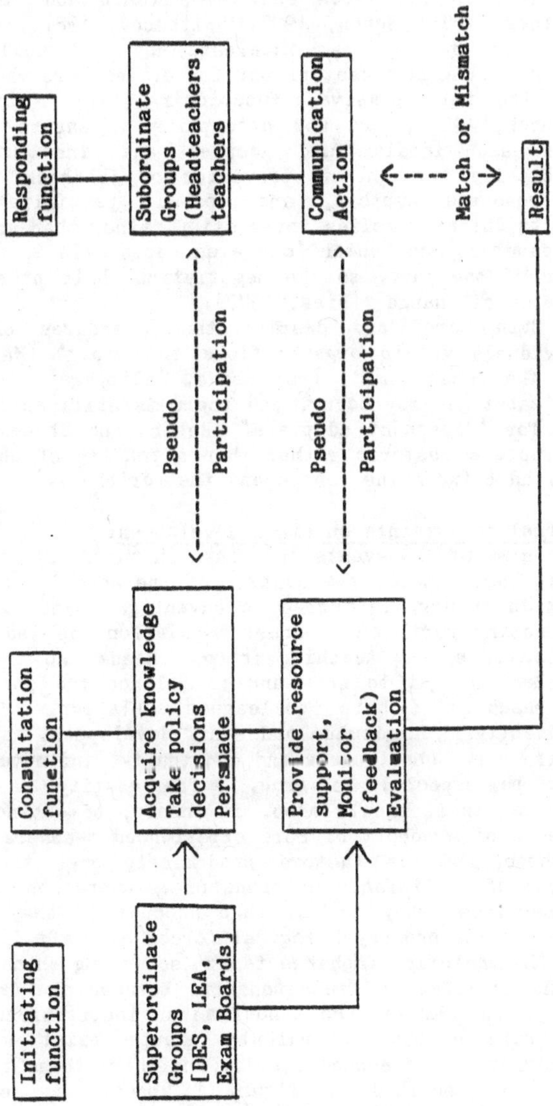

This kind of centre-periphery model has often been shown to result in token or temporary responses to change (Norris, 1974). However, Figure 1 above shows how the superordinate groups have now refined the original models, prevalent in the 1960s and 1970s (Chin and Benne, 1969; Havelock, 1971; Schon, 1973; Leithwood, 1981), and how in the light of their own interests and the knowledge that, 'there is a significant proportion of teachers who prefer to play the more passive, functioning role' (Reynolds and Skilbeck, 1976), are now attempting to ensure that their ideas and ideals are adopted and institutionalized, principally through the provision of feedback, monitoring and resource support, and 'pseudo participation' with clients which, 'implies interaction rather than equalisation of resources' and which 'may even succeed in increasing the power of one party to the negotiation while preserving the illusion of change' (Nias, 1972).

Even here, and despite the 'pressures placed upon individuals within organizations to comply' (Marsh, 1984) with the demands made from above, 'slippage', 'avoidance', and 'sabotage' may occur, and there is still ample opportunity for 'dissonant adopters' (Rogers and Shoemaker, 1971) to create a rhetoric rather than a reality of change along the road between the centre and the periphery.

Internal constraints on staff development

While some of the events described in the first part of this chapter are outside the control of the school, they may, at least in theory, be turned to advantage. For example, the contracting pupil and teacher population has led to a more stable, if ageing teaching force. Heads can therefore be expected to 'get to know and to balance the strengths and weaknesses of their colleagues' (Taylor, 1981) more efficiently. Curriculum and staff development may begin to acquire more cohesiveness and continuity, and mutual support might be expected to grow. The quality of classroom teaching itself should also, in theory, be enhanced by the presence of a cohort of more experienced teachers. Yet even if these positive factors predominate over the negative effects of declining conditions of remuneration, resourcing and services, they do not take account of the effects of socialisation and psychological forces on staff development.

The rhetoric of change is not something which is unique to the interface of relationships between the DES and the LEA, or the LEA and the school as an institution. Indeed, superordinate and subordinate groups exist within the boundaries of the school itself, and where these take on the functions described in Figure 1 above, the results are likely to be equally problematic. However, for the head-teacher who is committed to staff development, there are other potential hazards which exist almost regardless of the approach (s)he adopts.

There is evidence that socialisation acts as a restraining factor on new learning. New teachers, for example, quickly develop a series of implicit expectations and norms of thinking and behaviour which allow them to cope with both the complexities of teaching and membership of a staffroom community. They develop, 'routines and decision-habits' (Eraut, 1977) to keep mental and emotional effort at a reasonable level, and reach a personal solution which allows them to perform their tasks as teachers 'successfully' within the context in which they work. Although writing in the context of student teachers, Lacey's (1977) identification of the teacher's possible responses to the struggle between his or her vision of how teaching should be and that of the school has relevance for all involved in staff development. The three responses to this tension between individually and institutionally perceived needs are:

> 1 strategic compliance, in which the individual complies with the authority figure's definition of the situation and the constraints of the situation but retains private reservations about them;
>
> 2 internalized adjustment, in which the individual complies with the constraints and believes that the constraints of the situation are for the best;
>
> 3 strategic redefinition of the situation which implies that change is brought about by individuals who do not possess the formal power to do so' (Lacey, 1977)

It is likely that at any given time all three responses will be present in every staffroom. The problem may be, however, that the external pressures which have been identified have caused more and more teachers (and headteachers) to strategically comply while in private seeing themselves as 'victims' of a system over which they have diminishing influence and control. The consequence of this may be a growing disillusionment and a lessening commitment.

Moreover, professional practice is made up of a number of interrelated theories of action that specify for the situations of the practice the actions that would, under the appropriate conditions, yield intended results, and much of these theories of action (Argyris and Schon, 1974) are at an implicit level. If teachers and headteachers do develop a series of implicit expectations and norms of thinking and behaviour, these are in a sense rules of action and theories of control which allow them both to maintain a stable view of, for example, the classroom and school and give priorities to certain kinds of information whilst ignoring others. Few people will readily abandon a relatively stable constant world over which they have at least some control -be it in the classroom or through established curricular, assessment procedures, academic and pastoral core structures, or communication patterns - unless they can see advantages for themselves, their staffs and their pupils. If they cannot, then they may use a repertoire of devices in order to protect themselves. They may:

1 Adopt the language of change, but retain old behaviour.

2 Become selectively inattentive to information that points to problems (ie ignore it).

3 Change jobs or change roles within the same institution.

4 Make marginal changes to behaviour.

5 Use authority to elicit the desired behaviour from others, so that they conform to desired change.

These have been characterized elsewhere as 'Games Educators Play'. Here are some examples.

1 <u>I Remember When</u>. This is a typical game played by old-timers in the field. No matter what the idea may be to effect change, they are always ready to knock it down by proclaiming there is nothing new about the idea. It is something which occurred 20 or 30 years ago and was unsuccessful then, so why bother with it now? This type of game is most pronounced in a stable staff of individuals who have "died on the vine" in their jobs.

2 <u>Smoke Screens</u>. This type of game consists primarily of diversionary manoeuvres by an adept individual who subtly throws out smoke screens of seemingly related but actually unrelated topics which confuse the issue. He confuses everyone in the group until the idea becomes lost or bogged down and the group decides it is not worth pursuing any further.

3 <u>If Only I Had Time</u>. This is a typical rationalization, so an individual or a staff does not even have to become concerned with considering change at all. This excuse of If Only I Had Time can, in some cases, be very realistic, but for many it is their game. When one analyses this game, he finds the type of person who uses it is absorbed in minutiae and activities of low priority which do keep

him busy and provide a seemingly logical excuse for him to use.

4 **The Poor Teachers and Children.** The person who plays this game is adept at using a maudlin, sentimental attitude. He proclaims teachers and children are confronted with so many things - what are we trying to do to them now? Who wants to be the dirty dog who hurts teachers and children?

5 **He Means Well, But.** The technique here is that the one who proposes change means well but doesn't really understand things. This is also a typical response of the "experienced" to the young educator. It is a beautiful technique to negate the proposal in a seemingly pleasant manner.

6 **Now I've Got You.** This is the game which can be played by someone who has a great deal of sophistication. Typically, he will allow the idea of change to progress along to a certain point where he will then come out with his "sword of Damocles" through statements such as, "Well, you know what research says about this", or "You know that so-and-so, an authority in the field, feels this way about this type of idea", etc. In this game a proposer of change is led down the primrose path until the sword falls on his neck.

7 **It's All Mine.** This game is played by the kind of person whose ideas are solely his own, and he won't let anyone become involved with him either to assist or even to offer suggestions or criticisms. This person becomes so all-possessive about his ideas that it is impossible for him to implement them.

8 **If It Weren't for Them.** This is related to game No 3 (If Only I Had Time) in that the blame is placed upon someone else for change not occurring. This allows a person never to be at fault himself, and he can blame situations such as lack of working facilities, no time for pursuing ideas, poor salaries, or others' ineptness for preventing him from initiating change.

(Day et al, 1986)

These games are played for a number of reasons: to avoid self-confrontation, to conceal ulterior motives, to justify behaviour (and thus avoid changing it) or simply to avoid participation in change which is not self-generated, perceived neither as necessary nor desirable, or which does not conform to the 'practicality ethic' held by many teachers.

Doyle and Ponder (1976) identify three examples of responses to teachers who are 'invited' to change:

a) the rational adopter - someone who might be said to adopt a step-by-step approach to solving problems, this person will
   i clarify goals and problems
   ii collect information about how problems arise
   iii consider ways to resolve the problems
   iv implement these
   v evaluate (the success of strategies)

b) the stone age obstructionist - who neither accepts the need for change, nor responds to 'invitations' to be involved

c) the pragmatic sceptic - who expresses, 'a concern for immediate contingencies and consequences'. He will evaluate change proposals in terms of their validity for him in his classroom ie he will ask three questions:
   i What do I/my pupils get out of it?
   ii Can I relate it to what I do/how I teach?
   iii What is its cost (in time, energy and finance)?
   The pragmatic sceptic wants to see a return for his investment.

Essentially, both the 'games' and above reactions may be seen not only as representing personal and professional limitations among teachers, but a response to increases in internal and external pressures which, cumulatively, are perceived as demonstrating a loss of faith by others in their 'professionality'. The headteacher may therefore have to help motivate some teachers who are frustrated, apathetic and resentful. Hands (1981) divided the teaching force of the 1980s into three categories:

1 those who are frustrated in their ambitions
2 those who are happy to be in their terminal posts
3 those likely to gain (further) promotion

Not all schools will contain all of these extreme categories of teacher, but they do serve to draw the attention of headteachers and others concerned with innovation to the complex web of role expectations, institutional constraints, professional experiences, teaching attitudes and approaches, and personality factors which may influence the responses of staff towards any form of new idea or practice that s(he) may wish to introduce into the school.

It seems, then, that resistance to innovation may be caused because teachers need to maintain current systems, because of plain stubborness, or because they themselves have played no significant part in its creation and development. This issue of ownership is vital in planning for staff development, for if heads and teachers do not feel that the work belongs to them (in the sense that it matches their perceived needs and those of the school) then they may not be prepared to accord the extra time, energy and commitment necessary for its development.

However 'carefully articulated and realistic programmes of curriculum education' (Nunan, 1983) are, they must take into account the human factor. This is necessary first because development of any kind inevitably involves people in a reappraisal of values, attitudes and feelings as well as practice, and these are, by definition, not governed by rationality nor amenable to prescription; and second, because attempts to promote staff development are unlikely to meet with success unless there is an active consideration by the headteacher of the psychological and social dynamic in its planning, process and evaluation.

Leadership constraints

It has been suggested that the task of management, in an age when many schools feel as if they are being pulled apart by opposing interests, is to gather these interests together using the strengths of each (Handy, 1984). Yet the headteacher is faced with three dilemmas:

1 the potential conflict between the needs of the individual and the needs of the institution

2 the extent to which there is participation in decision-making

3 his ability to fulfil appropriate leadership roles

The Individual and the Institution

Staff development has been defined as:

> a systematic attempt to harmonize individuals' interests and wishes, and their carefully assessed requirements for furthering their careers, with the forthcoming requirements of the organisation within which they are expected to work. It can be seen that this is a somewhat broader concept than that of staff training. (Piper and Glatter, 1977)

Planning for staff development must, therefore, be both reactive (in response to the articulated needs of individuals and groups from within and outside the school) and proactive (as a result of systematic identification of individual and institutional needs). Inevitably this kind of planning requires the time, energy, and skilled commitment of head and senior management. It requires the development of systems of communication, consultation, support, review, monitoring and feedback which are credible and valid to all concerned, in which all concerned have an investment, and into which all concerned feel able to place their trust. The successful development of such systems will depend to some extent on the priority which is given and seen to be given to staff development by the headteacher. Two approaches may be identified which characterize different models of leadership in relation to staff development.

First there is <u>the peripheral approach</u> in which programmes of staff development are regarded as fringe activities. This is characterised by ad hoc provision for individuals to attend courses, conferences, etc according to 'here and now' interests and needs. Feedback from course attenders is not required. This approach needs a minimum of administration and often results in a growing resentment within staffrooms against staff for whom 'cover' has to be provided with little warning and no convincing reason, and against heads who allow this to happen. Second, <u>the integral approach</u>, is, 'characterised by developing co-ordinated policies, practices and procedures that aim to recruit, train and maintain staff in a way that satisfies both the needs of the individual and the needs of the organisation' (Lyons, 1976).

The integral approach is potentially the one which may win the active support of staff, though even this will be dependent upon the way in which the policies, practices and procedures are set up, maintained and reviewed. For example, the big temptations for the head who is enthusiastic but busy are to:

1 evolve a plan which involves <u>his</u> perceived needs for the school, staff and pupils in isolation or by consulting only with his senior management team

2 plan for too much without considering extra workloads, morale problems and other practical considerations

3 plan without considering support implications, feedback and outcomes

4 seek short-term 'sticking plaster' solutions to immediate problems rather than generate alternatives to help with decision-making processes.

This approach is likely to be viewed as an 'authority' or 'top-down' model of staff development in which, for example, any assessment of an individual's potential is more likely to be based on senior managers' guesswork rather than on knowledge and understanding based on observation and discussion (Braddick, 1979).

One starting point for inquiry is to embark upon an agreed programme of school evaluation as being a necessary prior stage to development. The case for school evaluation has been made by Simons (1982), and the underlying assumptions are that:

> 1 a better understanding of the organisation and policies ... could improve the opportunities and experiences provided in classrooms;
>
> 2 systematic study and review allows the (school) to determine, and to produce evidence of, the extent to which they are providing the quality of education they espouse;
>
> 3 a study of (school) policies can help teachers identify policy effects which require attention at school, department or classroom level;
>
> 4 many policy issues cut across classrooms and require collective review and resolution
>
> 5 there are many learning experiences (fieldwork and extra-curricular activities, for instance), which do not take place in the classroom and which require the cooperation and appraisal of the whole school
>
> 6 participation in a school self-study gives teachers the opportunity to develop their professional decision-making skills, enlarge their perspectives, and become better informed about the roles, responsibilities and problems of their colleagues. (Simons, 1982)

Normally, teachers (or headteachers!) cannot be expected to have the time or energy to engage in constant re-examination of their work. But there might be a policy in which, for example, teachers and groups of teachers agree to focus their energy over a limited time period to investigating a particular problem, applying a particular teaching method, or developing a specific aspect of the curriculum. Such an agreement is likely to produce commitment where a lack of one may only produce frustration.

There is a need for a policy because it is not assumed that change will be a continuous process, particularly where it involves self-evaluation:

> People have to develop implicit theories of action in order to make professional life tolerable. There are too many variables to take into account at once, so people develop routines and decision-habits to keep mental effort at a reasonable level. This evolution and internalisation of a theory of action is one aspect of learning to become a teacher and coping in the classroom. Hence to reverse the process and make the theory explicit for purposes of self-evaluation is to draw attention once more to myriads of additional variables, and to raise the possibility of paralysis from information overload and failing to cope ... to continue for any length of time at all ones actions as problematic is a sure recipe for mental breakdown ... (Eraut, 1977a)

Whether the first priority identified by the staff of a school is to agree on a staff policy for staff development, whether it is to review curriculum, or roles and responsibilities does not seem to me to be important. It is crucial, however, that the focus for the policy has been agreed through consultation so that all agree to commit themselves to the task in hand. The way in which this agreement occurs depends not only on the abilities and attitudes of the staff but also on the leadership roles and strategies adopted by the head, the skills which (s)he can apply, and the opportunities which he provides for teachers and departments to investigate systematically the nature of their needs, devise procedures, and acquire appropriate resources to implement and maintain the means of fulfilling these.

Participation in decision-taking

It is reasonable to suggest that the integral approach to staff development is more likely to succeed if it is established through the participation of all staff in the school so that senior management priorities do not always dominate decision-making. Despite the potential for conflict in this model, it is the one which provides the clearest support for the professionality of teachers. However:

> The precise balance would be for each institution to decide in full and open debate: anything else would establish a fertile breeding ground for uncertainty and suspicion which could wreck the partnership on the rocks of either side's mistrust. (Yorke, 1977)

If assessment of individual and institutional need is to be based on a gathering of perceptions of staff and knowledge of their practice, then this must be first for the purpose of understanding their individual, subject specific and departmental frames of reference. The head needs to find ways of engaging with staff in order to understand their beliefs, attitudes, motivations and behaviours so that any interpretations, decisions, judgements are informed. Headteachers who are committed to staff development are, in effect, 'managers of inquiry' in their own schools. Staff development, then, must be recognized as being, and reflecting in practice, a partnership of interests between the DES, LEA, the school, the department and the individual teacher. No single one of these has the exclusive rights to what is the 'best' way forward for another, and each must recognise this. Indeed, since all could legitimately claim to be serving ultimately the best interests of the pupils, then all must be taken into account. Where staff development activities are planned and perceived to provide a balance between the national need, the local need, the community, school, departmental and individual need as identified by the DES, LEA, school, department and individual teacher respectively, then they are likely to be supported by all concerned. Where the perceived staff and curriculum development needs of any one of these groups dominates for any length of time then this is likely to lead to a lessening of the commitment of the others. Indeed, where programmes of staff development have not been negotiated with those who are expected 'to develop' the resulting reticence or resistance of groups or individuals to embrace them, far from being an act of weakness which implies superordinate-subordinate, employer-employee relationships, may be viewed as an act of professional strength.

The implication of this for 'leaders' in schools is that their primary function is not to identify need for others, but to involve others in identifying needs by providing environments which minimise constraints upon learning and in which a variety of concrete, collective and personal experiences may be reflected upon, discussed, assimilated and accommodated.

There are four assumptions about professional learning, the nature of change, and the leader's role which underpin this view of staff development. These are:

1 Professional development is not something that can be forced because it is the teacher who develops (active), and not the teacher who is developed (passive) (Eraut, 1977).

2 Change which is not internalized is likely to be distorted and temporary. Hence, power-coercive strategies or external initiatives which rely on authority rather than encourage development may seem to work, but usually result in 'token' changes at the surface level only.

3 Change at deeper levels involves the modification of perceptions and attitudes, and this is unlikely to occur unless there is participation in the decision-making and planning of the in-service activity.

4 The leader's role is consultative and collaborative.

<u>Leadership roles</u>

Leadership style is the product of leadership roles, and any role will be the product of a constant process of negotiation, which involves not only the expectations of others, but how the individual perceives these expectations, which he perceives as legitimate, and the manner in which he responds to them' (Maw, 1977). Figure 2 below, though clearly applicable more to industry than education (in which the superordinate - subordinate dimension is complicated by the professional autonomy of individual teachers), does provide an interesting range of leadership roles which might be applied, for example, to a staff meeting. it is possible to speculate that the greater the area of freedom accorded to staff, the more sharing there will be of experience, information, and opinion, and the greater the investment of staff in applying decisions taken.

The headteacher who adopts the 'consulting' or 'sharing' modes of leadership behaviour will have a vision of organizational democracy in which there is:

> ... the development of trust among members of the group; openness and sharing of ideas, values and reactions among colleagues; emotional honesty or facing up to one's feelings; self respect and respect for the autonomy of others with whom one works; and belief in the

possibility of continual learning and staff-development ... (Gray, 1975)

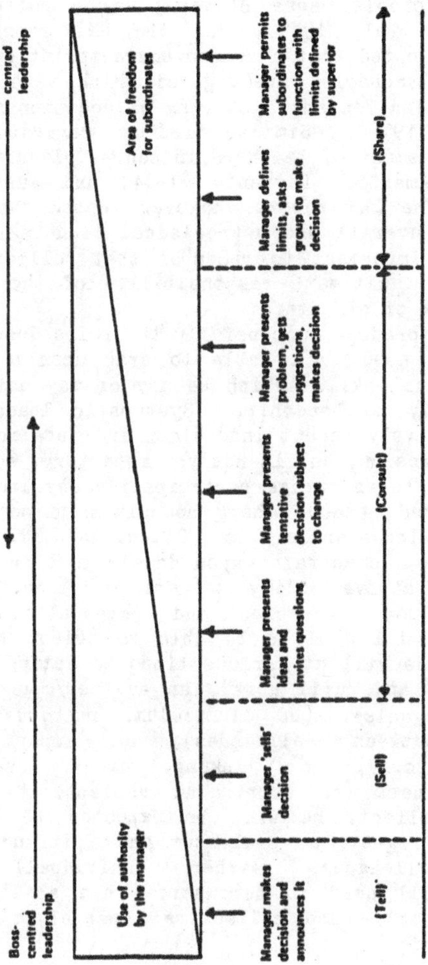

Fig. 2 Modes of decision-making open to a formally-appointed leader (from Tannebaum and Schmidt (1958;1973)

One of the principles-in-action on which this model is based is **participation by staff in the running of the school.** This is based on the assumption that if people are involved in making the decisions that shape their activities, then they are likely to be more committed to their work. The Rutter study, for example, found better results in those schools where planning was a collective activity (Rutter et al, 1979), and the HMI report on Secondary education noted that a common characteristic among those one third of schools investigated which were 'very well led' was consultation and a sharing of decision making among staff. (DES 1979). Similar findings regarding the collaborative involvement of teachers in course planning has been reported in America (Lawrence, 1974) and Australia (Batten, 1979). The DES report, however, noted that the head retained, 'an overall and acknowledged leadership' of staff - and it is important to remember that collectivity does not abolish the ultimate responsibility of the head-teacher for the work of his staff.

If a head is to adopt successfully the roles described above then he will need to be able to draw upon a whole range of interpersonal skills which he may or may not have acquired on his way to headship. Systematic leadership training is a relatively recent innovation in education, is by no means comprehensive, and is not yet mandatory, so that many heads who wish to encourage participation may lack the confidence to proceed because they themselves do not have the appropriate knowledge and skills. Often, then, the head himself will act as a constraint upon development in which staff are seen as active policy shapers. If he is to respond actively to the roles and personalities of colleagues then he will need to be able to select from a variety of roles. He will at various times be acting as an appraiser (of staff and pupil work), an adviser/counsellor (to staff), an organiser (of curriculum, resources), a linking agent (between colleagues); an expert (on curriculum, resources), a linking agent (between colleagues); an expert (on curriculum content, teaching techniques). In effect, he will be expected to be an innovator, a change agent, an evaluator and a friend! In meeting with colleagues, either individually or collectively, he will need to demonstrate his ability to account for individually and collectively perceived needs through his skills of:

1 Planning
2 Organisation
3 Communication
4 Negotiation and contracting
5 Guidance and counselling

6 Continuity and support (through monitoring and review)

Research has indicated that morale in organisations is high when most teachers have a) intrinsic job satisfaction, b) involvement in the immediate work of the group which constitutes the school, c) identification with the organisation, d) interpersonal relationships with 'superiors' in the organisation, and e) satisfaction from work status (Miller and Fom, 1966). Not all adults however have a need to be self-directing. Some teachers, like some children, may need to be 'told' things, or may have an expectation that they should be told (a 'felt incompetence' formed by such factors as role expectation, socialization or psychological needs). Indeed, when teachers are participants in their own learning, problems may arise because their inquiry skills are either undeveloped or underdeveloped. Among teachers, then, as among children, the need and ability to be self-directed will vary, and this need will depend upon factors such as cognitive and personality development, motivation, social development and role expectation.

Since, at its heart, much of staff development work is concerned with questioning the teacher's self-image, the affective relationship is of prime importance if one is to take into account such concerns as anxiety, status and identity. For example, changing one's teaching style may involve a temporary 'burden of incompetence' (Macdonald, 1973) so that there will be a considerable need for psychological and moral support (Day, 1981).

This affective role is rarely made explicit, yet the attitudes of teachers to the process of staff development and to the part played in this by senior management are clearly crucial to its success. How is the headteacher perceived? Is he an authority or a threat? Is he a process helper or a judge with alien values? The answers to these questions will to a large extent depend on the interpersonal relationships which the head forms with his colleagues, and these will be determined by how much he is seen to take into account personal individual factors in his management of people. It is not enough to make organisational changes without taking into account the amount of support which those involved in implementing those changes will need, for change of this kind, 'will not persist if some individual changes do not occur; and changes in the ways individual professionals think and work will soon regress without supporting organisational change' (Schmuck, 1980).

If the headteacher wishes to be perceived as a 'helper', then as well as possessing appropriate helping skills he must be aware of potential misgivings of staff which may lead to unproductive tensions. For example:

1 It is not easy to receive help.
2 It is difficult to commit oneself to change.
3 It is difficult to submit to the influence of a helper: help is a threat to esteem, integrity, and independence.
4 It is not easy to trust a stranger and be open with him.
5 It is not easy to see one's problem clearly at first
6 Sometimes problems seem too large, too overwhelming, or too unique to share easily.

(Brammer, 1973)

He needs to be perceived as trustworthy and this trustworthiness needs to be demonstrated in his behaviour. Gerald Egan (1982) suggests that this can mean a number of things:

> **Confidentiality** ... 'If I tell this person about myself, she will not tell others'
>
> **Credibility**. 'Interpersonal trust is defined ... as an expectancy held by an individual or group that the word, promise, verbal or written statement of another individual or group can be relied on (Rotter, 1971, p444) ...
>
> **Consideration in the use of power**. The assumption here is that the helper is perceived as having power and as being the kind of person who will not misuse it ...
>
> **Understanding**. The client can say, 'If I tell this person about myself, he will make an effort to understand me'.
> (Egan, 1982)

Egan suggested a number of first steps in helping 'clients' which may be usefully applied to the school staff development context:

1 Attend carefully, both physically and psychologically, to the messages transmitted by the (teachers)

2 Listen especially for basic or core messages.

3 Respond fairly frequently, but briefly, to these core messages, but be flexible and tentative enough so that the (teacher) has

room to move (to affirm, deny, explain, clarify, or shift emphasis)

4 Be gentle, but don't let the (teacher) run from important issues.

5 Respond to both feeling and content unless there is some reason for emphasising one or the other.

6 Move gradually toward the exploration of critical topics and feelings.

7 After you have responded, attend carefully to cues that either confirm or deny the accuracy of your response. Does the (teacher) move forward in a focused way?

8 Note signs of (teacher) stress or resistance and try to judge whether these arise because you have lacked accuracy or have been too accurate.
(Egan, 1982)

Possession and sensitive application of such helping skills is by no means guaranteed in the holders of senior management posts in schools. And so they themselves may be said to constitute another potential constraint upon staff development. In the end, this is the most crucial of all the areas of constraint identified in this chapter.

More than ever before, schools need leadership which can both provide moral support for teachers who have sometimes become 'punch-drunk' by external pressures on the curriculum and on their own perceived professionalism; and intellectual support, so that the staff development policies which LEAs will require annually from every school from 1987 may accurately reflect the particular needs of the individual as well as the collective needs of the school. It is, therefore, incumbent upon all who hold leadership roles in schools to identify for themselves and to seek help and support in identifying both areas of strength and areas for improvement in their own helping skills. Even helpers need to be helped.

References

ACSET (1984) The In-service Education, Training and Professional Development of Schoolteachers: Report to the Teacher Training Sub-Committee, DES mimeo
ACSET/INIST (1980) In-service education and training: Some considerations, DES mimeo

Argyris C and Schon D A (1974) Theory in practice: increasing professional effectiveness, Jossey-Bass

Auld R (1976) William Tyndale Junior and Infants Schools Public Inquiry: A Report to the Inner London Education Authority, London, ILEA

Batten M (1979) National Evaluation of the Development Programme, Schools Commission: Canberra

Berg L (1968) Risinghill: death of a comprehensive school, Harmondsworth, Penguin Books

Bolam R (1982) School focused in-service training, Heinemann, London

Braddick W A G, Smith P J (1979) The design of appraisal systems, Ashridge Management College

Brammer L (1973) The helping relationship: Process and skills, Englewood Cliffs NJ: Prentice Hall

Chin R and Benne K (1969) General strategies for effecting changes in human systems. In Bennis W; Benne K and Chin R (eds) The Planning of Change, Holt, New York

Day C (1981) Classroom-based in-service teacher education: the development and evaluation of a client-centred model, University of Sussex, Education Area, Occasional Paper No 9, 1981

Day C, Johnston D and Whitaker P (1986) Managing Primary Schools: a professional development approach, Harper and Row

Doyle W and Ponder C A (1976) The Practicality Ethic in Teacher Decision-Making, Mimeo, North Texas State University, Denton, Texas, USA, 1976

DES (1972) Teacher Education and Training (James Report), HMSO

DES (1975) The Bullock Report: A Language for Life, HMSO

DES (1977) Curriculum 11-16, HMSO

DES (1978) Primary Education in England, HMSO

DES (1978) Making INSET Work: In-service Education and Training for Teachers: A Basis for Discussion, DES, London

DES (1978) Special Educational Needs (Warnock Report), London HMSO

DES (1979) Aspects of Secondary Education in England, HMSO

DES (1980) A View of the Curriculum, London, HMSO

DES (1981) The School Curriculum, DES: Welsh Office

DES (1981) The Secondary Curriculum 11-16: A Report on Progress, London, HMSO

DES (1982) Mathematics Counts: Report of the Committee of Enquiry into the Teaching of Mathematics, (The Cockcroft Report), London, HMSO,

DES (1985) Education for All (The Swann Report), HMSO

Egan G (1982) The Skilled Helper, Brooks/Cole Publishing Co, Monterey, California, USA

East Sussex Accountability Project (1979) Accountability in the Middle Years of Schooling: An Analysis of Policy Options, University of Sussex, mimeo pp 96-107

Eraut M E (1977) Strategies for Promoting Teacher Development, British Journal of In-service Education, Vol 4 Nos 1 and 2, Winter 1977

Eraut M (1977a) In-service Courses: their structure and functions, in Richards C (ed)(1977) New Contexts for Teaching, Learning and Curriculum Studies, Association for the Study of the Curriculum

Gray H L (1975) Organisation development in education: Educational Administration, 4, 1, pp 21-26

Hands G (1981) First catch your adviser: the INSET role of advisers, in Donoughue C et al (1981), In-service: The Teacher and the School, Kogan Page, London

Handy C (1984) Taken for granted? Understanding Schools as Organizations, Schools Council/Longman, London

Havelock R G (1971) The utilization of educational research and development, British Journal of Educational Technology 2(2)

Henderson E S and Perry G W (1981) Change and Development in Schools, McGraw Hill, London

Holt M (1971) The Underachieving School, Penguin Books, Harmondsworth

Illich I (1972) Deschooling Society, London: Penguin Books

Lacey C (1977) The Socialisation of Teachers, London, Methuen

Lawrence G (1974) Patterns of Effective In-service Education, Department of Education, Tallahassee, Florida, USA

Lawton D (1981) The Politics of the Curriculum in Gordon P (ed)(1981) The Study of the Curriculum, Batsford, Studies in Education

Leithwood K A (1981) Managing the implementation of curriculum innovations: Knowledge: Creation-Diffusion-Utilization 2 (1981) pp 341-360

Macdonald B (1973) Innovation and Incompetence in Hamingson, Donald (ed) Towards Judgement: the Publications of the Evaluation Unit of the Humanities Curriculum Project 1970-72, Centre for Applied Research in Education, Occasional Publication 1

Marsh C (1984) Disseminating Curricula: a Look from the Top Down, Journal of Curriculum Studies, Vol 16, No 1, pp 53-66, 1984

Maw J (1977) Defining Roles in Senior and Middle Management in Secondary Schools, in Jennings A (ed) (1977) Management and Headship in the Secondary School, London: Ward Lock Educational

Miller D C and Fom W H (1966) Five Major Dimensions of Morale in Organisations, Industrial Psychology, Harper International

Norris N (ed)(1974) SAFARI, Innovation, Evaluation, Research and the Problem of Control, Centre of Applied Research in Education, University of East Anglia

Nunan T (1983) Countering Educational Design, Croom Helm

Piper D W and Glatter R (1977) The Changing University: a report on staff development in universities, NFER, Windsor

Reynolds J and Skilbeck M (1976) Culture in the Classroom, Open Books, London

Rogers E M and Shoemaker F F (1971) Communication of Innovations: A Cross Cultural Approach, Free Press, New York

Ruddock J (1981) Making the most of the short in-service course, Schools Council Working Paper 71, Methuen Educational

Rutter M et al (1979) Fifteen Thousand Hours: Secondary Schools and their Effects on Children, Eastbourne, Open Books

Schmuck R A (1980) Interventions for strengthening the schools' creativity in Bush T et al (eds) (1980) Approaches to School Management, Harper Row, London

Schon D A (1973) Beyond the Stable State, Penguin, London

Simons H (1982) Process Evaluation in Schools, in McCormick R (ed)(1982) Calling Education to Account, Heinemann Educational Books Ltd

Tannenbaum and Schmidt (1958:1978) How to choose a leadership pattern, reprinted in Harvard Business Review, 1978, 51, 3, pp 162-180

Taylor W (1981) Contraction in context, in Simon B and Taylor W (eds)(1981) Education in the Eighties, Batsford Studies in Education

Taylor Report (1977) A New Partnership for Our Schools, London HMSO

Yorke M (1977) Staff Development in further and higher education: a review British Journal of Teacher Education, Vol 3, No 2, 1977

White J (1981) Enigmatic Guidelines, in White J et al (1981) No, Minister: a Critique of the DES Paper 'The School Curriculum', Bedford Way Papers 4, University of London Institute of Education

Chapter 9

A STRATEGY FOR SCHOOL-BASED STAFF DEVELOPMENT

Ben Kerwood and Simon Clements

This chapter provides an optimistic view of the support and the positive opportunities for staff development of all kinds which are currently available for teachers and schools. The author leads the reader on a 'Cooks tour' of school-based staff development, short and long course opportunities and those presented within the national specific grant training scheme; IT-INSET work; and action research (a theme which is developed in the next chapter). He calls on schools to make use of external consultancy where appropriate, and describes flexible programmes of secondment on which course content and structure is negotiated between teachers, local authority and higher education institutions. Throughout the chapter, the teachers' own perception of need and ability to manage their own learning are taken as the twin starting points for effective staff development.

Coping with change

Perhaps it is because teachers spend most of their time dealing with young people, helping them learn, assessing their needs, looking after their personal and social development, that schools have often neglected to look after the needs, welfare and professional development of their own staff. Many teachers who have experience of industry through exchange or secondment are surprised to find how closely concerned firms are for the welfare of their employees; it is not that schools lack systems of pastoral care, but they use them almost exclusively for the welfare and development of their 'product', their pupils.[1] This is

---

[1]If readers are squeamish about using the word 'product' to refer to pupils, they should read Charles Handy's reply to the question he poses on page 24 of his book 'Taken For Granted? Understanding Schools as Organisations'. Are children workers, clients or products? (Handy, 1984a)

something that simply could not happen in a business whose product is computer software or baked beans. The problem is, predictably, equally observable in the USA.

> Teaching is characteristically viewed only as meeting with students. Very seldom are the activities of planning, evaluating, reflecting or engaging in professional and intellectual pursuits noted in definitions of teaching, although these and other sets of behaviours are considered essential to the maintenance of effective teaching-learning situations. Consequently, teachers and others in schools become preoccupied with the adult-child relationship at the expense of the potential power of adult relationships. (Griffin, 1983)

A period of rapid change sets up tensions and produces fears and self-doubt which can stop us from seizing opportunities, experimenting and taking the risks we need to take in order to develop instead of regress. As teachers we give to young people the extra help and support they need as they experience the rapid changes of adolescence. We need to devote just as much help and support to teachers as they cope with the radical demands made of them by a society in the throes of drastic technological and social change. Where the only constant is, arguably, the state of change itself, we need to come to terms with it, cope with it, manage it. Above all we need to come to terms with it psychologically so that we perceive change as presenting opportunities, not as a threat.

If we really want to make change appear alarming, we can call it metamorphosis, conjuring up Kafkaesque images of identity; but if we want to make it appear more positive and progressive, then we can call it development. This is altogether less threatening, since to remain alive is to develop. This chapter is about development, about managing it in our schools in such a way as to make full use of the opportunities a rapidly changing world presents for teachers. Embarking on new developments involves risks, and this chapter aims to give reassurance to those who read it, to encourage them to launch out and move with the current. A canoeist learns how to let the current do the work, prussicking across a stream by deft use of paddle and water pressure. There are similar skills to those of the canoeist which we hope at least to identify here.

What a school-based staff development strategy means

The chapter title is significant. The use of the word 'strategy' implies planning which is long term, broad based and coherent. It is about a plan of action, and as such it presupposes commitment to generally agreed policies, for it is not possible to develop a strategy without clear, long-term aims. How many schools have yet given sufficient time to developing school-wide staff development policies?

'Staff development' is a broader and more coherent concept than say, staff in-service training which implies a more passive role for staff, a more limited attempt to improve their performance in specific areas. Staff development embraces not only individual education and training, individual appraisal and career enhancement, but also whole-staff development as part of a dynamic and changing organisation. Unlike curriculum development which can be subject specific and limited in scope, staff development is more than improving teaching technique within a subject area; it includes all-round development of the individual and the inter-relationship of teachers' different subject areas and levels of responsibility. It is about teachers "creating 'thinking schools', that is to say, schools in which all members of staff participate fully in seeking solutions to those problems which they themselves define as being of the highest priority" (Merritt, 1981).

> Staff development efforts involve <u>people</u> in <u>interaction</u> with one another in particular <u>contexts</u> to accomplish professional growth and school improvement goals. (Griffin, 1983)

For us the significant features of the term 'school-based' are that instead of teachers being seconded to other institutions where they develop in isolation and out of the school context, the staff development takes place within the school so that ownership of change remains vested in the teachers. The development process is an organic one which starts from the school's own perceived needs, relates individual needs to those of the whole and ensures continuing development through practical outcomes and immediate feedback. Most importantly, the school is seen as a major resource in material and above all in human terms. The staff are the central resource, their expertise and creativity tapped through individual encouragement and through working in teams. The changes of role and exchange of ideas which are the essence of teamwork make it one of the most dynamic forces for development.

<u>Working in the context of the school</u>

The chief advantage of working in context is that development begins with identifying concrete problems, bringing to the surface key preoccupations which are of major concern to the school itself. Beginning with real issues and practical concerns and only later applying theory produces much less resistance to change from people who see their job as essentially practical. Motivation is increased by emphasising the problem-solving nature of development, encouraging the sharing of individual problems and identifying concerns common to all or to certain groups. Many teachers will have been unaware that their own problem is shared by others and will be more willing to face it given colleagues' support and co-operation.

An in-service day, or half a day, may be used very effectively as a workshop in which staff share their concerns with one another and support each other in producing creative solutions and plans. After the briefest of introductions, people break up into working groups of ten or so members to discuss and pool their contributions, recording them with felt-tipped pens on flipchart paper. If the creative resources of all teachers are to be tapped, it is important to avoid the inhibitions of hierarchy. To this end, groups may be leaderless but it is usually more effective to choose as leaders people from various levels who are secure and confident enough to enable the group to function without any one person dominating it and with everyone contributing something. The briefing of group leaders is crucial, as is prior briefing and consultation of the whole staff about the purposes and parameters of the day.

Once the working groups have identified and discussed problems, they record the most significant of them on flipcharts. They go through the same process with suggestions or plans for action. it is usually advisable to limit the number they record to six or perhaps ten of each. The flipcharts are then blue-tacked up for display in a central area where everyone can look at them over a cup of tea. Meanwhile the co-ordinator of the day, perhaps a deputy head, an adviser or an outside consultant, collates all the ideas from the groups, either taking them from the flipcharts or asking group leaders or scribes to hand in duplicate lists on A4 paper. For the final plenary session, the co-ordinator feeds back the collated ideas using an overhead projector. Because the groups are working in the context of the school, they will tend to identify concrete problems and barriers and to produce practical outcomes. A skilful collator can turn data into information, can begin the process of showing how the specific and the practical relate to more general and theoretical contexts, can point towards the possible ways forward which might have been dismissed or received with scepticism had they been proffered in theoretical papers.

This model of in-service workshop achieves a high level of feedback. Inevitably problems are bound up with people and there will be views expressed which could be perceived as threatening by a range of people including the head, deputies and heads of department, but also governors, parents and the LEA. It is important to involve as many of these interested groups as possible in the workshop, a point we look at in more detail later in this chapter. There is a degree of risk here which needs to be anticipated and consciously taken, just as there is risk in allowing pupils or teachers to contribute self-assessment to profiles or appraisal schemes. Because the element of risk to a headteacher is high, there is an important part for the LEA to play here in providing support. Many heads may only be deterred from undertaking a new project by the fear that it may fail. That fear is greatly reduced if the project has LEA support, national support, or the support of a consortium of schools, very probably brought together by the LEA. Credit for any success needs to be given to the individual school, otherwise it will not be able to take a pride in owning its achievements, but it is important that the risk of failure is shared more broadly.

The risk is worth taking because feedback is a crucial process in any sort of development but it needs to be two-way. This is ensured where the whole staff is involved in an in-service workshop day, each person both contributing and listening, but where smaller working groups are operating over a longer period they need both to consult the rest of the staff and to keep them fully informed, sharing with them every stage of development, involving them in every decision that affects them. The impact of a single in-service day can easily be lost if it is not followed up by feeding back to the staff a paper recording the main issues of the day and using this paper as a basis for continuing activity by working groups.

Secondment as a complement to school-located INSET

In-service training days and regular meetings of working groups both rely heavily upon teacher goodwill, something which is understandably in short supply at the moment. Recurrent industrial action on top of levels of resourcing which rule out the possibility of finding time for working groups within the timetabled day makes it unlikely that effective staff development will be achieved without use of teacher secondment. And here lies a serious problem, because most secondments take the teacher out of school and teachers returning from secondment are commonly treated with suspicion and a certain amount of envy or resentment, their suggestions for changes being greeted with scepticism, suspicion or hostility. Change is likely to be perceived as sudden, imposed from outside and more concerned with the advancement of the returning change-agent than with the development of the institution and all its members. If change is to be unthreatening it needs instead to be continuous and organic, not necessarily steady or gradual, but a process in which all are involved, whatever stage it is at.

Some teachers will resist change simply because it forces them to think afresh, to try things that are new; some will feel that their personal standing depends upon maintaining the status quo and will see a threat in any sort of movement; others will feel they have built up a subject department or some other empire, possibly at the expense of other developing empires and will see any sort of sharing or whole-staff development as a potential threat. Such people are more likely to be infected with enthusiasm for change, or at least be less resistant to it where it comes from within rather than from a colleague returning from a course, where everyone is involved, and where different people are invited to contribute in their own particular way. Attempts have been made to lessen the re-entry problem by seconding more than one teacher from the same school at a time so that they can give each other mutual support when they return, but the problem of off-site in-service courses remains. Plans and solutions developed out of context are hard to adapt to the reality of the situation, which has probably changed since the teacher was last in the school. Alternatively, plans may be theoretical, needing translation into specific and practical terms.

A more radical approach to secondment has been adopted by some LEAs who have wished to encourage school-based staff development programmes through allocating secondments to those involved in school-based INSET. They have been able to do so by negotiating flexible programmes of secondments with universities, polytechnics and colleges of higher education. Under these arrangements, proposals made by individual schools or groups of schools for collaborative work involving teams of teachers are tailored to fit Diploma or Certificate-bearing courses. The work is mainly school-located, but involves access to higher education facilities, including seminars and tutorials. Assessment is based upon individual submissions which may take the form of a fairly traditional dissertation or may bring together a collection of more practical work completed within the school. In some cases, a submission in the form of a videotape of practical, school-based activities has been accepted. It is not yet possible to enter a joint submission for certification, but the requirement that work be submitted individually does not preclude it originating in a group or team project.

An example of this sort of school-based secondment is Oxfordshire's 'New Learning Initiative', NLI, their DES funded provision for low-attaining pupils. Staff from eleven schools have been seconded, one in each school for a year, more for a term at a time to develop new and varied curriculum programmes. The project has been to investigate why some pupils respond unfavourably to schooling, but "once you start asking questions about the ways pupils behave and respond, you have to start asking questions about the ways teachers behave, what they do in the classroom and how they do it. It has been important that teachers involved in the project have engaged in this process of self-evaluation and review" (Oxon CC, 1985). In that the project involves groups of teachers in planning, discussing, reviewing, evaluating and developing the project, exchanging ideas and acquiring new knowledge and skills, it is a project as much about the professional development of teachers as about low-attaining pupils. In short, NLI teachers become change-agents in "school-based internal development, working from individual schools' existing strengths", a model consciously based on the thinking of HMI in 'Aspects of Secondary Education' (DES, 1979). It is the teacher's reflexive account and evaluation of his or her work which forms the basis of the dissertation each submits for accreditation to Oxford Polytechnic.

DES and LEA short courses are a further, but more limited way of providing time for staff development. The tendency has been for courses to be geared to the training of trainers who will return to their schools and feed back their expertise by running programmes of staff training and development. Typical of this approach have been the courses set up under the Governing Inservice Training Grant Scheme, GIGS, (Circulars 3.83, 4.84 and 3.85). Teachers have been trained in priority areas of management for heads and senior staff, special educational needs, mathematics, science and pre-vocational education in order to return and train others. The expectation is that the schools and the LEA will find time for these trainers to do their work and the logical course is to anticipate that as much time will be needed for the trainer to work in school as was given for his or her release.

Time has also been 'bought' for school-based staff development by rethinking the relationship between initial teacher training and continuing in-service training. Increasingly there is a move towards basing initial training more firmly in the schools, involving teachers more closely in the process and blurring the distinction between teacher and learner. Where tutor, student and teacher work together, all three parties contribute towards one another's development, and where a number of students are present in one school, a sizeable number of teaching staff can be involved in development. In effect, the university, polytechnic or college tutor's time is being 'bought' by the school, the student is a further resource, and teacher-time is released through co-operative teamwork, allowing opportunities for testing theory in the context of the particular organization. The school becomes the testing ground for theories of classroom interaction, small group work, teacher/pupil negotiation, subject integration or whatever developments are being considered. By observing and analysing other teachers and classes at work and by trying out and evaluating ideas with groups of pupils, whether these involve changes in the process of learning or in the content of the curriculum, teachers can benefit from action research as an integral part of the staff development programme. Probably the best example of this type of scheme is the IT/INSET project based at Leicester University, but the Cambridge University PGCE course and the Oxford University PGCE 'Internship' scheme are on similar lines.

It seems likely that these schemes will prove to be the pattern for the future, rather than the exceptions, since the Government has made clear its intention of ensuring that contact between training institutions and schools is close and continuing: "a sufficient proportion of each training institution's staff should have enjoyed success as teachers in schools, and their experience should be recent, substantial and relevant. Many of the staff do not now have such experiences. Those of the staff who are concerned with pedagogy should also have continuing regular contact with classroom teaching ... The training institutions should therefore now take steps, in consultation with LEAs and schools, to ensure that there is sufficient recent teaching experience among relevant staff through, eg secondments, the use of joint teacher/tutor appointments and schemes of teacher/tutor exchange. The establishment of close links between training institutions and suitable schools in their vicinity will facilitate arrangements along these lines" (DES, 1983).

Recognition that "a dynamic, highly motivated and skilled teaching force is directly dependent on recognition of the needs of teachers already in service for further training and professional development and the provision of opportunities to meet those needs" (ACSET, 1984) has led to commitment by the Government to change the secondment system in March, 1987. The current 'pooling' arrangements under which LEAs are able to recoup most of the cost of secondments to long courses is due to be replaced by a new scheme on the lines of the ACSET recommendations. If the scheme reflects the interim arrangements of the TVEI-Related In-service Training (TRIST) Fund introduced in 1985, then it is likely to prove considerably more flexible than existing arrangements. The criteria for funding include, for example, "group work in other schools, on employers' premises, in colleges or in teaching centres", (TVEI Unit, 1985) reflecting the tendency in LEAs where the system of secondments has been used to the full, which has been for higher priority to be given to County-wide projects involving teams of teachers and advisers and to school or College-based In-service Training than to individual secondments to study for higher qualifications.

The new scheme includes incentives for LEAs to use the scheme fully, including budgeting for costs for administration and funding at 90% instead of 75%. This is important because under the present system of poolable secondments there are huge disparities in the amount the scheme is used by different LEAs. Some LEAs currently have 200 teachers on secondment to long-term courses whereas others have no more than 4 or 5, a difference which gives teachers in some LEAs far greater chances for professional development than in others. In its recommendations to the Secretary of State ACSET noted:

> We are aware of the disparity which exists between different LEAs in the financial provision made for INSET and hence in the opportunities for teachers to undertake INSET activities. We regard it as unsatisfactory that geographical location and ability to pay should be factors in determining whether or not teachers have access to INSET. (ACSET, 1984)

The need for recognition, accreditation and reward

It is important that In-service education and training which is school-based should carry with it the reward of external accreditation at Degree, Diploma or Certificate level in just the same way as other full-time secondment. Not all teachers are motivated by this sort of formal recognition, as witnessed by the popularity of schoolteacher fellowships, but the importance of rewards is one that should not be played down, nor can it be dissociated from the problem of greatly reduced promotion prospects within the profession.

> One of the great strengths of school-focussed INSET is also a potential danger. By stressing the needs of the educational system (for example, the school or department) more teachers will certainly be motivated to participate in INSET but, in a time of economic cuts, it will be only too easy to elevate the needs of the system above those of the individual teacher. (Bolam, 1982)

What is required is a careful balance between the two, for they are complementary rather than mutually exclusive.

School-based staff INSET tends to put a high emphasis on the process of the course and on its practical outcomes. The Certificate takes second place to the tangible achievement of curricular packages, new procedures, systems of time use, groupings or other innovations. It may be enough to record a teacher's participation in such work, or to refer to their contribution and achievements in a subsequent job application. On the other hand, Certificates and Diplomas are important incentives and currency for many people, and school-based staff development needs to ensure that certification is provided, or that alternative forms of accreditation or public recognition are given by the LEA or by the school, perhaps through its governing body. At present, DES regulations tend to equate secondments with the gaining of further formal qualifications, but after March 1987 it may be that LEAs will be able to choose forms of secondment in which the process and the practical outcomes are the justification and reward.

Staff development needs to consider alternatives to financial rewards and to encourage teachers to be more aware of the various aspects of job satisfaction that appeal to them and the ways they can seek rewards and recognition within existing constraints. Just as pupil profiles are being developed which celebrate a wider range of success than do conventional exam certificates, so ways of recognising and celebrating staff successes need to be included in any development programme. A more flexible approach to role which does not link responsibility automatically with financial reward can allow creation of posts of responsibility and changes of role which are both rewarding in themselves and valuable preparation for later promotion, and which release new sources of talent within the school.

Teacher motivation and reward are, of course, not the only reasons for external certification of In-service Training and development. Another is the need for some external yardstick to apply so that only high standards are accorded recognition. This is part of the public accountability of schools. If money and time are to be spent on staff development, then there needs to be some evidence that resources are being well used. It would be helpful if whole-school, or group achievements could receive whole-school, or group accreditation, but at present it remains impossible to attain academic awards other than individually. Even where teachers work on joint projects under secondment arrangements at a higher education institution, individual submissions are required for certification. It would be good to think that plans for group certification were under consideration, but we have yet to find evidence of them. In the meantime, there are two ways in which whole-school development can achieve national recognition. The Royal Society of Arts 'Education for Capability' Recognition Scheme welcomes applications from all sorts of educational establishments whose work encourages in learners the four capacities of competence, coping, creativity and co-operation. The Society of Education Officers 'Curriculum Award Scheme' is intended to be the educational equivalent of 'Awards to Industry'.

No school is an island

School-based staff development needs to be open to outside influences for other reasons than that of accreditation. Access to theoretical input is probably the most important contribution a university, polytechnic or college can make, and it is a contribution which is likely to be made stronger and more welcome where it has grown naturally from identification of a problem in the practical school setting. There is often a reluctance among teachers to believe that theoretical models can be helpful or useful, just as much academic research is couched in such forms as to be virtually inaccessible to practitioners. But it is often impossible for a school staff to see their problems with enough detachment to seek other than short-term solutions. It can come as a considerable surprise to find that your problem is not unique, and that much of that most treasured commodity, time, has already been spent by others on analysing it, researching into it and investigating possible solutions. To ignore wider theoretical research often leads to re-inventing the wheel at considerable cost in time and resources. It also leads to short-sighted solutions which are based on hunches rather than on painstaking professional research.

HMI noted the dangers of schemes that are inward-looking in their 1981 Discussion Paper, linking the problem to the employment of an external agent, an aspect of staff development we consider in this chapter.

> There is by now ample evidence of the success of school-focused In-service training, but there is the obvious danger that self-nurture is limited in the insights that are available to it. Someone from outside can often act as a Socratic figure, in posing the questions as well as helping to arrive at solutions. Certain of the questions that should be asked may be more obvious to the outsider than to those fully involved, and some external agent who knows the school is well placed to advise on the range of resources best suited to what has been decided upon. This is a function to which the local education authority adviser and the college lecturer can both contribute. (DES, 1981)

The reverse of this coin is that solutions and theories introduced from outside are seldom successful in bringing about change within an institution. Teachers in a school need to feel they have found their own solution to their own problem, that they own the means of change, if lasting innovation is to be achieved. Needs have to be assessed, problems formulated, the relevant theoretical inputs absorbed and solutions reached which are based on sound theory and research but which are unique to the particular school and its staff.

At the same time, staff involved in school-based development have access to considerable resources for action research. Attachment to a college or university ensures not only a theoretical input, but tutorial help in making use of the school as a source of empirical research to match against the theoretical. It may prove hard for a teacher to step out of role to carry out research within their own school, but this is another area where LEA help can enable co-operation between schools so that research can be carried out in another or in several schools in the Authority.

Comparison with other practice is another important reason for encouraging cooperation between schools. The LEA can facilitate the sharing of practice within the Authority. ILEA, for example, is setting up a databank to further this process and Oxfordshire has had a databank of work done by teachers on secondment for some time. The CSCS national databank in York was set up to fulfil this precise function, collecting information about interesting practice from schools all over the country, storing the information on micro-computer and making it available to enquirers. The CSCS databank puts enquirers in touch with schools who are willing to share examples of practice in a particular area of interest. Recently more specialised databanks have been established like the one for schools and industry at St Mary's College, Twickenham, but the CSCS databank remains a model which is continuing to develop and is now available by direct access through Prestel and the Times Network (CSCS 1 and 2, 1985).

Any scheme would do well to find out what local, regional and national networks exist. Through subject associations like the Geographical Association, cross-curricular associations like the National Association for Pastoral Care Education, NAPCE, LEA Resource Centres and orgnisations that specialise in setting up networks like Understanding British Industry, (UBI), and The Centre for the Study of Comprehensive Schools, (CSCS), a school-based project can gain access to a wide variety of other practice. Accessing is even more direct where Prestel or the Times Network facilities are available. Already many schools are linked to computer networks via their own modem. The use of, say, the Times Network provides a source of staff development in itself through the facility for teachers to gain micro-computer experience through using it in a real situation, a model for acquiring competence which can then be applied to pupils' learning.

A Policy of Openness

The need for school-based staff development to involve other 'stakeholders' has been alluded to earlier in this chapter in connection with reaching the agreement of all interested parties to a whole-school policy. It is also relevant to accountability and accreditation which we have discussed. By stakeholders we mean all those who have an interest in schools - parents, members of the local community, including the business community, elected members, governors, pupils, HMI, and LEA officers and advisers. This is a formidable list, and we are not suggesting they all be involved all the time, but that their interests should be respected, they should be used as a resource and there should be as much openness towards them as possible.

The Ruskin Speech of 1976 was only one of several landmarks along the route towards relevance in education, more answerability to the needs of society. Recent Government statements have been concerned, if not obsessed, with the need for education to be instrumental in meeting the nation's needs, above all its economic needs. The view that education is valuable per se, and needs no justification, eloquently expressed by Enoch Powell in his speech to the Merchant Taylors' Company, was greeted in this Times Educational Supplement leader:

> There could hardly be a more opportune time to make this case, and make it without compromise ... If education is a self-justifying good in a good society, it follows that access should be as wide as possible for reasons which relate not just to the growth of GNP but to the enrichment of our civilization. Mr Powell's broadside is timely and wise. (TES, 4.1.84)

Education <u>may</u> be a self-justifying good, but not since the 1960s has it been perceived as such by the general public. Instead schools are increasingly likely to be judged by their ability to turn out a useful product, and teachers by their ability to contribute effectively to this end. Developing the policies outlined in 'Teaching Quality', the Government White Paper 'Better Schools' suggests while "Every teacher needs a repertoire of teaching styles" (p 134), "The principle of relevance means that teachers should be skilful in drawing on pupils' experience and helping them to apply what is learnt to life outside school, so preparing them more effectively for working life" (p 137) (DES, 1985). Staff accordingly need to be sensitive to their 'market'.

Marketing is not something that schools have traditionally been good at. Instead they have been more concerned with passing on a body of received wisdom. Once they are seen as serving a community, however, they need to find out what it is the community wants before deciding how best they can provide it. This is the equivalent to the practice of market research, and it is something school-based In-service work is in a good position to undertake. Market research involves openness to criticism and to constructive suggestions. It is the very opposite to working on plans behind closed doors and then unveiling completed plans to the interested parties. People who have not themselves been involved in planning change are much less likely to welcome it. CSE, for example, would probably have received a warmer welcome from industrialists had they been involved in its preparation from the outset. Staff development involves a change which will gain more support and understanding from governors and parents, for example, if they are involved on working parties, invited to attend In-service training sessions.

Involving people from outside the school

Professional and managerial development are common concerns to teachers and members of industrial firms. Inviting people from firms to contribute to staff development in school can help teachers see themselves as others see them, help mutual understanding of each other's needs, help overcome isolation and lead to growth in teamwork. Schools can take advantage of the fact that many of their pupils have parents who work in industry and the majority of adults in firms have children of their own, to build on this mutual interest. It is particularly helpful for teachers to work alongside parents, forgetting their particular role and the formal teacher/parent relationship and instead working together as adults who are faced with common problems.

The Schools' Council (now Curriculum) Industry Project, SCIP, made extensive use of adults other than teachers as an extra and particularly valuable resource in working with children. The Project was as much about changing teacher attitudes and approaches to learning as about developing children's understanding of industry, and much of the staff development was achieved by the use of outside change agents. Lesley Bradshaw's recent work with the North Yorkshire Schools' Industry Association, NYSIA, exemplifies the role an outside facilitator can play in school-based staff development. Her paper 'The Schools Industry Liaison Officer' is a detailed analysis of the role (Bradshaw,

1985). The outside facilitator can adopt a relatively narrow focus or be of general use to the school as a change agent.

When a business organisation embarks on a course of action which involves change, it is quite likely to employ an outside consultant. Where a school embarks on a staff development scheme, something which also involves change, it would do well to consider engaging someone in a similar consultant role. The main problem for a school is shortage of cash to reward a consultant on anything like the scale regarded as normal in the industrial world, but there are ways of overcoming the problem, at least on a small scale.

We have come across a number of ways in which schools have been able to bring in outsiders in the consultant role. SCIP and NYSIA have already been mentioned. At Adeyfield School, Hemel Hempstead, the secondment of a bank manager to the school was successfully negotiated between the school and the Banking Information Service, BIS. The manager brought a different viewpoint to the school which gave new insight into staff development, and the day-to-day contacts during his time with the staff were as valuable as the final report he produced. Michael Beloe, the Head, wrote:

> When we came to review his recommendations, we felt we needed to tighten up on our procedures for in-service work. It is difficult to ensure that the school as a whole benefits from the experience of individual colleagues returning from courses. We also decided to proceed with annual discussions/interviews with all staff on a pretty informal basis ... Have we any recommendations for others , thinking of taking in an 'outsider'? We feel it was very worthwhile. BIS has considered it successful enough to make a further secondment on similar lines, and CSCS is planning to hold a seminar on secondments from industry into schools. It should prove an enlightening discussion.

It was. The seminar, mounted jointly by CSCS and BIS took place on 24 May, 1985, and is to be followed by a second seminar.

Within a Local Authority, advisers can be brought in as consultants and arrangements can be made for a teacher from one school to act as a consultant in another. But LEA advisers and teachers from other schools, particularly if they are in the same Authority, are not ideal for the consultant role. Havelock defined five characteristics of the consultant, viz

1 The client initiates the consultancy.

2 The consultant-client relationship is temporary and specific to the immediate problem in hand.

3 The consultant and client come from different professional disciplines.

4 The consultant is advisory only.

5 The consultant has no administrative relationship to the client (ie he is not a superordinate or able to assess the client).

Several of these criteria are not met. In short, these people could be seen as either threatening, or influential, or both, as would members of HMI for example. It is hard, if not impossible, to combine consultancy with a monitorial role because it is about helping people cope with change, not about judging or changing people.

There is a very small number of former teachers, headteachers and lecturers who offer their services as consultants, and we have ourselves been involved in several consultancy roles with school staffs as part of our work for CSCS. Feedback suggests that an outside consultant can play an invaluable part in helping teachers to bring focus to a whole-staff INSET day or to evaluate what they are achieving in school over a longer period. As yet demand for consultancy in education is but a tiny fraction of demand in the industrial world and this appears to be more due to lack of awareness of the function than to lack of resources. If the demand were to grow, then the function could be exercised not only by retired teachers, but by seconded teachers and heads. It was as seconded teachers that we provided our consultancy service to CSCS members, and we have come across LEAs who are using a seconded headteacher for the same purpose within the Authority.

The management of time

Of all the requirements for a school-based staff development strategy probably the most essential is time. It is only too easy to use lack of time as a reason for inaction, for delay or to lay the blame for inaction at the door of those accused of making unreasonable demands on the time available - Exam Boards, Local Authorities, the Government or whoever. Once again a comparison with industrial approaches is helpful. Any firm that used shortage of time to justify inaction or delay would soon go out of business. Instead businesses accept realistic time constraints within which careful management and ordering of priorities can put the time available to most effective use.

Teachers' time is the prime resource in a school. Teachers' salaries account for over 60% of the costs of education. Staff development programmes need to start from this premise and to ensure that strategies are designed to maximise its use. To this end development programmes would do well to include investigation into alternative structures for the school day which allow more flexible use of time, and into curricula based on modules within a common core where subjects are brought together into areas, clusters, or faculties. Both investigations would seek to find ways of releasing teachers during normal school hours and of encouraging teachers to work cooperatively in learning, so that they can undertake development work. Detailed consideration of alternative approaches to timetabling and structuring the day are not possible here, but several alternatives are considered in 'The Oxfordshire School Day' (Oxon CC, 1982) and Stantonbury Campus, Milton Keynes, and Countesthorpe College, Leicestershire have put several alternatives into practice. Primary practice has much to teach secondary schools about cross-curricular work and effective use of teachers' time.

Nor is consideration of the vexed question of contact time possible here. Presently contact time means teaching time, but if staff development and the management processes of running a school are to be given the sort of priority that would be accorded to them in an equivalent industrial organisation, then contact time needs to include planning time, thinking time and meeting time, both formal and informal, between staff at all levels. It may be that one good thing to come out of the present struggle between teachers' unions and employers over conditions of service will be a re-definition of contact time to include day-to-day management and staff development. After all, "Wages are money paid for time. The individual sells his or her time. The employer then organizes the efforts of the individual during that time" (Handy, 1984b). There seems to be a growing realisation by teacher employers that valuable human resources are being wasted by failing to ensure that sufficient time is devoted to the continuing professional development of their employees.

Certainly any agreement over a new contract of service for teachers will have to take into account the time needed for teacher appraisal schemes. The recent study of teacher assessment commissioned by the DES from Suffolk LEA, in recommending that classroom observation be "seen to be central to the process of appraisal" and that it should be followed by an informal interview of at least 45 minutes to establish teachers' views of their own performance, and ways of improving it, concludes that appraisal would take up to 12 hours per teacher and that appraisers might spend up to half their time in school carrying out the task. It also recommends three-day training courses for heads of department, followed by yearly one-day refresher courses (Suffolk CC, 1985). This gives some idea of the sort of time that will need to be invested in school-based staff development if it is to be accorded the priority it deserves. The welcome this report has received from the teacher unions and the Secretary of State gives some grounds for optimism.

Getting the message

Conscious development needs feedback. To give this, there needs to be a continuous process of evaluation. There is likely to be a requirement for a summative evaluation to be submitted to the LEA as part of ensuring they get value for money, and by the University or other provider to enable them to plan appropriate future programmes and to contribute towards wider research. Where the school has mounted its own programme, it, too, will benefit from a summative evaluation at the end of each stage of development. There also needs to be formative evaluation matched by enough flexibility in the development programme for changes to take place during its course in response to feedback from participants. Where the participants know that feedback from them is listened to and results in change, this strengthens their commitment to and sense of ownership of the in-service programme.

In our experience, participants' self-assessment is best coordinated by an evaluator, who needs similar characteristics to the consultant role which we considered above. The consultant is "an 'outsider', ie is not part of any hierarchical power system in which the client is located" (Lippitt, 1959). Likewise, the evaluator needs to be seen as a 'helper', someone sufficiently informed who is, as it were, on the side of the participants and who ensures that the scheme is meeting their needs in the most effective way possible. Through informal discussion, more formal questioning using interviews and questionnaires, and through participant observation, the evaluator can articulate the reactions and criticisms of participants, feeding them back and directing them to programme providers and organisers. (For more detail on the means available for evaluation, see Henderson, 1978.) The evaluator gains credibility and the confidence of participants by becoming their spokesman and agent for change.

Longer-term evaluation is altogether harder to achieve. Ray Bolam comments gloomily that "At present, there is a dearth of good ideas for ensuring effective feedback about, and follow-up to, INSET activities and programmes" (Bolam, 1982). We have found it quite possible to assess, feed back and follow up the perceptions of the participants and we have found the role of participant observer very valuable, but we have yet to find an effective way of evaluating the way staff development programmes influence the school as an organisation, or the way they affect the subsequent practices of the participating teachers, individually or as a group. It is of little comfort that precisely the same problem has been noted in the United States (Griffin, 1983). It is our belief, however, that what is most important is that teachers' perceptions should change and develop. It should be possible to record their perceptions of key issues at the outset and compare them with their perceptions of the same issues later. Have they, for instance, grasped the central message?

The message the teachers should receive is that it is their own perception of their needs which is the starting point; that they are being trusted to formulate their own problems; that they are being valued as the principal resource, that they are being given the power to manage their own learning and develop their own solutions. In short, the message is one of empowerment. Instead of being removed from the organisation to learn from outside experts, it is recognised that the organisation contains sufficient talent within itself for development. The confidence that this realisation brings to the staff enables them to look for expert and theoretical help from outside when they need it, and to be more open in the way they approach their work and their problems, evaluating, appraising and consulting one another and sharing ideas, successes and failures. At no point do staff lose the power over their own development and in consequence they feel a sense of ownership of all the changes that take place. In short, they and their school have the power to develop through identifying and solving their own problems in a continuous process. That is the message.

References

ACSET (1984) Report of the Advisory Committee on the Supply and Education of Teachers The In-service Educational Training and Professional Development of School Teachers, London, HMSO.

Beloe, M (1985) Contributions 8, York: Centre for the Study of Comprehensive Schools

Bolam R (1982) (ed) School-focussed In-service Training, London, Heinemann

Bradshaw, L (1985) The School Industry Liaison Officer, York, Centre for the Study of Comprehensive Schools

CSCS Broadsheet 1 (1985) Concerned with Comprehensive Education?, York, CSCS

CSCS Broadsheet 2 (1985) Databank Services, York, CSCS

Department of Education and Science (1979) Aspects of secondary education in England, London, HMSO

Department of Education and Science (1981) *Teacher training and the secondary school. HMI discussion paper*, London, HMSO

Department of Education and Science (1983) *Teaching Quality*, London, HMSO

Department of Education and Science (1985) *Better Schools*, London, HMSO

Griffin, G A (1983) *Staff Development*, Chicago, University of Chicago Press for National Society for the Study of Education

Handy, C (1984a) *Taken for granted? Understanding schools as organizations*, York, Longman for Schools Council

Handy, C (1984b) *The Future of Work*, Oxford, Basil Blackwell

Henderson, E S (1978) *The Evaluation of In-service Teacher Training*, London, Croom Helm

Lippitt, R (1959) Dimensions of the Consultant's Job, in *The Journal of Social issues* Volume XV

Merritt, J (1981) in Donoughue, C (ed) *In-service: The Teacher and the School*, London, Kogan Page

Oxfordshire County Council (1982) *A Change in the Oxfordshire School Day?*, Oxford, Oxon CC

Oxfordshire County Council (1985) *New Learning Initiative Occasional Paper 2. In-service training and staff development*, Wheatley, Oxon CC

Suffolk County Council (1985) *Those having torches ... Teacher Appraisal: a study*, (The Graham Report) Ipswich, Suffolk LEA

TVEI Unit (1985), *TVEI Related In-service Training* (TRIST), MSC

Times Educational Supplement (4.1.85), *Back to First Principles* page 2 leader, London, Times Newspapers

Chapter 10

ACTION RESEARCH FOR STAFF DEVELOPMENT

Brian Wakeman

In this chapter the reader is invited to consider the merits and possibilities of applying action research techniques to the management of professional development. The author uses his own school as a case study for this, drawing from examples of practice, and argues that, particularly in a time of resource contraction and attacks on staff morale, heads and senior managers must promote openness, respect for persons, participation and questioning if they are to nurture a staff and curriculum development policy which is perceived by all parties to be relevant to their needs and to have practical outcomes. He sees whole school, department and individual action research as offering a practical way forward, and in doing so, reinforces the calls of the authors of the previous chapter for empowering teachers and schools to take more advantage of the whole range of opportunities for staff development.

What is action research? This expression is heard in various contexts of medicine, tutorial work with pupils, and in educational research. John Elliott describes action research as the 'systematic reflection on practical problems experienced by teachers with a view to arriving at what ought to be done about them' (Elliot, 1977). Stephen Kemmis and Robin McTaggart writing in "The Action Research Planner" say that the concept of action research has its origin in the work of social psychologist Kurt Lewin, (1946).

> Two of the ideas which were crucial in Lewin's work were the ideas of group decision and commitment to improvement. A distinctive feature of action research is that those affected by planned changes have the primary responsibility for deciding on courses of action which seem likely to lead to

improvement, and for evaluating the results of strategies tried out in practice. (Kemmis, McTaggart, 1982)

Action research, then, is essentially practical. It is about the day-to-day activities of teachers and learners. It is about surviving in the hurly-burly of the classroom, but more importantly it is about improving teaching and learning. Action research is not an activity which is esoteric, remote or jargon-ridden, but it is about 'what teachers actually do'. As Jon Nixon remarks,

> By investigating and reflecting upon their own practice teachers may increase their understanding of the classroom ... action research informs the teachers judgement about such things as how children learn ... These kinds of enquiry may increase the knowledge and understanding of teachers in such a way that they are able to respond more sensitively to the needs of their pupils in terms of both face to face classroom interactions and more formal aspects of curriculum planning and school organisation. (Nixon, 1981)

Action research, then, has three motifs: 'practicality'; 'problem-solving'; and 'professionalism respected'. These three notions relate directly to staff development, and to the optimism I have toward action research as a worthwhile strategy in management. Before I explore these motifs and describe the techniques of action research a discussion about the notion of "staff development" is appropriate, particularly in these times of declining resources, promotion prospects and declining morale.

"Staff development" or "professional development" are expressions we meet at conferences about management in schools, or in the rhetoric of handbooks for new teachers joining our schools; and yet familiar though we are with the expressions, I suspect interpretations may vary. Staff development may mean 'getting on a course to climb the promotion ladder' to junior colleagues in the staff room, but to deputy heads it may mean 'manipulating colleagues to fit in with the boss's plans!'. A parody perhaps? Consider your LEA perspective. That application for a summer school in pastoral care for pupils may be grant-aided as an investment for the authority, but a teacher may regard it very differently. There are political and personal dimensions to these notions which may be complementary or in opposition. Before passing on, these need to be acknowledged. Conflicting interests exist, and it is not always possible or desirable to disentangle the personal from the professional motives.

To take account of these issues and acknowledge the difficulties I will use the terms 'professional' or 'staff development' in their broadest sense. Individual teachers or groups of teachers may wish to improve their own professional knowledge or develop the quality of learning in their school. Managers may wish to improve or develop particular aspects of the organisation, curriculum or pastoral care of the school. There may be weakness in procedures, communication, or control in a school which a new head wishes to remedy. Innovations such as TVEI, 'Life-skills' teaching, or new examination syllabuses may demand changes in pedagogy, so a management team may wish to develop new teaching skills. An LEA or group of HMI may perceive a need for co-ordination of the personal, social and moral education in several individual schools, and so they set up a special conference or regional DES course. These examples all illustrate genuine concern for professional or staff development. It may be more directed to the personal achievement, acquisition of skills and knowledge, and self-esteem of the individual teacher; or it may be more directly concerned with curriculum development, or school organisation. Both these directions are legitimate, because staff or professional development is concerned with the improvement in the quality of teaching and learning in schools. Thus I see a direct link between professional development and curriculum development.

Writing from my view as a deputy head, staff development policies and plans for training, or the development of new skills which are imposed in a power-coercive way, can be fraught with difficulties both for manager and colleagues. Teachers are irritable and sceptical about even the most well-meaning suggestions that 'surely we all need to develop our skills', or a more direct 'we really should improve this or that'. Resentment is particularly strong when the manager is none too competent in the area he is proposing for development in others! It seems to me that negotiation with colleagues about their own interests and problems, about their estimation of what they would like to develop is a more cautious and potentially fruitful strategy. Teachers feel vulnerable enough without the implicit criticism contained in the suggestion that we 'need' staff development.

In our work at Rotheram High School and further afield we have found the impact and uptake of staff development plans have been more successful where we have identified a real need (not just a bright idea or the latest gimmick from the County Hall or elsewhere). This "need" may be perceived by the LEA, the school management or by a small group of colleagues, but it is important that it is perceived by the majority of colleagues too. The best intentions can be misunderstood, and well-laid plans ambushed by cynical "chalks" if the justification is not clear, and there is not at least some measure of agreement about the plans. I am not suggesting that staff room talk should be the sole arbiter of management plans for staff development, but there is certainly a need for participation, consultation and justification.

Now I want to return to the central thesis of this chapter, that action research does promote staff development. Teachers are willing to co-operate in the discussion of practical problems in school. Control, examination results, the learning difficulties of particular children, pastoral or behavioural problems, parents, home backgrounds, racism, gender, problems that children are experiencing in understanding, motivation and constraints perceived are all part of the practical conversation of teachers. Deliberation about our professional concerns, "where the action is", trying to improve what we are engaged in each day is where professional development should start. Teachers can identify and co-operate with plans that help them solve their own problems, help to improve teaching and learning, and where their own professionalism is respected. If we impose a foreign research language upon teachers, or make them insecure about the skills they demonstrably have, they are not likely to develop any further understanding or acquire any new skills.

Teachers think about their practice intuitively, or perhaps in a more self-conscious way as part of their everyday work. They have little time to step back to think more analytically about their everyday affairs. This is the normal intuitive reflection about school life. 'Why did that lesson go so well?' 'What was it that was causing Sheila's difficulties with her Geography mock exam ... she does so well in class?' 'Why do these thick kids always put the lathe tool upside-down in the machine?' Headteachers, LEAs and the more substantial in-service courses can help teachers by providing the time or resources to aid the disciplining and focusing of their thought and reflection. The steps of review, diagnosis, planning, implementation and monitoring, structure thinking and give a problem-solving strategy for busy teachers to apply to their everyday practical concerns.

The level of systematic reflection where teachers work together needs a deliberate management policy. If headteachers want colleagues to think, plan, review and develop teaching and learning then there are implications for management. We can pay lip service to the notion of curriculum development, but if we want collaborative action research, or the much talked-about 'critical community' of teachers then there are strategic implications .

I believe we need to move more than half way toward providing the opportunities and resources for the fulfilment of lofty aims. Departmental meetings can be timetabled in to the school day, either permanently or for occasional reviews. The staff at Rotheram requested this after a conference on 'Problems and Possibilities in Mixed-ability Teaching' The head built opportunities for review and discussion into the school day the next year, and the staff responded with an increase in discussion, review and planning. If we build in times when colleagues can work together, exchange views with other departments, explore honest doubts and reservations, and design new courses, then they are much more likely to want to spend their own time exploring major problems or aspects of school self-evaluation. Some years ago when introducing termly staff conferences we were able to curtail the school day, provide the opportunity for discussion in attractive accommodation with a buffet meal, and create a sense of enquiry and community about common problems.

There is more chance of practical outcomes if our colleagues see that the notion of the "reflective practitioner" is given priority in the management of the school, and illustrated at the highest level. The measure of success we have at my own school is largely due to the head creating a more open, questioning climate. Teachers spend a lot of time outside the normal school hours meeting, talking, reviewing and planning in spite of some comments in the press and by politicians. I believe we should not take this for granted, but actively encourage and foster it by creating "possibilities" during the normal school programme.

This is where action research is such a help for professional development. It involves stages of REVIEW, DIAGNOSIS, PLANNING, IMPLEMENTATION, AND MONITORING EFFECTS. Teachers become involved in the decision-making processes of the school both at the individual classroom level, or in major reviews about whole school issues. They can tackle practical problems about ways of improving the quality of learning, and also grow in their personal understanding of the task of the teacher.

Review meetings, case conferences, working groups, curriculum committees and departmental meetings all form part of the management of comprehensive schools. The reader may be querying, 'What's new here?'. Well we do not wish to make any pretentious claims, but the action research strategy does provide a tool for professional development policies. It aids both aspects of staff development: personal growth and curriculum renewal. An illustration of this second level of action research may be of help.

At present, like many schools, we have working groups on matters of concern. One of these is a group reviewing our assessment of learning procedures and reporting to parents. We started out with the "general idea" that it was time to look at the way we assess and record pupils' learning. The REVIEW involved a discussion of how we assessed and recorded learning at that time generally, and specifically in departments. There was much discussion about the present procedures, the weaknesses, the need for a common system. We had a paper presented on issues in assessment, examined other schools' ideas and a particular Scottish scheme. Out of this review of our own situation, of other literature, and our own needs, a DIAGNOSIS emerged of the problems involved in criterion reference assessments - particularly the problem of designing an effective system which was relatively easy to operate in terms of time and simplicity. Early on the group wondered whether computers might be a help, so another review and diagnosis of the problems associated with the use of computers took place. After several months of these reviews and diagnoses we reached the PLANNING stage of working out our own system based on categories of attainment: 'knowledge', 'understanding' and 'creativity'; work-related attitudes of 'perseverance', 'enterprise' and cooperation'; and general skills of 'writing', 'oral', 'number' and 'coordination'. We then asked Subject Departments to work out the criteria for grades 1 to 4 for their pupils. This planning took many months of hard work before we reached the IMPLEMENTATION phase of some trial runs using mark sensing cards for the computer print out. We were able to iron out teething problems, write an instruction manual for users, run more trials, and constantly MONITOR the trials and tribulations experienced by the users!

As John Elliott (1981) points out, action research is not just one cycle of Review, Diagnosis, Planning, Implementation and Monitoring, but several cycles or spirals as the focus of study shifts as in the case of the group's task I have just described. There were several cycles of action research over the years of developing and improving the scheme. We still have problems with it, and are monitoring its effectiveness. The great merit of action research is that it has a mechanism built in for "renewal" in the 'institutionalisation' phase of innovation. Action research also guards against jumping to conclusions about complex organisational and learning issues. The reconnaissance or fact-finding phase is important at the outset.

Perhaps the most familiar level of action research is that represented by the Classroom Action Research Network (CARN). This approach was exemplified by the Ford Project which extended over two years from 1973-1975 involving 40 teachers concerned with implementing inquiry/discovery approaches to learning and instruction in classrooms (Elliott, 1976-77). More recently the Schools Council Programme 2 Project: Teacher-pupil Interaction and the

Quality of Learning (TIQL) (Schools Council/Longman, 1985), adopted action research techniques to enquire into the possibilities of teaching for understanding, while at the same time teaching for assessment (Elliott, Ebbutt and Crossley, 1983). My own school was involved in this project. Six teachers were closely involved with research but this extended to other colleagues who were drawn in through interest and to the whole staff at two conferences.

Action Research - a case study

Group discussion and problem-solving will be going on from time to time in every school, but I want to describe some of the techniques involved in a different level of action research and illustrate these from our experience at Rotheram. Reflection about our practice should be going on all the time, I believe. This level is more focused, disciplined and specific. Teachers do not have the time or energy to do this continually, but for specific purposes, for extending professionalism, re-awakening jaded motivation, for increasing understanding of classroom processes and for genuine research and enquiry this level of more rigorous reflection is excellent. The majority of our staff have been involved in this more disciplined action research at some time. In addition to this, short courses, certificates of further professional studies, advance diplomas, in-service BEd's, and masters degrees have involved pieces of research over the eight years or so that interest in action research has developed. Figures 1 and 2 provide examples of whole school and individual action research. The TIQL Project I mentioned earlier drew in further colleagues and our own evaluation group involved others. Two or three times a year the school is the focus of research from one of our local colleges or from the Cambridge Institute of Education. I now want to illustrate some techniques colleagues have employed.

Case 1

One colleague teaching Biology was concerned with the poor level of motivation and behaviour in a 4th year CSE group, so he started out with a general idea of packaging the biology course in a similar way to other science courses. He used a tape recorder in the lesson (which incidentally he found quite threatening). Later he adopted the triangulation procedure which involves gathering accounts of a teaching situation from three quite different points of view: those of the teacher, the students, and a participant observer who on this occasion was an outside consultant from higher education (but who could equally well have been a friendly colleague). The idea of triangulation is to get a much wider or rounded view of what is going on in the classroom. It is, for example, most interesting to compare

Fig 1 Examples of Action Research at Rotheram High School Conducted by Individuals

TITLE	AREA OF CONCERN/TOPIC	METHODOLOGY	RELEASE: ACCESS: DISSEMINATION
VALUES AT RHS (BRIAN WAKEMAN)	- What are the STATED VALUES? - What values are the pupils able to perceive - What discrepancies exist	- 'COVERT' Field Notes - Interpretative - Written replies from pupils - Interviews - Participant observation	To HM To Pupils To staff interested To conference
MIXED-ABILITY AT ROTHERAM (LESLEY COLLINS)	Impact and problems arising from innovation. An attempt to identify some issues, problems, strengths, weaknesses and implications of this innovation	DEMOCRATIC EVALUATION - document collection - historical account - memories of staff - observation of teachers, methods and pupils - interviews - triangulation - questionnaire - analysis	Negotiated simultaneous release to HM and staff
SOCIAL EDUCATION AT ROTHERAM (BRIAN WAKEMAN)	- Description of innovation - Impact on staff and pupils - Congruence of aims and outcomes - Tracing effects on attitude and behaviour	CASE STUDY - Portrayal - Field Research - Document analysis - Interviews - Surveys of staff and pupil opinion - Analysis - interpret	- Copy available to colleagues in School and in Institute Library. - All case study cleared for release

KEY FINDINGS	IMPACT: TAKE-UP: INFLUENCE	PROBLEMS
- The actual and stated values - Pupils able to identify stated school values - Pupils identified interesting shortcomings - Value implicit in organisation	- Staff meeting on values - Generated a lot of interest and discussion - Subsequent discussion paper and proposed staff coherence	- Democratic procedures not adopted - Writer's interpretations - Ethical framework dubious
- Need for more understanding of Readability - Need for diverse resources - m/a organisation but little m/a teaching methodology - Identified lack of depth of understanding of n/a - Need for INSET	Findings and implications of such importance: Reports and action held in abeyance for future staff INSET conference. Identified pupil's point of view. INSET conference on m/a teaching was organised in May 1982. Colleagues now working on improvements	- Release to Staff not implemented - "Shelving" - Will it gather dust ... or raise the dust! - Getting other colleagues to read the study
- Staff attitudes have become more positive over five years - Pupils identified key areas of interest, attitudes and influence - Growth in language skills; social confidence; self-awareness; ability to handle conflict; and prep for exams	- Helped justify S/E in School - Legitimised the consulting of pupils about their own learning - Led to on-going curric. review - Courses changed and improved - Follow-up study by John Crossley of Cambridge Institute of Education	- Getting adversay accounts - Over-identification of writer with topic

Fig 1 (Continued)

Fig 2 Examples of Whole-staff Systematic Reflection - 'School-based INSET in Action' at Rotheram High School, Luton, Beds.

TITLE	CAUSE OR STIMULUS	CONTENT/PROCESS	OUTCOMES
'Pastoral Care and Form Tutoring'	- management concern to develop quality of tutoring - linking the pastoral concerns of the school with Social Education	- lecture by K Blackburn - discussion of issues raised about tutoring, pastoral care and our Social Education programme	- raising consciousness of the importance of FT - reinforcing of value placed on FT by an authority from outside school - drawing off of hostility to the policy
'Spelling and Readability'	- management desire to increase awareness of 'language across the curriculum' - stimulus of a colleague's research into spelling, and another's into readability	- report by colleague on her 'spelling' research - lecture and practical exercise for staff on assessing readability by C Cripps, CIE	- adoption of 'A Spelling Policy' - real impact on colleagues' understanding of relation between readability of work-sheets, and texts, and the pupils' understanding
'Discussion methods in Social Education lessons'	- desire of Co-ordinator to develop colleagues' skills in conducting different kinds of discussion with pupils	- simple paper on discussion prepared by Co-ordinator - the practice of methods in group work with the staff involved	- difficult to assess: certainly an increase in skills for some, and an enlargement of possibilities for others

'The Problems and Possibilities in Mixed-ability Teaching'	- management wish to review - the follow-up of a colleague's case study of the introduction of mixed-ability groupings in the school	- the use of Nominal Group Technique to identify the real problems of m/a teaching - using NGT to identify strategies for improvement	- a collegiate experience - various organisational outcomes: Department meetings, and a 'supervision room' - departmental intents
'The Values of Rotheram High School'	- generation of thought by two action-research projects: one on values and the other on ritual - management desire to enquire into congruence of aims and outcomes, philosophy and practice	- paper exploring the notion of values - examination of our practice as a school in the light of stated philosophical aims in groups of staff across departments	- raising of understanding of school philosophy and hidden curriculum - generation of heated discussion
'Bullying and Racism'	- increasing number of incidents - pressure group of staff - management desire to tackle problem, and improve situation	- papers prepared by colleagues on numbers of incidents, and types, and another on possible ways forward - discussion groups on responses to the papers and what action should be taken	- planning content of pastoral curriculum - development of knowledge and understanding of area - raising awareness of the purposes of Pastoral Curriculum

Fig 2 (Continued)

Fig 2 continued

'Report by Colleagues on their involvement with the Schools Council TIQL Project'	- to report on what colleagues had been doing - to widen discussion about insights, skills and processes participants had developed	- reports on the individual case studies - faculty discussion groups on the issues and questions about teaching for understanding that had emerged from TIQL	- dissemination of information about research project and TIQL - development for staff reporting to colleagues - discussion of learning issues

what you think as a teacher is taking place, with a friend's account, and perhaps more importantly compare yours with the pupil's to see what the received curriculum actually looks like. The focus of Simon Aspray's study shifted as he began to take interest in the relationship between teaching for higher levels of understanding and his own anxieties about control. Through the triangulation and interview of pupils Simon began to investigate the relationship between understanding, interest and control.

In his short case study he analysed the transcripts of his lessons and the triangulation interviews, and posited the hypothesis that 'the link between interest and understanding is not so much the obvious one that interest improves understanding, but rather that understanding leads to interest'. He discovered that his explanations (with humorous illustrations and playful banter) led to understanding, and that understanding to interest, with this new group of 4th Years he was studying. He discovered that in the previous group his anxiety about loss of control had inhibited his ability to take risks in engaging the children in discussion, so he also concluded that 'understanding tasks' which Walter Doyle (1979) notes are 'high risk' for pupils, are also high risk for teachers unless they are confident in their own ability and the control sanctions.

This small scale project illustrates the process of action research, and the techniques of classroom recording, transcriptions, pattern analysis, and triangulation. The teacher analyses his evidence, seeks to understand it, posits and tests possible explanatory hypotheses in the light of the evidence, writes up his conclusions tentatively and applies his insights to other lessons. Furthermore, the process of enquiry can lead him to discuss his ideas with others, to read more theoretical literature, to grow in his understanding. It involved Simon in sharing his ideas with other teachers further afield in his own LEA and elsewhere. The small scale research which he felt had little worth, has extended his own professionalism and been of benefit to others. This is all the more interesting when you realise Simon had no teacher training, coming from a hospital laboratory into teaching.

<u>Case 2</u>

The TIQL Project furnishes us with several examples of action research techniques. Another teacher, Peter, started with an initial concern about the number of pupils who were not completing their practical projects in their external Examinations in Technology. Our point of departure in this study was to interview pupils who were just leaving or who had left school to find out what problems they had experienced in doing Technology. This revealed a number of insights about learning difficulties. Some of these were thought-provoking, when fed back to Peter. Later we looked at the Technology examination papers to see what cognitive demands were being made of students. We adapted a typology from Smith and Meux (1970) and a typology of understanding from Kemmis, Atkin, Wright (1977) to see whether these questions were demanding high levels of understanding and conceptual competence. They were, of course, and this gave Peter an important insight into his work. He has written up a case study 'Problems with Problem-solving' (TIQL mimeo CIE, 1982) and collaborated with an external consultant on a paper entitled 'What to do with my data: reporting action-research' (see Prideaux and Bannister, 1983). This paper illustrates two problems of action research common to many teachers: how do you cope with the information you collect and how do you present your findings in a written form? Peter found it a lot easier to talk about his ideas than to write about them, so one strategy we used was to tape record and transcribe a conversation about his problems in Technology and his ideas about the problems. He then had written access, recorded data of his own ideas on which to work.

There are several excellent guide books to action research. Anything written by John Elliott on action research is worth reading because of his long experience in research and his work with teachers in action research (see Elliott, 1981) Colin Hook's book 'Studying Classrooms' (Hook, 1981) is the best practical guide I have read. It is full of ideas about observational skills, interviewing, questionnaires, sociometry, recording media, and recording and reporting information. 'Field Research' (Schatzman and Strauss, 1973) is very helpful on a strategy for research in the 'naturalistic' school of sociology. Jon Nixon's "A Teacher's Guide to Action Research" (Nixon, 1981) gives some interesting illustrations of action research, and "Uttering, Muttering" is very helpful (Adelman, 1981). The Deakin University's "The Action Research Planner" (Kemmis and McTaggart, 1982) and the companion volume "The Action Research Reader" (Kemmis, 1982) are essential reading.

Fig 3 below provides a useful summary of approaches to studying classrooms.

Practical Effects of Action Research

There is no doubt that action-research leads to professional or staff development. I base this statement on extensive experience both at my own school and in working with teachers in my own LEA and further afield in other parts of the country. Some colleagues have participated in action-research through in-service courses which lead to higher or further qualifications. In this more limited sense of personal professional development teachers benefit. However I want to give examples of some effects on the

Fig 3 Summary of Approaches to Studying Classrooms

METHOD	PERSONNEL AND EQUIPMENT	ADVANTAGES	DISADVANTAGES	EXAMPLES OF USE
Observation instruments	By teacher, colleague or outsider. Note book, recording sheets	Fits in with regular school activities Selective focus Economical as regards money and equipment First-hand information about actual behaviours Adaptable to individual classroom situations Can be used in live situations or with audio or visual records	Can interfere with teaching and classroom management Difficult to be fully objective May need support equipment for complete analysis eg tape recorder Colleagues or outsiders may not be available to help May need to be carried out over an extended period	Analysis of teacher questioning, pupil response, pupil-pupil interaction Pupil participation in activities Use of equipment by pupils Estimation of pupil achievement and performance levels Teacher and pupil movement Playground behaviour

Field notes, anecdotal records and diaries	By teacher Note book, record cards or sheets, diary	Personal viewpoints Can be compiled by the participant observer at any time Uncomplicated and cheap Can be incorporated into self-analysis of day's work and future lesson planning Cumulative records enable analysis for patterns, trends, etc. Other evidence easily added to notes or records	Subjective impressions and accounts may be biased. More objective analysis may need other data collection techniques Detailed or long conversations are difficult to record by hand	Implementation of new curriculum package Account of pupil's behaviour at school camp Self-reflection about own teaching techniques Introduction of team teaching and effect on teachers and pupils Workings of school council
Interview	By teacher or outsider with teacher, pupils, parents, etc. Note book, tape recorder	Face to face contact with informant Comfortable, informal approach Can use during school or after school Suitable for in-depth probing and/or identification of problems or needs Direct approach - can be adjusted to respondent(s) age or language level	Time-consuming Some pupils may have difficulty expressing their views or may be reluctant to reveal true feelings Outsider may be unfamiliar with pupils or parents	Obtaining pupils', other teachers' or parents' views about classroom and school matters, eg reading scheme, new equipment, school rules, teaching methods, etc.

Fig 3 (Continued)

Questionnaire	By teacher with pupils, other teachers, parents and community Question sheet	Easily distributed Can be quick to fill in Focussed and adaptable to specific needs Provides feedback for action Respondents familiar with questionnaire procedure	Preparation can be lengthy Clear and relevant answers require careful preparation and trial runs Analysis of responses is time-consuming May get poor rate of return Difficult to get in-depth responses - may need to be supplemented by interview Problems of obtaining true or honest responses from pupils	Expectations of pupils about a new curriculum or subject Pupils' comments about instruction or school organisation Parents' views about school policy, curriculum content, etc. Teachers' opinions about school equipment, organisation, etc.
Sociometric methods	By teachers with pupils Question sheet	Reveal pupils' interpersonal relationships Adaptable to specific circumstances and needs Ease of construction and administration	Pupils may be reluctant to reveal true feelings unless confidentiality is assured Do not give reasons for pupils' choices Short-term - need to be repeated periodically Unsuitable for groups who do not know each other	Groupings of pupils for cooperative work Seating in classroom Deciding partners for classroom activities

Fig 3 (Continued)

Unobtrusive measures	By teacher Note book, camera	Inexpensive, straight-forward approach Can supplement other methods through triangulation Do not affect school or classroom environment - non-reactive Draw on a variety of evidence	Some evidence may be inaccessible, eg confidential documents Need to develop skill in being unobtrusive! May be accused of invasion of privacy	Pupils's attitude to school Quality of school-community relations School organisation and administration
Photographs and slides	By teacher or outsider Camera (possibly plus synchroniser, slide projector and tape recorder)	Fresh perspectives on familiar settings Enable illustration of school and classroom activities Promote understanding and stimulate discussion Can be viewed by a variety of audiences	Cost of equipment Possible disruption of classroom teaching Difficult to show whole classes Selective focus of photographer Processing time - delayed feedback Purely visual, no sound (can be overcome with tape-slide methods)	Record of teacher and pupil behaviour, eg non-verbal expressions, co-operative work Classroom activities and out-of-school excursions and visits

Fig 3 (Continued)

Audio recording	By teacher or outsider Tape recorder, microphones	Easy to set up Records all conversation within range of equipment Portable - can be placed in different parts of room Relatively unobtrusive Allows repeated analysis	Recording is unselective - extraneous noise may make conversation High cost of quality equipment Transcription costly and time-consuming No visual record - periods of silence convey little information	Analysis of teacher and pupil talk Recording of interviews Analysis of team teaching conferences - instructional planning Record of pupils' work
Video recording	By teachers, pupils or outsider Camera, video recorder, TV monitor, operator	Extensive coverage of classroom activities - sound and vision Attractive to viewers Video recordings can be viewed repeatedly, allowing a variety of analysis	Very expensive May be difficult to borrow or hire equipment Difficult to make unobtrusive	Analysis of teacher and pupil behaviour, eg teacher instruction, pupil group discussion, classroom movement. Out-of-classroom activities, eg playground behaviour

Fig 3 (Continued)

Case study	By teacher or outsider Equipment and techniques previously described	Permits focus on an individual case, eg pupil, teacher, classroom, school, curriculum scheme In-depth analysis possible Draws on a wide variety of research methods Suitable for longitudinal or developmental approaches	Investigation in depth requires much planning, collection of information and analysis. Very time-consuming if extensive coverage required. Feedback to teacher may be delayed until case study completed	Study of single case, eg pupil, new instructional approach, maths curriculum package, school assessment procedures, etc.

(Hook, 1981)

Fig 3 (Continued)

action-researcher beyond the acquisition of qualification or certification, to address the question: 'What are the practical outcomes of this action research?'. I want to summarise these under three headings: the effects on the teacher/researcher; the practical effects on teaching and learning; and the motivation effect on the pupils.

Effects on the teacher-researcher

One marked effect on several colleagues was an increase in self-esteem and prestige. 'Who can possibly be interested in my problems with thick kids who can't tool a lathe?', asked one colleague, only to find that many teachers outside the craft world and even in primary schools have shown interest and admiration for his work about difficult concepts lurking behind deceptively easy language (Nolan, 1982).

The recognition that colleagues gain from discussion of issues across the lunch table, from giving reports of their work at staff conferences or further afield is considerable. Action research puts professional knowledge back into the hands of teachers. It is important that we do not underestimate the worth of a process that builds self-esteem in a period of low morale among teachers.

A second effect on teachers which both our own advisory and inspection service and visitors from other LEA's have noticed is summed-up by the word 'awareness'. Action research leads to a heightening of awareness about issues in teaching and learning: spelling; readability; language; teaching styles; conceptual demands in craft; the logical dimensions of examination question papers; the attitudes of pupils toward personal and social development lessons; non-verbal communication; the problems of pupils from ethnic minority backgrounds; what learning looks like to pupils. Not only are teachers noticeably conscious of educational issues and prepared to talk about them to colleagues, but they are actively engaged in relating their awareness to the practical tasks of teaching and learning. 'Awareness' is perhaps a vague term, so let me give some illustrations. When you have been observing lesson profiles and timings or the interaction between teacher and pupils there is a 'flash-back effect' when the researcher resumes teaching. He becomes conscious of talking too much, or balancing a lesson differently as a result of insights gained through research. I have been conscious of insights creeping-up on me as I teach, after studying the strategies of a teacher in discussion lessons. I have become more aware of the type of questions I am asking the learner, and the way I am receiving the learner's responses.

This awareness or consciousness can be unpacked further as 'deeper levels of understanding'. Teachers gain understanding of the processes of learning, of the complex social milieu of the classroom, of instructional techniques, and of the substantive area of enquiry. They begin to clarify their own theories about teaching and learning, as well as consulting the library on more academic theories of the history, psychology, sociology or philosophy of education. The study of education becomes rooted in their own practical knowledge rather than in academic theories alone. (See Day, 1985, for further evidence of this effect.) These comments rooted in Rotheram's practical experience reflect the notions of Hoyle's "extended professional", Stenhouse's 'teacher researcher' and Elliott's 'teachers gaining control over what is to count as relevant and valid knowledge in education'.

Practical effects on teaching and learning

Any raising of self-esteem or deepening of understanding of professional practice among teachers should have a corresponding pay-off in the classroom. Here are a few examples of practical outcomes. We have had a number of studies of aspects of our Personal and Social Development work. These have led to further INSET on skills in the classroom and to colleagues experimenting with different techniques. For example, in a recent survey of pupil-opinion about their learning in PSD and in follow-up interviews discussion is frequently mentioned as being helpful in their learning. There has been an increase in discussion, and the use of case-study material in values education. A project on mixed-ability teaching led to the alerting of management to a number of problems, which were further explored in a staff conference. This was a less direct effect, but perhaps broke up some impervious layers so that the ideas could 'percolate'. Some studies have an effect for a time, but only a residual impact after the passing of years. A study of techniques for teaching spelling became a policy document after discussion and INSET work, but now after the passage of time, the detailed suggestions have evaporated leaving the "look-cover-write-check" technique as a skill in the practice of several colleagues. A 'readability' survey of Humanities worksheets led to direct improvement in the match between learner and print in several departments. A package of Geography materials for classroom use was developed after a review of the extent to which we were meeting the needs of ethnic minority pupils. A similar thing happened in the science department. Several staff are much more conscious of their use of spoken and written language, and others of the concepts demanded by Craft teaching since the TIQL Project. Short-term effects can be quite dramatic in terms of new skills practised, insights gained and put into practice, and the positive effect on the pupils' motivation at the time. Longer term effects are more difficult to evaluate. Many of these projects or studies have directly informed management, contributed to decision-making, and some have formed the basis for policies.

Effect on the pupils

Some headteachers are anxious about the justification of the time used in making these evaluations, with parents knocking on our door asking for accountability. Action-research or school reviews like the GRIDS Project (Guidelines for Review and Internal Development in Schools) (McMahon et al, 1984) can be a tool in giving accounts to our parents of what we do and how we try to improve our work. Our experience both at Rotheram and further afield is that action-research not only motivates the teacher but it also motivates the pupils in their learning. Rather than be put-off by the 'stranger in the classroom' they begin to take more interest. This has been true of studies about language, technology, spelling, truancy, PSD and Biology. I find that when pupils see that teachers are really interested in their ideas, learning and opinions, this enhances teacher-pupil relationships, builds pupils' self-esteem, and creates an interest in their own learning.

Conditions for the success of action research

I want now to try to identify factors which led to the growth of action research studies in the school - to explore the conditions that facilitated the growth of action research at my school, and how have we tackled the problems associated with initiating and sustaining this work? Undoubtedly the most important factor is the ethos of the school which the headteacher, David Taggart, has built over the years. At Rotheram there is an openness to the style of management, an emphasis on respect for persons in the school's philosophy both towards staff and pupils, and an atmosphere of participation and questioning. This may not always be so (practice often belying ideals), but as I travelled around meeting more teachers and visiting schools as part of my own research I believe openness, respect for persons, participation and questioning are identifiable characteristics of the school. These factors have been important for action-research.

If a school is not open to questioning, is not responsive to suggestions for improvement, is not willing to enter dialogue with junior colleagues, and not even willing to listen to criticism then action-researchers will have a hard time. If we really have 'got it all right' then perhaps there is no need for enquiring studies. Questioning, reflection and debate should emanate from the top of the hierarchical structure if we wish it to succeed. I am not talking about negative destructive criticism, but a willingness to tackle real problems of organisation, communication, curriculum development, and practical improvement in teaching and learning. Cooperation with colleagues to improve the quality of our pupils' education is called for.

A second cluster of factors in our school is more sociological. There is a lot of social distress, family break-up, and low self-esteem among our pupils as in many urban schools. This brings acute behaviour problems, and learning difficulties into the classroom. Our intake is not fully comprehensive in the spread of ability. We have more pupils of middle and lower ability. Add to this an inhospitable attitude by some local white children to minority groups, and you can see that crises and problems frequently arise. This stress in the school makes colleagues more willing to seek alternative solutions to problems which keep presenting themselves. I believe this facilitates enquiry and reflection for daily survival and for improving what we are doing.

The history of curriculum development and major innovations, and evaluation in the school has made reflection and action-research part of the normal procedures of school life. (I suspect some colleagues long for a quieter life!) Further, the head's policy of encouraging INSET work both within the school in our own INSET programme, and outside the school in short courses, and further professional and post graduate studies does encourage thoughtful dialogue in the school and an atmosphere of professional development. We have education cuts and a falling roll, and, like other colleagues, have varying degrees of success in solving our problems and maintaining our direction and momentum as a school. Some of our staff feel frustrated and challenge our progress.

Undoubtedly our links with higher education have sustained our action-research and helped discipline thinking in several colleagues. Significantly, we now have colleagues who act as internal consultants giving advice and direction to colleagues. Ideally the aim of a school should be to diminish its reliance on higher education for evaluation activities by growing expertise on home ground.

Problems of initiating and sustaining action research

I summarised these for a conference in a chart which I reproduce in Figure (4). In brief, credibility, receptivity, priority, special skills, and institutionalisation are the main problems. 'Credibility' is concerned with questions such as: "Why be bothered with action-research?", and "What practical use does it serve?" While it is true that several colleagues still have this healthy scepticism because the teacher's life is full enough with all the demands in their normal busy lives, it is also true that we have a core of staff who are convinced of the merits of this

Fig 4 Some problems and solutions in the initiating and sustaining of Action-research

PROBLEM	PRESENTATION: DETAILS	SOLUTIONS: STRATEGIES
CREDIBILITY	- 'Why be bothered with it?' - 'What use does it serve?' - 'Not more educational jargon?' - 'What's in it for me?' - 'It's only conference fodder for you!' - 'Why are you interested in evaluation?'	- Practicality ethic - A Problem-solving strategy - Sell as a means of professional development - External recognition brings esteem - Consider the work of colleagues
PRIORITY	- 'We've enough to do already!' - 'Not more bumph! .. Oh OK then ..' - 'Sorry, I can't make it' - I'll have a go later in the term. Ask me then' - 'Will you cover for me?'	- Picking your moment - Persuasion - Patience - Finding rewards - Management policy - Making time available
RECEPTIVITY	- 'Not now, I'm writing 180 reports!' - 'Nag, nag, nag, what do you want from me, blood?' - 'I've nothing worth saying' - 'We all know this ... who is kidding who?'	- Tact - Bounded time - Being the 'gate-keeper' to alient concepts - Encouraging participants to make a personal investment

SKILLS	- 'I don't know what I want to do?' - 'How do I go about collecting data on the social background of 1200 pupils?' - 'What do I do with all this data?' - 'Help I can't write!' - 'Why was Mrs X so angry when I asked her class why they were so bored in her lesson?' - 'How can we implement these findings?'	- Practical suggestions - Photostat key articles for them - Do it with them ... show them how - Build-up a library for staff - Act as internal consultant - Get outside help from experts - Give colleagues the credit

Fig 4 (Continued)

work, some who participate but would not be happy with the terminology and others who can be persuaded that it has value on occasions, for certification or staff conferences. As I said earlier, the practicality ethic has direct appeal in the staffroom. When colleagues can see that action-research has relevance and application and that it is worth investing their valuable time then they are more likely to respond. When they perceive there is 'something in it for them' if I can put it rather crudely, that they can have another strategy which helps survival and leads to problem-solving, they are more interested. When one or a group of colleagues report on their action-research at a staff meeting, the others are able to see its worth in terms of certification, the growth in understanding in the presenter, and the practical effects on the task of the teacher. Action research has a user-fascination and brings recognition to teachers from within the school and further afield.

'Priority' arises out of credibility. Teachers genuinely have enough to do already. Even if a colleague is convinced of the credibility of action-research or any other staff development strategy for that matter, picking the moment is an important skill. Some colleagues participate because they are self-motivated, or have the carrot of a course certificate. Account needs to be taken of the school calendar, of peaks and troughs in activity, demands of reporting, examinations, assessments, parents evenings, the amount of naked energy tired teachers have toward the end of term and so on. Consultation and collaboration rather than imposition and authoritarianism are necessary. We need to invite colleagues to say when, what and how they wish to evaluate. After all, evaluation and action-research as one mode of professional development activities will come fairly low on the priority list of even the most enthusiastic teacher. Face-to-face teaching, marking, discipline problems, report writing, school extra-curricula activities loom large in colleagues' minds. There is a gentle art of popping 'evaluation and action research memos' in the top of colleagues mental in-tray filing system every so often to promote the priority of reflective practice. Management policy can build-in time for action-research so that it is seen as a higher priority. We have found the civilising influences of comfortable accommodation, simple things like attractive refreshments, the recognition by the head of the work and worth of extra activities go a long way in keeping good will. Finding extrinsic as well as intrinsic rewards for colleagues is as important for teachers as it is to the learner, in motivation and good will.

"Receptivity" was a notion I soon learned in connection with the TIQL Project. You could pick the wrong moment, misjudge the pressure in the staffroom, or let impatience, or lack of sensitivity, animate you at the wrong moment and then even the most reasonable 'bright' idea could receive a stony response. One further problem is that some teachers believe they have little or nothing worthwhile to say, or that what they have found by reflection is common knowledge anyway. I can only comment that it is worth persuading teachers to make their practical knowledge explicit, because it is of so much benefit and interest to others. This practical knowledge locked-up in teachers needs to be shared so that new generations of teachers can benefit. Some colleagues are not receptive to writing-up their ideas because of a different reason. It is considered to be pretentious, or somehow "not cricket" to write-up knowledge about teaching and learning. I encourage colleagues to write-up their ideas for others, because writing first focuses and clarifies thinking, and then makes this practical professional knowledge accessible to teachers. So much educational writing is jargon-ridden, unintelligible and remote to teachers.

When teachers have made a personal investment in their research I have found they are more willing to continue with the activity.

There is no doubt that there are skills which can be learned. Helen Simons helpful 'Suggestions for a School Self-evaluation Based on Democratic Principles' (McCormick, 1982) enunciates practical principles for teachers conducting action research. References were made to other literature earlier which provide helpful insights into the 'how?' of conducting your own action research. The problem with books is that teachers find little time to read masses of print, and are suspicious of alien words and action research jargon. During the TIQL project I acted as a 'gatekeeper' to articles and working papers coming from the central team letting in only those I judged my colleagues would have patience with.

There are special skills involved in selecting a focused and manageable topic of enquiry, of collecting information which is recognisable as having some validity and reliability and not hopelessly biassed. Skills of data collection can be learned fairly quickly, but it is much more difficult to know what to do with the information you collect. I have found practical workshops which take colleagues through the processes of 'description', 'making sense of the data', 'interpretation and the formulation of explanatory hypotheses', 'the designing of action steps' the most productive way of introducing the skills of action research. An experiential approach can anticipate practical problems in conducting research, and encourages teachers to enquire further into writing about research. I believe schools interested in action research for professional development need either an internal consultant or a coordinator who can help colleagues with their enquiries, or there is need for contact with the 'expert' or 'enabler' from higher education or the LEA.

The management of action research

The 'management' of action research is a very contentious issue. It is doubtful if systematic reflection can be imposed on colleagues in a power-coercive way. Indeed the action-research movement is much more a 'bottom-up' than 'top-down' model of educational change. It is about teachers who are prepared to question their own approaches in order to improve the quality of teaching and learning. It is not about the imposition of policies. Brock-Utne writing in the CARN Bulletin No 4 says that the ideology 'underlying action-research is definitely democratic ideology' (Brock-Utne, 1980). Writers who link critical theory in social sciences with action-research talk of 'enlightenment' and 'emancipatory knowledge'. Critical theory and action research, says Kemmis:

> share an interest in liberating communities of inquirers from the dictates of tradition, habit, bureaucratic systemisation and individual expectations. But the emancipatory interest is far from a sceptical response which breaks free of systemisation without establishing an orderly process for social and intellectual reconstruction. On the contrary, action-research and critical social science embody <u>participatory democratic processes for social and intellectual reconstruction</u> (author's emphasis) (Kemmis, 1982)

Not all action-researchers would agree with the linking of action-research with critical theory, indeed many would find the neo-Marxist intellectual framework repugnant. Action-research is, however, about teachers gaining control over what is to count as relevant and valid knowledge to inform decisions about classroom practice. There are motifs of 'collaborative or cooperative discourse' about practical problems, and of 'professionalism respected' about action-research which have far-reaching implications for the management of schools.

In this chapter I have indicated that action-research has developed at my school within a more open style of management. Participation in the formulation of policies and decision-making, a more consultative approach to management, and a genuine respect for teachers grouping together to enquire into their practical problems with a view to improving the situation are necessary pre-conditions for the management of action-research. Action-research can be perceived as disruptive, antagonistic and even possibly subversive in a school with a more authoritarian or 'line-management' philosophy.

However there are still issues, policies, and strategies which need to be considered in the more open democratic institution. Is this organic self-evaluation part of a wider programme that reviews the whole school over a period of time, or is it spasmodic, individualistic, and fragmented? How do individual classroom studies relate to across the curriculum issues or whole school structural implications? What procedures exist for the communication of ideas and criticisms generated by colleagues? Do we have a platform for the discussion of the implications of action-research? Many action-researchers are frustrated by their inability to discuss the implications of their work with management let alone have any effect on structural or policy changes. Many schools have an immune system ready to deal with any virulent strain of action-research which threatens the status quo in the school. A school needs rational procedures for reporting action-research, and for debate of the findings. Rather than filter-out ideas generated by colleagues, managers need to channel creative and constructive thought for the improvement of our schools.

Further, there are questions of 'who?' 'when?' 'what?' 'how?' and 'why?' which should be considered as part of management policy about action-research. The 'who?' concerns personnel. Which colleagues will engage in this work and how will that be decided? Is there a need for someone to act as a coordinator or internal consultant to enable colleagues to carry out their enquiries? Such a person could support colleagues with technical skills, outside help from higher education, the LEA, or other contacts in schools further afield. The 'when?' concerns the timing in the school calendar. There are peaks and troughs of activity, some periods better than others. There are points on the timetable when cooperative work in departments or in pairs is easier to organise than at other times. The 'what?' concerns the topics or issues for enquiry. There will be areas of school life which need review by common consent, some will be sensitive and possibly open to hurtful personal criticism some will be safe and undramatic in implication. A school needs some kind of policy about what areas of the school life will be reviewed, and who will decide those areas. The "why?" concerns the justification for this activity. Is it worthwhile? Do not colleagues already have enough to do without further demands?

Finally the 'how?' is very important because it concerns the way in which these reviews, discourse, and action-research studies (whichever level we are talking about) are actually conducted. There are technical skills, procedures, group activities which guard against these activities deteriorating into negative 'hit sessions', or into reinforcing existing prejudices, or the viewing of school through 'rose-hued spectacles'. Enquiry should be rigorous and self-critical, creative and 'possibility-thinking' rather than depressive and negative. Ideally schools need colleagues who have some experience in facilitating systematic reflection, and who have acquired action-research skills who can assist colleagues. Where this is not possible at present LEA advisers and INSET units at institutions of higher education can assist schools to acquire the appropriate skills. There are certificates of further professional studies, and the possibility of workshops in a school which will close school early for part of the afternoon for INSET activities.

Enough has been said to indicate that schools need a clear policy about action research and INSET activities for staff development. However, a policy is not enough. There need to be procedures, communication systems, strategies and the will and patience to see plans implemented. Action-research activities can survive as marginal activities without management support, but with active support as part of policy they can inform decision-making, and contribute to both the development of the life of the school and to individual teachers' professional development.

There has been interest in the institutionalisation of action research recently at CARN (Classroom action research network) conferences. Presumably activities which become continuous or are repeated within a regularised pattern that is normatively sanctioned may be said to be 'institutionalised'. In this sense action research has become part of the life and practice of Rotheram High School over eight or so years. That is not to say that all teachers regularly engage in this activity, however. It is worth repeating though that if action research is not to be a fringe, esoteric, or even a subversive activity in a school it does need sanction, encouragement and support from the school management. There is need for structures to facilitate the work.

In conclusion then, I have tried to invite readers to consider the place that action-research might have in secondary school management in promoting staff development. I have argued that action research in any of the forms I have described does promote staff development, but that a school needs the policies and structures to promote this activity. There are many approaches to staff development, and strategies which can be implemented in our schools. It is the contention of the writer that action research provides one approach which can have a remarkably fruitful effect on the professional development of colleagues and curriculum development in a school.

References

Aspray S (1982) 'Interest Understanding and Control', TIQL Project mimeo, Cambridge Institute of Education, Cambridge

Adelman C (1981) 'Uttering Muttering', Grant McIntyre, London

Bannister P (1982) 'Problems with Problem-solving', TIQL Project mimeo, Cambridge Institute of Education, Cambridge

Brock-Utne B (1980) What is Educational Action Research?, Cambridge Institute of Education, Cambridge

Day C (1985) Professional Learning and Researcher Intervention: an action research perspective, British Educational Research Journal, Vol 11 No 2, 1985

Doyle W (1979) 'The Tasks of Teaching and Learning in Classrooms', R & D Report No 4103, North Texas State University, USA

Elliott J (1976/7) 'Developing Hypotheses About Classrooms from Teachers' Practical Constructs; An Account of the Ford Teaching Project', Interchange No 7(2)

Elliot J (1977) 'Rationale and procedures' Classroom Action Research Network Bulletin No 1, January, Cambridge Institute of Education, Cambridge

Elliott J (1981) 'Action-research: A Framework for Self-evaluation in Schools' Schools Council Prog 2 'Teacher-pupil Interaction and the Quality of Learning Project' WP No 1, Mimeo Cambridge Institute of Education, Cambridge

Elliott J and Ebbutt D (1985) 'Issues in Teaching for Understanding', The Schools Council TIQL Project, Longman/Schools Council, London

Elliott J, Ebbutt D, Crossley J (1983) 'Professional and Staff Development. Action Research into Teaching for Understanding: a Guide to the TIQL Project', Mimeo Cambridge Institute of Education

Holly P and Whitehead D (1984) 'Action-research in Schools: Getting it into Perspective' CARN Bulletin No 6, Cambridge Institute of Education, Cambridge

Hook C (1981) 'Studying Classrooms', Deakin University, Victoria, Australia

Kemmis S (1982) 'The Action Research Reader', Deakin University Victoria, Australia

Kemmis S, Atkin R, Wright E (1977) 'How do Students Learn', CARE Occ Pub No 5, University of East Anglia, Norwich

Kemmis S and McTaggart R (1982) 'The Action Research Planner', Deakin University, Victoria, Australia

Lewin K (1946) 'Action research and minority problems' Journal of Social issues, No 2, 1946

McMahon A, Bolam R, Abbott R, Holly P (1984) '<u>Guidelines for Review and Internal Development in Schools</u>', GRIDS Project, Longman/Schools Council, London

Nixon J (ed) (1981) '<u>A Teacher's Guide to Action Research</u>', Grant McIntyre, London

Nolan E (1982) '<u>Workshop Pedgagogy</u>', TIQL Project, Cambridge Institute of Education, Cambridge

Prideaux D, Bannister P (1983) '<u>What to do with my data; reporting action research</u>', TIQL Project, Cambridge Institute of Education, Cambridge

Schatzman L, Strauss A (1973) '<u>Field Research</u>', Prentice-Hall, Englewood Cliffs, New Jersey, USA

Simons H (1982) 'Suggestions for a School Self-Evaluation based on Democractic Principles' in '<u>Calling Education to Account</u>', McCormick R (Ed) 1982, Open University Press and Heinemann Educational Books, London

Smith B O, Meux M (1970) '<u>The Logical Dimensions of Teaching Behaviours</u>', University of Illinois Press, USA

Wakeman B E (1984) '<u>Personal, Social and Moral Education</u>', Lion Publishing, Tring, Herts

Wakeman B E(1984) '<u>Curriculum in Action</u>', Open University, Milton Keynes, Bucks

SECTION 5: WORKING WITH INDUSTRY

Chapter 11

THE REACTION OF HEADTEACHERS TO INDUSTRIAL MANAGEMENT SKILLS TRAINING - ONE COMPANY'S EXPERIENCE

Paul M S Kibbey

The chapter provides evidence of the successful application of a range of human resource management techniques used in the training of industrial managers to education. The author describes a series of company organised workshops for headteachers on the theme of managing change, which are a joint initiative of Rank Xerox and Understanding British Industry (UBI). He gives examples of the material used, and personal testimony of headteachers involved regarding the success of the initiative and perceived appropriateness of the work to the training experience back in the school environment. The initiatives described began in the late 1970s, when the author discovered that few opportunities existed for senior managers in schools to acquire basic management skills as part of their own career development; and that at that point education had apparently failed to devise procedures for identifying the right people for promotion or to provide appropriate training. The chapter establishes a useful context, not only for the increasing possibilities of industry-education collaboration in the 1980s and beyond but also for the discussion by Joan Dean in Chapter 2 on the responsibility of the LEA for promoting staff development.

The background

The origins of my Company's involvement in Management training for secondary school headteachers are to be found in the late 1970s when a series of largely unrelated happenings occurred. Rank Xerox had a long tradition of community support in the UK but we made a conscious decision that our contribution to schools - industry liaison lacked both direction and co-ordination. As a significant supplier of information technology products we realised that we had an important information-giving and awareness role to play with those in schools concerned with its impact on the curriculum, and on the way in which schools are managed.

Equally the fact that Rank Xerox had for 20 years been almost exclusively - and uniquely - a supplier of reprographic products but was by then transforming into an office systems products Company as well (in a marketplace where fierce competition was now widespread) gave us some credentials with which to discuss with others the theme of Management of Change. The third happening was a discussion with the education foundation 'Understanding British Industry', prior to 1980 unknown to us, who had heard of Rank Xerox's desire to contribute more to education liaison and were seeking a sponsor for an Awareness of Industry Workshop for teachers.

UBI's proposal appealed to us because of the opportunity it afforded to work with a nationally structured 'link' organisation and through them with schools drawn from all parts of Britain. Our work with schools had been confined to liaison with those near to the Company's offices and factories, and important as these contacts were - and still are - we sought the means to extend our support to schools more widely. Rank Xerox had the concern common to most businesses that too few able school leavers chose a career in industry and that this originated from a lack of understanding of the role of industry and commerce in the generation of wealth. UBI's philosophy of concentrating their efforts on teachers rather than pupils made sense to us over the long term and it was with some enthusiasm that we agreed to organise and sponsor our first residential teachers workshop in July, 1981. We were fortunate to have limited spare capacity at our Company training centre in Newport Pagnell, Buckinghamshire, in which to accommodate the Workshop. Newport Pagnell has since become the temporary home for some three hundred heads and their subordinates over a four year period.

Awareness of industry module

There was clearly a link between the first workshop and its primary aim of putting over the message about the wealth creation system, and the development of management skills training 'modules' for headteachers. In order to make that link, I will briefly touch on the Awareness of Industry 'module' with which we began. It aimed to give delegates an overview of the tasks and challenges facing a modern business and an in-depth look at the key functions of a business and their interrelationship. The heads also would explore the effect of information technology on the office environment and obtain practical ideas for helping school-children to acquire a better understanding of the world of industry and commerce. Sessions were led by Company Managers on Personnel and Industrial Relations, Manufacturing, Selling, Business Finance and the Changing Office environment. Feedback suggested that delegates found all the topics useful and thought-provoking. (Intense interest in the information technology session and the implications it had for education led to a Workshop series for headteachers exclusively on this theme, which began in 1983.) However, the session which undoubtedly created most interest - and which was to have the most lasting impact on most delegates - was the five hours on 'Management Skills'.

Management skills module

The Management Skills module was presented to a group comprised largely of heads of departments and deputy headteachers, with a sprinkling of headteachers present as well. Clearly it was not possible in one half day to give more than an overview of the Company's approach to management skills training or to give more than one practical exercise. In Rank Xerox, managers are evaluated once a year on a range of Management Skills using an open appraisal system in which both appraiser and appraised openly share and record their views on past performance, agree future objectives, and devise action plans to attain objectives. The results over time highlighted the importance of human relations skills. Internal company research suggests that the most effective managers are those who, firstly know how they are perceived by their peers, subordinates and boss, and secondly are strong on team building and development. The consequence for training was to concentrate more on training in human relations skills, to create a higher order of these skills among managers, and thus to effect organisational change.

The basis of much of the human relations training in Rank Xerox is the interactive skills module. It is a system of categorising, recording and analysing observed behaviour in order to provide individuals with an objective profile of their performance in a group situation. Effects on the group of certain patterns of behaviour are analysed and individuals can learn to modify their own style of contribution. The implications both for greater individual effectiveness and for building stronger more effective teams are significant.

The system was explained before delegates took part in a group exercise during which their contributions were recorded and individual profiles drawn up. They were advised that at least five hours of observation are required before a reliable profile can be produced. Our aim was to introduce the model to the delegates, to give them experience of operating in a group with this new awareness and to provide some initial feedback. Not only was the exercise enjoyed by most participants, but teachers at all levels represented found the material and approach both useful and appropriate to their own situation. Many expressed a desire to have spent longer on this session and some recommended further training along similar lines for those in positions of management in education.

This early experience persuaded us that an appropriately designed workshop exclusively for headteachers focusing on the management of change and the management skills necessary to effect that change could make a valuable additional contribution to our work with schools. At the same time I recall feelings of disbelief as an industrialist that senior managers in schools had had so little opportunity to acquire basic management skills as an integral part of their own career development.

Development of management of change module

In assessing with my UBI collaborator, Ruth Howell, and my Rank Xerox colleague John Edwards (now Principal of Singleton Management Associates, and the indispensible tutor of our Management of Change series) how best we could structure such a workshop, we used as a startpoint an analysis of what my own Company was trying to develop in human resource management training. (As has been noted already in this chapter, managing change - with all the implications inherent in that process - was a priority Rank Xerox had been forced to embrace during the 1970s to protect and grow its business.) We identify four key elements in our management training which together equip our managers to be effective. Firstly, we are concerned with Performance Management - managing people to achieve adequate results for the enterprise. Beyond this we are seeking leadership in our industry through a process of "Quality" - something we define as "fully conforming to customer requirements, internal and external". It has a number of elements, which include a management style with clear and consistent objectives, and a predominantly participative and disciplined approach to problem solving and decision making. We term the participative process 'Employee Involvement' - by which Rank Xerox people at all levels participate in influencing their work and worklife. It recognises that we have good people and that we should make better use of them. We aim to create an environment where employees can be involved in bringing about beneficial change both for themselves and the Company. The change process is activated by problem solving groups, effective meetings, and communication. Thirdly, we train managers to be efficient in monitoring and controlling their sphere of responsibility and this includes the process of staff appraisal. Finally, we emphasise in our training the importance of team building - groups of employees formed and developed to accomplish specific tasks based on shared and mutually agreed objectives.

Input at this design stage from two practising headteachers confirmed that the theme of change was highly relevant to the experience of people managing schools, as were the notions of 'success' and 'failure' and the fact that achieving the former 'label' had much to do with getting the best out of people - with effective human resource management. Management training sessions in our Company are based on a highly participative approach, using group exercises, case studies and role plays and it seemed important to retain this style in offering a workshop to teachers. Our aim would be to avoid lectures about industrial management practice and try to use school situations as the focal point of discussion about good management practice. The elements of human resource management which we felt ought to be covered included leadership, style, interpersonal skills, team building, interviewing, meetings management, coaching and problem-solving. This was endorsed by our two consultant headteachers.

At this point it is worth recalling that an alternative approach to giving heads an insight into management skills practices in industry was suggested to us by Understanding British Industry - providing places on Rank Xerox in-house management courses - and we were happy to proceed with this approach in parallel with running 'tailor made' workshops. We felt it would be useful to compare feedback on the effectiveness of the two methods. Reference is made later to the provision of places on in-house courses - suffice to say at this stage that three years later both options are being taken up.

Management of change 1

For the Management of Change Workshop three primary themes were chosen. These were team building in an atmosphere of change, the management of human resources and the application of management skills in the context of schools management. It was intended that by the end of the Workshop, delegates would have reviewed and examined the relevance of some modern business practices and management skills to the management of change in education, and have exchanged formally ideas and experiences relating to the management of change in schools. Thirdly, they would have received input from senior executives in industry and education on the major issues facing our industrial and educational future.

Heads were given the opportunity to study the Company's management training approach, which is carried out on the basis of identification of need - present or future. All managerial jobs can be synthesised into five major elements, each of which embraces a range of skills, all of which in turn are trainable. Each year every manager is assessed against the range of skills, and strengths and weaknesses are identified. Every employee has objectives for each year against which his or her performance is assessed at the year end. From this appraisal training needs are diagnosed and appropriate training is provided. Potential managers are identified, a career route is agreed, their existing skills are assessed against those they will need in the future, and relevant training is planned.

In offering this approach to heads in terms of its possible relevance to Education the common reaction has been that the obvious logic of the approach underlines the frequent failure of Education either to identify the right people for promotion or to provide appropriate training. Many heads feel there is much that Education can learn and adapt from this approach. The view has also been voiced that the difference between the local education authority's perception of the heads role and his or her own perception of it constitutes a fundamental divide, and heads, like the industry based manager, have the task of taking conflicting messages and interpreting them for their staff, while at the same time developing managers who in turn can handle that task.

In reviewing with heads the relative importance of interactive skills, we use as the start point the three main areas in which our managers constantly identify a need for developing their own skills - managing stress, managing time and managing change. The management of change thus represents a major emphasis in their development programmes. We explore with heads an interpretation of the 'management of change' and a consideration of some of the factors which lead to success or failure in the change process. The successful change process requires firstly the creation of an environment in which change can take place positively and constructively, and secondly the formation of strong and powerful teams. Within this process the most important element is that of managing people. The interactive skills module was developed in the Company some years ago to help managers be more effective in meetings and in the skills of influencing, negotiating and communicating.

The reactions of heads to the practical 'testing' of this module has been consistently positive. It is based on extensive research and observation of managers in their working environments from which it has been possible to draw certain conclusions about the most effective profile to aim for in different situations - as appraiser, as chairman of a meeting, as negotiator, and as a leader of a team. Subsequent contact with delegates has revealed that some have applied the ideas successfully in their own schools and have achieved more productive meetings as a result. The approach often results in clearer identification of purpose within a group, clarification of individuals' roles, more constructive listening to others and greater commitment to and understanding of final decisions. The benefits are deeper individual involvement and satisfaction and strong, committed teams. Recent reactions to this experience include the following:

> The focus encouraged close examination of one's personal interactive skills in terms of strengths and weaknesses. I think personal reflection encouraged by this exercise is a very useful tool in terms of becoming more sensitive to behaviour back in my own situation and thus the opportunity to modify it.
>
> As we progressed so it became more and more apparent that what we were looking into had a direct relationship with education.
>
> I can't get enough of this. How I wish heads were trained in these techniques before headship. It would make things so much easier.

The following session considers the theme 'Influencing Skills and Management Styles'. It comprises an examination of management styles, an analysis of the factors affecting the choice of style in the context of change, the implications of verbal behaviour profiles for management style, and completion of individual profiles. The two main styles of management - 'push' and 'pull' - are explored and discussed and heads complete a questionnaire to identify their predominant style. The most effective managers are those who can use either style uncompromisingly in the appropriate situation so that others in the team know exactly where they stand. Within the two main categories there is a range of management styles and a range of behaviours associated with those styles which can be used in different proportion to suit the context in order to bring about change. The skill of the manager lies in choosing the appropriate option for the situation. An effective team should be composed of 'pushers' and 'pullers' and an awareness of the range of styles and their implications can provide the manager with a useful tool in selection interviewing, in defining and choosing the style of person needed to fit the team.

The practice in my Company is to send profile questionnaires to delegates in advance of the training programme, and also to their subordinates, their peers and their managers. Experience and research has established a correlation between the closeness of perceptions of one manager by the various parties and that person's success in managing change. Although a high risk activity, the potential strength and usefulness of the questionnaires are only realised when the results are shared. The sharing process itself is conducive to establishing an environment where change can take place, and complements and enhances other practices within the Company such as appraisal and counselling.

The intention of this session is to increase the desire of headteachers to make specific, on-the-job changes and to provide some tools to help them manage those changes successfully. If good intentions are to come to fruition the problems inherent in managing change have to be directly confronted. Excellent ideas and a high degree of motivation are insufficient on their own to combat the inevitable personal, group and organisational resistance.

Our experience indicates that headteachers find this analysis and exercise useful. The profile questionnaires provoke considerable interest, not only from a personal point of view but also for their potential usefulness in in-service training and staff selection. It has helped some of them to identify clearly and rationally what they had previously believed and practised intuitively. Typical reactions have been:

> An eye opener, providing insight for me into areas of my management style previously governed almost entirely by intuition.
>
> This session allowed me to think clearly concerning my own and other methods of management. The concept of appropriate style was one I shared but had not heard explained before. This session also offered a good method of actually examining one's own style and analysing where one was ineffectual and at times actually blocking action.
>
> The self awareness instruments were of great value as a means of introducing staff appraisal. This session clearly related appropriate management styles to tasks in the education field.

The final session of the initial Management of Change Workshop explores "Influencing/Negotiating for Change". Rather than solely applying the concept of influencing (dictionary definition: "to modify to any end or purpose; to bias; to sway"), my Company prefers to operate on the principle of 'negotiating' - "the ability to persuade and bargain to get agreement and commitment". Our training in this area is based on developing those skills demonstrated by successful negotiators. They show significantly higher than average use of certain strategies, including particularly those concerned with time in planning and preparation, flexibility, creating a conducive climate, and establishing trust. The profile of the successful negotiator in terms of the verbal behaviour patterns of the interactive skills model is markedly different from the not-so-successful.

The details of the profile are analysed and discussed. Following this the heads take part in a group negotiating exercise where they are encouraged to put the various tactics into practice. The exercise highlights the importance of establishing the process (agreeing objectives and criteria, avoiding personal judgements and assessments) and roles, thus drawing together all the process and style elements connected with the principles of managing change. Heads have generally found the role play activity useful and rewarding. The need for change in schools also makes the session highly relevant.

In the design phase of Management of Change we decided that an important output of the Workshop - for both the delegates and organisers - would be the development of personal action plans by the heads, based on specific ideas which they had gained from the workshop which they felt had practical application back in their schools. The following themes frequently recur in headteachers plans for action.

* Team Building
  - applying awareness of management styles and group interactions to building strong teams
  - reducing the size of management teams

* Staff Appraisal
  - introduction or improvement of staff appraisal systems

* Meetings
  - establishing a clear purpose for every meeting

* In-Service Training
  - introduction of management skills training with senior staff/new non-probationary staff.

Personal Management Style - adjustment of style to suit specific circumstances/people
- greater awareness of effects of own style on others
- more awareness of others perceptions of own style
- observation of management styles of other staff

Monitoring Control - setting clearer objectives for change and methods of measuring results.

Management of change 2

From the production of personal action plans evolved a virtually universal wish on the part of headteachers to reconvene as a group some six months afterwards, both to review and assess progress with the action plans identified at the first workshop, and to explore in more depth some of the techniques touched on at this Workshop. The pattern of an initial Workshop followed by a further session later in the year has now become established practice. The content of the follow up Workshop was based entirely on the feedback from the headteachers who formed the 'pilot' Management of Change. A firm wish was expressed that the second Workshop be based again on group exercises, self analysis and discussion.

The objectives identified for the follow-up were:

* to review and evaluate the practical effect of the first Workshop
* to devise a generic approach to a management/staff development programme, concentrating on selection and appraisal systems
* to share with senior executives in industry and education their views on the responses their respective worlds should be making to the challenges of change
* to receive further input on industrial techniques and processes for managing change
* to initiate action plans relating to their immediate current issues and concerns

The first main session of the follow-up Workshop is Human Resource Development I', and is designed to cover the first stage of a Staff development strategy - selection criteria and processes - and to highlight industrial approaches to person/job match, the interview itself and post interview actions. The start point is a description of my Company's approach to selection, and headteachers can observe in detail the various stages followed, from guidance notes and actual examples. The entire process depends on the integration between job/person/application/interview.

The process begins with the production or revision of three documents - the job description, the employee specification and the application form. The job description states the purposes, duties, responsibilities and relationships of the job and lists the physical, social and economic factors that affect it. The employee specification utilises the information contained in the job description and is drawn up around the framework of the Seven Point Plan developed by Professor Alec Rodger. The seven points (physical, attainments, intelligence, aptitudes, interests, disposition and circumstances) are themselves divided into a number of sub-sections, not all of which will be relevant to every job eg physical - appearance, health, speech. The Plan ensures that no aspect of the person is neglected and aims to diminish subjective irrelevance. Attributes need to be categorised as either essential or desirable. The application form and interview structure need to be closely linked to the employee specification and hence Rank Xerox again make use of the Seven Point Plan. The successful completion of the selection process then depends on the skill of managers in interviewing techniques. The process gives the manager a procedure for compiling a dossier of information and for identifying the areas to explore. The video 'Manhunt', featuring John Cleese, is shown to heads as a tool for focusing on the practice for interviewers to adopt - look, listen, speak - in order to establish what they need to know.

The importance of the team role profile is discussed based on the approach evolved by Dr. Meredith Belbin in his work at Henley Staff College, which by profiling eight predominant team roles (company worker, chairman, shaper, innovator, resource investigator, monitor, evaluator, team worker and completer) and their potential contributions, helps identify the chemistry of a team and provides a method by which to improve it. The greater the awareness and agreement among individuals of their respective roles, the more effective the team is likely to be. Psychometric tests can be used with a high degree of accuracy to measure an individual's role predominance and, armed with an awareness of that together with the other role possibilities, one person can fulfil different roles in different teams. The process is thus not only a useful selection tool in ensuring an appropriate balance of people, but is also a powerful tool in team building.

Sample forms, guidance documents and explanatory notes are distributed to the headteachers to encourage discussion about their potential use in education. On the one hand the perceived constraints within education are seen as considerable barriers to the introduction of this approach, but set against this are the perceived strengths many feel exist. Generally the constraints are seen as the frequent absence of power for the head to make decisions on appointments because of the involvement of the governing body, the dearth of people sufficiently skilled in interviewing to extract the kind of information proposed in the Seven Point Plan, the unacceptability of some of the areas of questioning in the education environment, and the structures in education restricting development and change. The benefits are felt to lie in the systematic nature of the process, the power inherent in such a well defined system, the clarity of purpose and method, the potential for building strong effective teams, and the basis it provides for monitoring and controlling.

Particular comments from Heads about this session have been:

> I was impressed by the systematic way in which the selection process is carried out - we could take that on board.

> Valuable input - I appreciate the systematic approach to what is usually done by instinct.

> Some valuable analytical tools introduced here.

The second main session on the follow-up Workshop, 'Human Resource Development II', covers the main stages of an industrial staff development programme - objective/target setting, key result areas, performance review and appraisal processes, together with a review of self-development initiatives as practised by a number of private and public sector organisations. The focus is on effective performance as the goal of effective management.

To perform effectively an individual has certain requirements of management. Surveys in industry have shown that, whereas ability and motivation are often high, role perception often lacks clarity. The job description can be used as the basis for identifying key result areas and objectives for the subsequent year. These then become the subject of constant reappraisal, with an annual review of past performance and reassessment of future targets with agreed criteria of measurement. The process highlights training needs to which management should then respond. Role and task clarification are essential ingredients for effective performance, with appraisal seen as the central feature in the process.

Whilst recognising and ascertaining the necessity of clarifying people's roles and tasks the culture of education is seen by some headteachers as a barrier to introducing any formal process. The culture is such that individuals are not to be judged by colleagues, the head has responsibility for everything, and heads of department have no real responsibility in management terms. It is apparent that many heads take the view that there is a marked difference in perception by those in education and those in industry of a system which encourages the formulation of objectives and constant assessment of the achievement of those objectives. To the industrial manager, such a process is seen as giving help and feedback; to the educationalist it is seen as "sitting in judgement". In general comments have been positive, if cautious:

> It will take time to implement such a scheme but I shall consider how best to find time for what must be a crucial part of the job.

With the object of making the Workshop experience as practical and relevant as possible for the heads, before coming to the follow-up series they are asked to identify in writing one critical issue currently facing them which requires resolution in a twelve month time frame. The problem must be either directly solvable by the head or dependent on a major influencing intervention by the head. Its successful resolution will have a positive impact either on the head's individual effectiveness or on the school's performance. As a prelude to discussing their problem delegates are offered a variety of approaches to creative problem solving including the use of a task planning model, force field analysis, (a delineation of helping and hindering forces as they affect a given situation), brainstorming, and a personal consequences window. Each approach emphasises the importance of clarity of objectives, and prioritising, as a basis for drafting an action plan.

Subsequently, delegates are able to work with their colleagues in identifying ways of resolving the issues they had identified, making use of the techniques and processes of problem solving offered in the previous session. Our experience has demonstrated the value of this, providing the opportunity as it does to address real problems systematically with a peer group. In general the techniques offered for problem solving are seen as directly relevant or useful. Feedback from heads has included the following reactions:

> The small group and the previous knowledge of the problems made this a highly practical, much valued session with all of us taking away ideas for tackling our current issues 'back on the ranch'.

> Most useful - it was possible, using the help/hinder model, to identify the issues/problems and present to each other a possible solution. The collective experience of other headteachers is a powerful tool.

As with the first Workshop delegates are asked to identify outcomes in terms of actions they plan to take and ideas they will implement. Typical examples of what they consider practical tools for use are material offered on staff development, problem-solving and management style and operation.

In the case of staff development, material on job descriptions, role clarification, task clarification, interactive skills and staff appraisal is found to have ready application.

To assist with problem solving, the techniques of force field analysis, contingency planning, the developoment of preventive and protective actions in order to safeguard the main action plan, the task force approach, the use of a Company designed structured process model to crystallize and focus team action planning and brainstorming are perceived as useable in school management.

The consideration of management style and its implications for operational effectiveness has resulted in a number of significant developments back at school. Some examples are more careful organisation of teams, improvement of time management, the involvement of Governors in interview training, and more careful preparation for staff appointments.

Some conclusions about management change

The foregoing in-depth account of the style and content of the Rank Xerox/UBI Management of Change Workshops for headteachers and the reaction they have received, indicates to us that much of the training received by our Company managers is transferable to the school management training system. We do not force feed our methods and style; they are presented as an offering, which headteachers clearly find have useful - if variable - applications to their own managerial function. Most headteachers who have attended 'Management of Change' have subsequently joined us for a third workshop to explore the use of information technology in schools and its implications for education. Without exception they have found the earlier experience of 'Management of Change' helpful in thinking through this topical and important issue. They have used team problem solving techniques to work through the issues with promising results.

An alternative menu for headteachers at Rank Xerox

An alternative route which a number of headteachers have taken to consider the relevance of industrial management techniques is by joining Company managers on in-house management training courses - the "table d'hote" option rather than the "a la carte". We are pleased to offer places to heads on these courses, in parallel with our workshop series, and the reactions have been generally most positive and have reinforced our belief in the universality of much of the knowledge and many of the skills required to manage effectively. One example of such a course is 'Managing Tasks Through People', which combines all of the "core" skills of management into an integrated approach to the management of major tasks and projects through other managers. The main output is a series of Action Plans related to personal management improvement. The emphasis is on learning by doing and receiving feedback on performance from professional management trainers.

To illustrate the perceived value of this particular experience I will in large part draw on the conclusions of Derek Bowden, Headteacher of Leftwich High School, who attended MTTP as part of a sabbatical term as Research Fellow attached to the North West Educational Management Centre at North Cheshire College. His thoughts are incorporated into a highly comprehensive and perceptive paper entitled 'Prepared to Manage'.

The course embraces much of the content of the two Management of Change Workshops, notably task management, job structure and performance standards, negotiating skills, team building and roles, management style and interpersonal skills. Many of his reactions reinforce those made by his colleagues on the Workshops - particularly those associated with working in teams - despite the fact that he was working exclusively with industrialists.

On the use of systematic problem solving techniques, Derek writes:

> My first reaction to the structured approach was that the simple and obvious was being clothed in a pseudo-scientific methodology. When working through a recall school issue with industrial managers taking the parts of colleagues, governors, parents etc. I realised how intuitive and uncontrolled my normal approach was. Most problems we tackle in school require concerted action by a number of people. It is not unknown for significant people in school to ask me or a deputy what is going on or to point out a serious consequence of proposed action which no one had thought of.

Reference was made earlier to the identification of key results areas in a job as an integral part of a staff development programme. Here Derek comments:

> Dialogue about job performance between a teacher and a head is often rendered ineffective because of mismatch of perceptions and expectations (accidental or deliberate). This is frequently because the conversation focuses on 'activities' rather than 'purposes'. I see 'KRA's (key result areas) as a possible way forward on appraisal because they view the job as a transaction relating the person and the organisation rather than as a sterile set of tasks to be carried out and assessed in ways which can dehumanise the person and the job.

This course utilises a range of personality and psychological tests about which Derek concluded:

> The information derived from the (various) questionnaires is, of course, interrelated and provides different viewpoints of the same phenomenon - oneself in action. I think an attempt to coalesce all the results to one great synthesis and action plan is bound to fail. I enjoyed doing the tests and thinking about the results. They helped me better to appraise and understand my own performance and those of colleagues. I can learn which weaknesses have to be accommodated, and where changes and improvements might be possible in the way we work as individual teams. If I accept my responsibility as a manager to develop those around me and myself, I know of no better starting place.

What has been revealing for us is the extent to which headteachers have not felt out of place alongside Company managers - underlining that many of the training needs are common to both. The indications in fact are that some have found this feature positively beneficial. One wrote to us last year:

> An industrial training course is an experience. Not only is there the new experience of working with people from a variety of fields but this in itself gave one the opportunity to examine the restrictive attitudes self-imposed by always working with those in the same profession.

Nor should we overlook that Rank Xerox managers have derived benefit from working alongside a headteacher. The same head went on:

> I was grateful that the course members recorded their appreciation of the contributions of someone from outside, and suggested that such a presence had enhanced the course.

Our Process Management Course was joined last year by a Senior Master whose comments suggest that middle managers in schools derive benefits just as heads do also.

> My overall impression was that it was excellent, and as valuable for me as a "manager in school", as for the industrial delegates. I certainly learnt a lot during the course, first and foremost that a manager is a manager wherever he works.

Some final thoughts

From Rank Xerox's point of view, which I am certain my colleagues in Understanding British Industry would endorse, we are not concerned either to prove or disprove the relevance of industrial management training to school management training. What interests us is that there are tools, materials and techniques used in industry which headteachers believe can help them to do what they do better, and which we are able to see put to practical use in schools. We have welcomed the creation of the National Development Centre at Bristol and have been pleased to offer support to its work in developing a national provision of management training in schools. We are equally encouraged by the considerable interest in industrial approaches and techniques shown by local education authorities and the institutions providing management training for senior school staff since the publication of DES Circular 3/83 and have welcomed the opportunity to be among those Companies sponsoring 'Providers' Workshops.

An attempt at summarising and drawing conclusions about our experience of working with headteachers can conveniently start with the premise that both schools and industrial organisations have a common objective: being successful. Success is of course measured by different yardsticks but in considering for a moment what makes Companies successful, a recent publication entitled 'The Winning Streak' attempts to identify common characteristics of management style among a sample of successful businesses. Interestingly among the eight common characteristics observed, four strike a familiar note: leadership, the involvement factor, the innovation factor, and the integrity perception.

Top managers in successful companies, it concludes, "recognise that leadership at lower levels thrives where managers have and explore understandable objectives, and the resources and support to pursue them". Involvement is defined as including "stress on the importance of information, both what is needed just to do the job, and provide feedback, and what is needed to give people a broader understanding of the Company and their role in it". The innovation factor represents "a continuous interest and commitment to things new, the the process of change". The integrity perception, from an employee standpoint, "is largely a matter of ensuring that people know where they stand and that they are being treated fairly.

It is not by accident that my Company has espoused these approaches in its human resource management training programmes. They are part of being a "quality" Company - a term referred to at the beginning of this chapter. The reactions of our headteachers suggest that "quality" is as important in their institutions and that they readily identify with the characteristics in management terms which are most likely to ensure its achievement.

If one accepts, as we often read, that industry and education also share a common difficulty - that of presenting their role adequately and effectively to their external audiences - it does imply that much is to be gained by working together to overcome this difficulty. It is certainly the job of top management in both sectors to carry out this task. In education that means headteachers.

Headteachers have a multi-faceted job which in recent years has increased in complexity. They recognise that management consists largely of getting things done through others, and the interactive skills and team building experiences used in training have immediate application in their jobs. There is a recognition that obvious differences exist in the culture and climate of schools and industrial enterprises. Our experience has been that enough similarities exist to make a joint assessment of the respective managerial tasks mutually productive and certainly worthy of a lasting and close association.

References

Goldsmith W and Clutterbuck D (1984) The Winning Streak, Weidenfeld and Nicolson

Bowden D (1984) Prepared to Manage, Cheshire County Council

Chapter 12

SCHOOL-INDUSTRY MANAGEMENT PERSPECTIVES

Roger Moore
Maggie Pankhurst

This chapter develops the theme of the benefits to be gained by collaboration between industry and schools begun in Paul Kibbey's contribution. However, whereas in the latter case the initiative described was taken by industry, here the impetus was provided by an educational institution's one term management course. The main thrust of the argument is that school managers can learn by observation of their peers in commerce and industry. After a consideration of some of the theoretical issues, the chapter is largely concerned with an examination of the experience of four successive cohorts of senior teachers attending one term management courses in which short industrial placements formed a significant element. In evaluating the organisation, processes and relevance of these placements, the authors found evidence not only of the positive initial impact of the activity but also more long term beneficial effects on the individuals' management of their own schools.

Until relatively recently those involved in education did not talk about "management". The assumption was that schools, and indeed other educational institutions, either virtually ran themselves or were controlled solely by a head, or principal, whose word was law. At the beginning of each academic year, staff were given a timetable of their teaching commitment together with some very broad indication of what they were to teach and were then expected to get on with it. There was very little real supervision of staff nor was there much professional contact between colleagues except to a limited degree at such times as the annual examinations and the termly compilation of reports, and at times of extreme crisis.

Then, about twenty years ago, things began to change. Most immediately and obviously there was the rapid reorganisation of the secondary school system on comprehensive lines following the issue of Circular 10/65. Schools became larger, sometimes as a result of planned expansion on new sites but more often than not as a result of amalgamations of existing schools. These "marriages of convenience" produced all sorts of problems. There was of course the problem of resolving the competition for the senior and middle range posts in the new institution. Difficult as this might be, it paled into insignificance when taken alongside the often contradictory value systems of the schools to be amalgamated and this could be problematical even where they were similar bodies, not to mention those many instances where grammar and secondary modern and single-sex and mixed had to merge. Finally there were the long-term organisational problems of the split sites of so many comprehensive schools, in some cases as many as three or four, widely separated by distance. Thus, schools not only became larger, they also became more complex. In addition they found it increasingly necessary to look much more to their external relationships. Secondary reorganisation leading to the demise of the 11+ examination coupled with the new initiatives in primary schools following the Plowden Report, meant that a school had to take more seriously its liaison with the feeder institutions. Here there were some instances - and not necessarily in sparsely populated rural areas - where this might involve up to a dozen contributory schools. This growing problem of the need for more effective contacts was given a further twist by the fact that a significant number of LEAs had reorganised their schools with a break either at 12, 13, 14 or 16. Finally, if all this were not enough, the pressures from Society were demonstrably more insistent. The pace of economic and social change undoubtedly speeded up in the two decades after 1960 and schools found themselves having to respond to issues and problems which they would not previously have recognised as being within their purview or competence. Society as a whole was coming to expect more and more from its schools. The notion of accountability became increasingly popular during the 1970s and in the latter part of the decade, especially after James Callaghan's "Ruskin Speech" in the Autumn of 1976, there was a determined and sustained attempt to give it detailed precision.

Circumstances then were making it abundantly clear that schools could no longer be left to run by themselves nor were they any longer institutions where all the decision making and responsibility could be concentrated in one person. Equally, with this realisation dawned the logical sequel, namely that if schools had to be managed then some training for those staff in responsible positions was at least appropriate if not quite mandatory. It is difficult to be too precise as to where and when management training for education began, but one early experiment was to be found in the North East Midlands in the mid 1970s. Here, a group of LEAs, working with the Inset Unit of the School of Education at the University of Nottingham developed a regional management course for secondary deputy heads. From this has developed a major response to the DES In-Service Teacher Training Grants Scheme (Circular 3/83 and its subsequent annual updates), providing both so-called "basic management" courses of twenty days' duration and the longer one-term full time secondments .

A significant feature of these courses has been an attempt to build in a perspective on management drawn from the world of industry and commerce to see if this can provide some illumination for the senior teachers taking part. What this chapter now seeks to do is: (1) to present some sort of justification for this; (2) to describe the arrangement of the experience on four one term courses mounted during 1984-5; (3) to attempt to analyse and quantify what the teachers learned from the experience; and (4) much more tentatively, to see if there were any influences in the longer term when the course members returned to their schools after the term's secondment.

In the first instance, the need to justify what we were attempting was a very real one. Admittedly there was a good deal of tacit encouragement from the centre. For example, Circular 3/83 spoke of the value of drawing on the experience of the non-educational world, and it was also highly significant that when the National Development Centre for School Management Training was set up in 1983, there was significant representation from industry and commerce on its steering committee. Yet the likelihood was - indeed still is - that to many involved in education the whole idea was anathema. In part, this might be put down to unthinking prejudice, another example perhaps of that anti-industrial culture which is thought by some contemporary commentators to pervade the educational system. However, the argument could be given at least a semblance of rationality. Thus in Taylor (1973) the point is made that the underlying assumptions on which schools are based are so very different from those of industry and commerce that meaningful comparison is not possible. To see the relationship between staff and students in the same light as those between management and labour is simply not appropriate. Further, it is suggested that, at the highest level of management within the school the "authority of the head is legitimated not by his skill as a manager, but by his stature as an educator".

The counter-argument rests on two foundations. The first seems to follow logically from the points already made in this chapter as to the changing nature of schools as institutions. We are now aware of the need to manage schools in a more positive sense than hitherto; the non-educational world has been conscious of this need in industry for rather longer. Surely, then we can be permitted to draw illuminating parallels and utilise industrial experience without being committed automatically to the facile and erroneous view that the pupil/student population of an educational institution is in the same position as the shop-floor labour force. If we accept this, then the second plank of the argument must rest on a clear understanding of how industry sees its staff, and especially how it approaches the question of training and development. Of course at this point it would be wise to issue the almost ritual warnings concerning the dangers of generalisation. The terms "industry" and "commerce" necessarily cover a wide range of organisation with a variety of purpose, size, structure and activity. However, when all is said and done, there is evidence of agreement on general principles and not just in the handbooks on management. Thus, McIntosh (1985), in a paper on the development of secondary heads, looked, for comparative purposes, at the practice of six companies, ranging from a bank and a building society, through manufacturing concerns to a hypermarket chain. In particular, she found that all were concerned first with the identification of needs and then meeting those needs by short, intensive, in-house training, rather than seconding staff away for longer periods. What now follows here is hopefully a not too contentious summary of the best practice in companies and organisations sufficiently large to have a personnel department with an effective policy on staff appraisal, development and training.

In the first place, industry sees it as fundamentally important to maintain some sort of equilibrium or balance between the interests of the individual member of staff, the interests of the immediate grouping within which the individual works and the demands of the task of work to be achieved (see especially Adair, 1973). It might be argued that, in education, for too long we have been almost totally obsessed with the task and neglected the other two aspects quite shamefully. Only when a crisis situation develops do we realise suddenly that an individual may have been placed under some intolerable strain. Moreover, it is probably true that effective team-work is often non-existent in a profession whose members, in the words of a deputy head of the authors' acquaintance "so often want to paddle their own canoe". Team-building indeed looms very prominently in the literature on industrial training, especially noticeably in the publications of the Industrial Society (1982-3) and Woodcock (1984). To be fair, there does seem to be an increasing awareness among educationalists that teams are an essential part of the functioning of a large secondary school. Thus, Matthew and Tong (1982) have argued for the inter-relation of head and deputies in a senior management team, and there are indications that their suggestions have not fallen on deaf ears. However, perhaps inevitably, the notion of team-work and team-building has made most progress among those responsible for pastoral care systems and the implications for training can be seen particularly in the work of Blackburn (1983) and Hamblin (1984). A third important feature of industrial management training has already been referred to above: its timing and length. Commonly staff are trained before going into post and thereafter subsequent inputs are as a result of needs identified by a regular and rational system of appraisal and development. This input is invariably short, intensive, and designed specifically to plug a clearly identified gap in the member of staff's performance. Here education surely has a great deal to learn. Even now, it is comparatively rare for post holders to receive adequate training before they enter on their duties. Moreover, in the present climate of restricted promotion opportunities, some LEAs have apparently set their faces against this, presumably for fear that such training might arouse premature and unrealisable aspirations. Indeed, there have been cases where recently appointed deputies have either not been given additional training or have felt strongly that what was offered was inadequate or even totally irrelevant. On the issue of the intensity of the training activity, it may be noted that while the twenty day and one term management courses are rather more economical than the traditional diploma or degree qualification, they are still pretty leisurely affairs in comparison with most of what is offered in industry.

These considerations apart, in arguing the case for a comparative industrial perspective in school management training, it is worth drawing attention to the existence of a number of practical initiatives. Thus, there have been cases where industrial companies have provided training facilities for senior school staff and a good example of this is described by Paul Kibbey in this book. An equally fruitful approach has been where heads of schools have called in senior managers from local industry to advise on specific management problems. Sometimes this is done on a purely private basis of personal contact but sometimes it is worked via the local field officers and coordinators of organisations like UBI (Understanding British Industry) and SCIP (Schools Council Industry Project, now renamed Schools Curriculum Industry Project). Long term secondments of senior teachers into industrial organisations are also increasingly common and here companies like BP have taken the lead. Some indication of the scope and importance of this activity is provided in a recent article by Everard and

Marsden (1985) and valuable advice is provided on setting them up by Sutton (1984).

However, the weightiest piece of investigation into the points of contact between school and industrial management is undoubtedly that of Everard (1984). Interestingly one of his conclusions is that the best way for schools to borrow what is relevant from industry is via the local, informal networks, gradually building up and utilising the expertise of industrialists on an occasional consultancy basis. This is something that is already happening, as we have seen above. This is not to deny the benefit of a formal course which may be invaluable in the process of inspiring enthusiasts to go out and spread the message generally. In effect of course, this is precisely the purpose of the One Term Courses with their stated emphasis on "training the trainers". Otherwise, arguably his most notable finding is a comparison of the role of the secondary head with that of a typical manager in industry. The list of points of contact is impressively long but what is perhaps most significant is the similarity in the general style and nature of their work: under pressure incessantly to respond to situations and, as a necessary corollary, hardly ever able to settle to the achievement of a planned systematically ordered task. Everard's comparison concludes with the words:

> If the Head's role is really that of Chief Executive of a large and complex organisation, it is clearly of interest to study how people are selected and trained for such roles in industry.

This indeed is the essential explanation of our decision to organise a short module of industrial experience with special emphasis on staff development for teachers seconded to the One Term Management courses at the School of Education in the period 1984-5. Now it is necessary to look at the precise organisation of that module.

On each of the separate courses under consideration the module has varied in length from 5 to 7 days and its position within the course has been altered in the light of feedback from the teachers. The module currently takes place in the third week so that the teachers can draw upon their industrial experience throughout the rest of the course. The timetable is as follows:

Day 1 Workshop on staff appraisal organised by a local industrial training manager.

Day 2-4 The teachers spend the time in a company near to their school following a programme that will give them an insight into the company's approach to staff development, covering the whole area of recruitment, job descriptions, appraisal, training.

Day 5 Debriefing of the industrial experience.

The period of time given to the industrial view of management is very limited, but it is hoped that, having made contact early in the course, the teachers will use their "industrial tutor" on other occasions during the course and after it.

Some of the teachers on the first two courses expressed considerable doubt about the value of an industrial perspective and showed unease about undertaking the experience. However, without exception, each group has afterwards emphasised the very important contribution that this module has made to their learning on the course.

On the first course the industrial placements were organised by UBI, after consultation with the teachers. Since then the teachers have been responsible for organising their own placements, in consultation with their local schools-industry liaison officer, where necessary. There are considerable difficulties and risks involved in encouraging participants to negotiate their own placements, particularly when this has to be done prior to joining the course, as is the case now that the module is in the third week. The difficulties arise because the briefing of the teachers has to be done via the written word which is not always the best means of communication. Many of the participants have had little or no contact with companies local to their school and their knowledge of such companies is very limited, and so they find it difficult to identify a company which will be able to offer them a suitable programme for three days. Even if they are able to identify such a company, they may be inhibited in their approach because of a lack of a contact in the company, or because of uncertainty about how to negotiate a suitable programme. Some of the teachers are also hostile to the idea of an industrial placement as they feel that the industrial experience is not relevant to the education system; and this attitude obviously inhibits the organisation of a good placement. A further problem relating to the briefing is that hitherto many of the teachers have not known that they would be attending the course until very close to the starting date. This means that the task of finding an industrial placement becomes another burden during the short hand-over period prior to the course.

The risks involved with briefing teachers in this way are that a few get very anxious about not being able to find a suitable placement and start to get a negative attitude towards the experience. Those who already have negative attitudes about industry may have these reinforced by uncooperative local employers. Experience has shown that these risks are worth taking as ultimately only a few people have been affected in this way, and it has always been possible to arrange suitable placements for them after their arrival on the course.

In addition to the problems of briefing the teachers there is the further problem of ensuring that they brief their industrial contacts properly. While we hear a lot about industry's criticisms of education, it is not always the case that at local level individuals within a company can see how they can contribute to the development of heads and other teachers, or for that matter why they should be interested in doing so. It is therefore essential that the briefing papers give the teachers clear guidance for the placement so that they can confidently approach local employers and give them a view of what they hope to achieve during the three days.

The briefing papers include a participant's brief, with the names of local schools-industry liaison personnel for them to contact, if necessary, an employer's brief with details of a university and UBI contact should they need it, and short reports written by previous participants about their industrial placements. A typical placement programme is also now included in the papers. The papers not only try to guide teachers as to what type of company may provide a suitable experience, but also encourage them to build on, or extend, their existing contacts, with a view to future development of liaison between the school and company.

The first day of the module is the last stage of the preparation for the experience. The use of an industrial manager to cover the area of staff appraisal has proved a very effective method of bridging the transition from education to industry. The manager is well briefed on current education issues and is able to relate the industrial experience to the education world in a positive way. He is also able to indicate to the teachers specific areas that they should look at and gives them confidence to ask questions that they might otherwise have felt inhibited to ask.

The experience of each individual during the 3-day placement is unique although, as we will see shortly, the learning has many common themes. The extent of the learning which occurs during the placement seems to depend more on the ability to negotiate, and renegotiate, a good programme, and to extract from the experience that which is relevant to the individual rather than on the quality of the placement. As always, for the open minded, there is much to be learned in all situations. It would seem, however, that the companies that provide the best placements have their own personnel department and provide at least some of their own training in-house.

The design of the programme will depend, to some extent, on the structure of the company. However, the best programmes would seem to be those that allow the teacher to talk to a wide variety of people, mainly those involved in personnel and training, but also line managers who have to carry out staff appraisals, young people who are undergoing training, and others who are subject to regular appraisal. The teachers are usually very impressed by the quality of management training in industry and they are able to compare this with their current experience.

The last day of the module is spent in the university, sharing experiences. This is done through group work, each group being asked to discuss two areas: (i) what has been learned from the industrial experience that is common to all and (ii) what has been learned that is relevant as a manager of a school. During the final reporting back session the various areas are discussed and the teachers are able to identify colleagues who may have had experiences which they wish to explore further at a later date. They are also encouraged to see their industrial contact as one that will continue to have a role both during and after the course.

The process by which the teachers organised their impressions during the experience ready for feedback produced a minor methodological problem. Initially course members were asked to keep a diary and then to use this as the basis for writing a report for presentation to the group as a whole. This proved to be too time consuming, even with a relatively small group. We therefore reverted to a technique borrowed from the central training department of the Boots company. Course members were asked to keep merely a very brief note of each day's activity, indicating just what area of the company they were involved in as well as the topic under investigation. They were then requested to analyse or classify their impressions under three heads: what were the significant learning points; how did they themselves react; how might the learning be applied back in their school situations. For example, this is a record of a day spent with the training officer in a prominent electronics company:

Topics Covered	Significant Learning Points	Reaction to Learning	How Might I Apply it in School
Method of entry into the company. Channels of re-cruitment. Selection Training opportuni-ties at all levels. Scholar-ships, bursaries and university recruit-ment. In-house training for existing employees.	1.Willingness of the company to train personnel and help/ encourage all the time. 2.Facilities for re-training. New technology courses. 3. Use made of own personnel but also facilities of FE College. 4.Use of Differential Test Battery and Interview as selection tools.	The ease and eagerness of industry to further the learning and updating of personnel. NB: All expenses paid by the company!	1.Try to ensure that staff at least have the opportunity for Inset. 2.Need to keep up with current trends in education. 3.Retraining of staff if possible or necessary.

These notes would then be used as the basis for immediate feedback and later a more formal report. It is this material, drawn from four successive one term courses, representing some fifty teachers of head and deputy status, on which the following conclusions are based. Firstly we attempted to define initial reactions before drawing out the particular learning achieved in the area of staff development.

The immediate off-the-cuff response from all four groups was virtually the same. Very few had had "bad" experiences and even those individuals were constrained to admit that it had still been useful and worthwhile. In general, people were impressed by what seemed to be better conditions enjoyed by their counterparts and especially what one respondent described as "the caring environment". There were indeed several humorous and some rueful remarks about applying for a job when the next vacancy came up. More seriously however, the doubts still persisted in some minds as to the transferability of the experience. Certainly too there was clear recognition that industry was very different:

> Industry has to be 'quick on its feet' to face the dynamic situation caused by changing needs, demands and fluctuations in the market.

But equally there was surprise when some myths were exploded: that industrial concerns were not run autocratically and that genuine attempts were made to develop "democratic management" and to involve "the workforce in the setting of goals"; that "hiring and firing" was not done quite so ruthlessly as we are sometimes led to believe. However, perhaps the most important general impression was that the experience had further strengthened the belief in "a need for on-going training in management".

More precisely in the area of staff development where course members had been instructed to direct most of their attention, they noted particularly practices in appointment and selection, appraisal (including goal setting), team development and training methods overall.

In the process of appointment, the teachers were impressed especially by the practice of negotiated job descriptions and the care which industrial managers gave to the selection process. For example, some of the major points came in the case of one of the course members who went to the regional office of a large insurance company. Having had the opportunity to examine the firm's system of job grade evaluation, he declared himself highly "impressed by the idea of the employee having some form of control over the level at which he/she is employed". Although, since he had previously read Herzberg (1959), he then went on to wonder whether this was quite so successful a motivational tool as was being claimed. Further, he drew the obvious point that the nationally agreed, rigidly imposed salary levels for teachers virtually removed this from the potential armoury of senior management in schools. As to the company's internal recruitment methods, he noted how effectively large amounts of relevant information were brought to the notice of those involved in selection. In terms of his own position, it emphasised how under-informed he was generally in making appointment decisions.

The appraisal or performance review process was generally seen in a positive light. In particular it gave further emphasis to the need for clearer role definitions and not only more precise job descriptions but the possibility that such descriptions would be modified in the light of changing circumstances. It was also noted that a good deal of appraisal in effect was carried on informally and this was felt to be a good thing although it did not entirely remove the tensions inevitably associated with it.

There were however, two reservations about its transferability, one a matter of operational detail, the other rather more fundamental. Firstly, it was pointed out quite rightly that since the process could never be truly objective, then a good deal rested on the competence and integrity of the person carrying out the appraisal. Secondly, it was argued that the much more clear cut hierarchical structure of an industrial organisation resulted in a general acceptance of a "top down" model of performance review. Not unfairly, there was some scepticism as to how well this might work in an educational situation where a greater degree of independence might be seen as desirable.

Generally too, the teachers were quick to appreciate that appraisal not only looked backwards at a staff member's performance but also forwards, in particular to identify future goals and also define training needs. With goal setting often they expressed themselves envious of the clarity of aims and philosophy of the organisation although it may naturally be doubted whether so diffuse an organisation as a school can realistically hope to achieve this. (But see Trethown's chapter on appraisal and target setting for an alternative view of this.) The attempt to plan for eventualities was also much admired, probably again with a degree of envy by a profession which, not always as a result of its own misdirected energy, has become too inured to crisis management. But, there was criticism of some of the practice. One observer felt that, in his company the targets had been too much imposed (although whether by managerial quirk or outside pressures he did not say) and that there would have to be rather more negotiation in his school context. Yet for him the experience undoubtedly reinforced the need for clearer criteria for measuring achievement. He also came up with an interesting operational point of detail. Namely, that when discussing such matters with staff, it should be carried out when both senior manager and subordinate were fresh and clear headed and not jaded at the end of a tiring day.

As to the training patterns themselves, it was recorded that often this was provided on site, by the company's own personnel and frequently in a very informal way. However, there were some contradictory messages coming across as to the real importance some companies placed on this part of their activities. Thus one respondent commented on "the ease and eagerness of industry to further the learning and keeping up to date of personnel". This was based on an experience with a large, internationally known and highly successful electronics company. However, from a smaller organisation there came the observation "training is the first to suffer in times of recession".

Finally in the area of staff development, there came through the awareness of the importance placed by industry on team development. A head attached to a subsidiary division of a large nationalised industry recalled a discussion of the process of developing the cohesion of a management team by setting up a "compulsory" weekend away from the daily pressures of the workplace. The aim was to enable hopes, aspirations and objectives to be shared and, it was argued, the end result had seemed to show a significant improvement in morale and hence team performance. For the head, this re-emphasised the importance of the middle management level in his school, although in terms of effectiveness, he had found himself wondering how well the industrial team had known each other before they were closeted away together. From the point of view of applicability, he felt he must consider afresh the need to provide similar facilities for his heads of department and pastoral staff. A weekend away might not be appropriate but perhaps a whole day at a suitable venue "might do the trick".

However, while the emphasis of the exercise was on the development of staff, other aspects of the management organisation and process did not go unnoticed. Two areas in particular stood out: firstly that of accountability and responsibility and secondly, public relations and the business of image-building. In the area of accountability and responsibility, many noted again the existence of a clearer cut hierarchy than in schools, but that there was the advantage of knowing equally clearly what your responsibilities were and to whom you were responsible. Hierarchy of course did not mean autocracy, and the extent of delegation was noted with approval. The importance of accountability and what it means in industry came across very forcefully yet simply for a deputy attached to a medium sized heavy engineering firm. The "significant learning" was seen in four words encapsulating what the manager has to do: "Plan; Organise; Act; Check". These four words she felt should also be kept in mind in her own situation.

On the question of public relations and image building the message was positive. That most companies were concerned to put themselves in the best possible light came across in two ways. Firstly, in some cases companies sent their glossy publicity brochures as part of the pre-experience briefing process. Secondly, in rather more cases, returning teachers reported that, early in the experience, someone had taken the trouble to explain in some detail the company's history and development and its current position in the economy. In at least one case this produced interesting analogies with teaching. Schools are now giving much more thought to the PR side of their activities in terms of information brochures sent to new and prospective parents. But perhaps the most striking though less direct manifestation of the firms' concern for their image was instanced by the care taken with these teachers seconded to them. The point has already been made that an exceedingly tiny percentage felt that they had had a bad experience. It should now be reiterated in this connection.

What might be said in conclusion on the basis of this admittedly limited evidence? Firstly that a good deal of the learning was applicable from industry to education. Secondly that, in a significant number of cases, the experience renewed or re-emphasised what was already well known but which perhaps had been forgotten. Thirdly, it confirmed the importance of some of the issues raised in the existing literature and referred to earlier in this chapter. Two important things remain to be seen and both are crucial to the ultimate justification of the exercise. The first concerns the way the placements were set up and the underlying intention of enabling longstanding relationships to be developed. Such longstanding relationships should clearly benefit both sides of the equation. At best, one might hope for an easy informality which would enable senior and middle managers from the school and from the firm to visit each other with the minimum of fuss. From such an arrangement the school might look for consultancy while the company would be able both to update itself on what was happening in education and, quite legitimately, make its interest known in the process. At the time of writing, frankly there is no prospect of assessing this outcome but one might suggest it as a useful piece of future action-research.

The second concerns more the real effect on practice. It will be remembered that course members were requested in their diaries to indicate how they might apply the learning in school. In the circumstances, then, it would be appropriate to check out the course members 6-12 months after they have returned to their posts in school. Accordingly, a very small sample of the first two courses was followed up, and while the responses can scarcely be depicted as conclusive, they indicate positive long term influences being worked out.

In three cases the heads involved claimed that while long term thinking was still being influenced by the industrial experience, precise application had been difficult largely due to adverse circumstances. In passing it needs to be pointed out that this is hardly surprising given that the period in question (mid 1984 to mid 1985) was one of exceptional disruption as a result of the prolonged industrial action in the schools. But even here there were interesting spin-offs which individuals were prepared to ascribe directly to the experience with the company. Thus one had followed the industrial practice of a rather longer selection process for staff appointments, spreading over two days. This particular head had also maintained close contact with the host company and was hoping to be able to negotiate the use of some of its training facilities for staff development activities he had planned. Another head felt that his view of the management process had been so much broadened by the experience that he had suddenly realised the real importance of his ancillary staff. The immediate result was that both the school caretaker and the canteen cook/supervisor were brought much more immediately into the decision making sequence. As he pointed out, both of these people were leading quite sizeable teams on whose effective working the smooth running of the school depended to a considerable degree. Now, regular meetings between them, the head and his deputy were seen as crucial and necessary.

In two other cases it was possible to see the influences with greater clarity and in rather more detail. The first was that of a deputy from a large urban comprehensive. In his response he began by emphasising that his experience had to be seen in conjunction with the parallel industrial secondment for one term of another senior colleague. Their joint decision to work together on return to the school, and moreover in close cooperation with the head, had given them considerable influence that they might not have had otherwise. But, what of the long-term influence? Certainly he still retained his initial enthusiasm from the experience as to the importance of staff appraisal and development and, underlying this, the acceptance that, in some way or other, every member of staff should be seen as a manager. More interestingly, he felt there was a practical spin-off in handling pupils. During the experience he had met and talked at some length to three ex-pupils who had all bitterly complained that the school had largely ignored their personal abilities. Having reflected on this he then instituted a re-examination of the school's procedures for recording progress and felt that something was now being done to remedy the criticism. Equally he had found himself drawing long-term on the experience of sitting in on a "problem" interview where he had been impressed by the process of "contracting" and persuading the employee to become more responsive and accountable. Therefore he had begun to introduce this technique into the school situation and had discovered, perhaps slightly to his surprise as well as pleasure, that this adult approach had had successes even with what he called "serious behavioural problems". But possibly the most interesting spin off with significant long term implications had been the organisation of an Inset activity designed to improve in general the links between the school and local industry and commerce. Some thirty representatives, including those from the two companies the deputy and his colleague had been seconded to, spent a whole day in the school while it was working normally. In the first half of the morning, each of them undertook a pupil pursuit and this was followed by seminars, led by appropriate heads of department, looking at new approaches to the development of literacy and numeracy. In the afternoon, the seminar activity was repeated, first on the subject of the school's system of profiling and secondly, some major projected changes in the curriculum. Again, while the sessions were led by school staff, the purpose of the exercise was to secure the comments and constructive criticism of the pupils' potential employers. By all accounts the day went well and people worked happily and productively together until well into the evening. Whether this will lead to further interaction is of course too early to say, but even as a one-off it is likely to have opened up a few eyes all around and as such is surely worthy of note.

The second case to which special reference is made is if anything even more interesting and gives us cause for some thoughts both about the practice of school management and the training initiatives currently being mounted to improve it. This concerns a head who was in the rather unusual position of having been in the very first one term course and then, shortly afterwards, being seconded to a management course run by the Coverdale Organisation. This participant claimed that the combination of the industrial experience on the one term and the Coverdale experience had changed his approach quite significantly. He had, for a start, become much more receptive to new ideas and influences; he felt he was planning in a much more systematic way; and he became more conscious firstly of concentrating on the strengths of his staff rather than their weaknesses and secondly of attempting to identify staff more carefully for future development. In short, he was managing his school more positively. But more than that were his contrasting feelings on the two types of management training he had undertaken, the one university based, the other industrially so. The former had been far more leisurely, the latter had more pace; the former was more knowledge based, the latter more concerned with the identification of skills and techniques (Chater 1984). This finding indeed merely echoes to a large degree points already made in this chapter, but it should not surely be interpreted simply as anti-academic sniping. Indeed, one may see the two experiences as two essential complementary strands in management education - a call for a more balanced approach which will utilise the best professional and academic practice for the in depth study and improvement of school management.

Finally, the long term effects of the industrial experience on one other of the early participants may be referred to since it strikes the note on which this chapter most aptly closes. Although this concerned a primary rather than a secondary deputy, the general point is still valid. Soon after completing the one term course, this particular teacher found herself promoted to a headship. As she thought about her new post and its challenges, she found herself increasingly influenced by the methods of staff management and development she had observed in the industrial situation. This reached the point where she formed the intention to request the company's personnel manager to advise her on the introduction of staff appraisal into her new school. In essence what she was concerned about was the need for change, and the conclusion she had come to was that this would be best achieved by involving people in the process rather than by attempting to kick them into it. But this highlights a seeming paradox. In industry change often seems to come quickly, sometimes apparently brutally. Yet, in spite of some well publicised cases to the contrary, industry does generally seem more concerned to secure the active involvement of its staff. Educational managers on the other hand often take the negative view that change is something to be avoided if at all possible and, if it cannot be avoided, then they are entitled to assume that their subordinates will merely acquiesce and not ask too many awkward questions. This, in a very real sense, is a reversion to the old days of autocratic (albeit benevolent) leadership. But as the opening section of this chapter has made clear, those days have gone and seem unlikely to return. This particular teacher saw things differently. She wanted her new staff not only to be asking the questions but also actively devising the solutions. If those engaged in the management of schools, not to mention all educational institutions, could learn this lesson from industry, then, we feel, much good would flow from it.

REFERENCES

Adair J (1973) Action Centred Leadership, McGraw Hill

Blackburn K (1983) Head of House, Head of Year, Heinemann

Chater R(1984) Learning From the Other Side "Education", 7 December

Everard K B (1984) Management in Comprehensive Schools: What can be Learned from Industry, Centre for Study of Comprehensive Schools, 2nd Edition

Everard K B and Marsden C (1985) Industry's Contribution to School Management Training: A Matter of Mutual Interest, BACIE Journal, March/April

Hamblin D (1984) Pastoral Care Training Manual, Basil Blackwell
Herzberg F et al (1959) The Motivation to Work, Wiley
McIntosh M (1985) Towards a Management Development Policy for Headteachers in Secondary Schools, NDC/SMT: Occasional Paper No 2
Matthew R and Tong S (1982) The Role of the Deputy Head in the Comprehensive School, Ward Lock
Sutton A (1984) Teacher Secondment to Industry, British Telecom/UBI
Taylor W (1973) Heading for Change, RKP 2nd Ed
The Industrial Society(1982-3) The Head as a Leader, The Industrial Society
Woodcock M (1984) Team Development Manual, Gower

SECTION 6: WHAT THE FUTURE HOLDS

Chapter 13

EXPLORING THE FUTURE: PRE-REQUISITES FOR STAFF DEVELOPMENT

Robert Moon

In tackling the impossible task of predicting likely long term future developments at a time of such rapid and continuous change, the author has succeeded nevertheless in describing a vision which is both radical-utopian and realistic. Starting from the premise that the individual teacher is the pivot on which all educational reform must turn he argues that, as a result of technological change, teachers will enjoy ultimately freer and more flexible working conditions. He identifies three key areas in which teachers will need to have developed skills: learning and new technology, student-centred assessment, and working as a team member in order to enhance the quality of the client-customer relationships. The providers of staff development will need to involve teachers much more actively in the process of defining needs and traditional 'top-down' models will be seen to be neither effective nor appropriate. The definition of needs is not only the individual teacher's prerogative for there are also collective needs as defined by the school, the LEA and central government. In this situation, the author sees negotiation as being at the heart of effective staff management policy in the future.

Traditions to be questioned

In many things the English have a rather self conscious reluctance to be visionary. Those who meddle with grand designs are viewed with a mixture of envy and suspicion. Educationalists are no less guilty than others concerned with social affairs. Wherever teachers gather the idealists enter at their peril. There have, of course, been notable exceptions to such a generalisation. The 1944 Education Act, whatever the shortcomings today, reflected visionary thinking. This Act, however, like the National Health Service, was conceived in the trauma of a world war and implemented in the aftermath of a national victory.

Amongst Europeans the English are most frequently stereotyped as pragmatists. Neither the social planning of the Scandinavians nor the wholesale, sometimes revolutionary, upheavals of those countries closer to the Mediterranean is seen as appropriate to the historical and cultural traditions of an off-shore island. Ideas about schools reflect this. In many respects the changing role of the secondary school teacher during this century has evolved slowly in response to changing institutional needs. Many make a virtue of this stability. They have, of course, a case; the traditions of teaching are timeless whatever the social and technological changes in society at large.

In looking towards the future of teachers, the pragmatic, evolutionary model would seem to represent an unavoidable way of proceeding. Creating the structures for reforming teachers' conditions and performance require recognition of a host of interest groups. The proposition advanced here, however, is that we require far more daring and visionary contributions to guide institutional reforms. In particular there is a singular lack of ambition in seeking to improve drastically the environment in which teachers in secondary schools pass their lives. Arguably this could make the single most important difference to improving schools. There is little point after all in looking at ways of promoting staff development without some idea of possible futures.

In-service education, school-based or focused staff development, have come in recent years to occupy an important place in local and national policy making. The move from subject-centred to whole school related INSET is now well under way. Local evaluation schemes have sprung up all over the country to promote development at the institutional level. It is only indirectly that the plans and programmes are addressed to the working life of the teacher. In the progress of ideas about INSET it may be timely to redress the balance.

Staff development was a barely acknowledged concept in the late 1950s and early 1960s. Educational attention was directed at the structural reform of institutions. A decade later, for a few brief years (1967-72?) the debate about secondary schooling acquired a pupil or student centred focus. Schools such as Countesthorpe, early in the field, and Stantonbury, rather later, displayed some of the characteristics of this movement. The parallel growth of project based curriculum reform was overwhelmingly aimed at subject development. Lawrence Stenhouse was alone in seeing the teachers as the pivot for reform. Moving into the last quarter of the twentieth century institutions have again achieved pride of place. The focus is different, however, with school self evaluation and local or national inspection representing some of the untidy strands in a new approach.

The next few years will see a significant growth in staff development programmes. This contribution seeks, in a tentative way, to look beyond the immediate future to what teachers tasks and responsibilities might be at the beginning of the next century. Few would dispute that teachers are very persuasive in promoting or inhibiting school reform. The power of the professions in the industrialised countries has been recognised by more than one observer of contemporary affairs. Local and national political intervention to curb professional control is likely to increase in coming years but not to the extent that the teachers influence will be minimalised in any significant way. Memories of school days must often centre around memories of schoolteachers. There is increasing evidence that teachers really do make differences to individual and school achievements. Most people have a wealth of anecdotal evidence to support this. A large majority of those teaching in our secondary schools will be there at the beginning of the next century. What can they look forward to? And what, therefore, can staff development contribute to achieving a reform of teaching conditions? Imagine briefly the classroom and educational world fifteen to twenty years on.

The classroom of the future

Teachers now spend a maximum of ten hours a week in face to face teaching. Studies of teacher stress had, in the 1990s, shown conclusively that all round performance could be significantly improved by extensive reductions in contact time. Performance in these terms had included both teacher job satisfaction and student attainment. Three inter-related factors had enabled this reduction to take place without excessive resource implications. Firstly teaching aids had come of age with the rapid and startling developments in technology. The video and microprocessor facilities available in most homes and schools had, at last, taken on a significant role in transmitting information across the whole of the secondary curriculum. Secondly the stranglehold of age-related learning had, partly in consequence of technological aids, been broken except in a few rather old fashioned institutions. The realisation that for many students tasks, including public examination objectives, could be achieved in far shorter periods of time had been significant in convincing public and parental opinion of the need for reform. Thirdly the end of full-time employment below the age of eighteen and the widening of the school curriculum to include a range of new objectives required young people to look beyond schools for a part of their education and training. Overall, therefore, there was a shorter working week in classrooms for students as well as teachers.

The ten hours of teaching was spread over the week. At least two half day sessions were guaranteed as free of commitments although in return all staff agreed to work one evening or weekend session. It was rare for any teacher to have more than three contact hours a day. All classrooms, although many needed some redecoration, were carpeted in order to make maximum use of the equipment that was now available. At least three screens could be used to retrieve information about the range of programmes that could be used by individuals or groups. A study in 1989 had shown that forty per cent of the content currently being taught in schools would be redundant or irrelevant a decade later. With a relatively static teaching force in the schools a radical programme of curriculum development had been initiated in the early 1990s to remedy the deficiencies. The failure of teacher retraining schemes had pointed to the need for other approaches. Teachers, therefore, had to move towards a position where learning was managed rather than information transmitted. Individual discussions with students became an important part of the teachers responsibilities. The imperatives of professional survival had, therefore, realised the ideals of some radical teachers of the 1960s.

A teaching day might well comprise the following. An early morning teaching session with a group aged between fifteen and seventeen preparing for a public examination. The methods employed were traditional, although the convenience of calling up a short video had helped lesson planning considerably. Later in the morning after a brief period reviewing a new video and textbook series, a meeting had been called to look at the development of the schools community placements programme. Half an hour of discussions with individual students had preceeded lunch. The afternoon had been spent shopping. That day a final teaching session from 6.00-7.00 pm had included youngsters from a number of local schools who wanted to follow a particularly specialist interest.

Over the previous decade two changes helped improve the daily life of the teacher. Firstly the role of ancillary helpers, after considerable negotiation, had been substantially upgraded. It was now possible for ancillaries to work with groups of young people in certain specified conditions. Teachers no longer supervised playgrounds or dining area nor did they necessarily have to sit with groups watching video or using the school resources centre. All teachers came to call on ancillary help in the same way that science teachers previously had used technicians. Secondly the monolithic school day, everyone arriving at 8.45 am and leaving at 3.45 pm, had ceased to exist even in the rural areas where students needed school transport. Refreshment facilities were available throughout the day at most schools and the lunch hour varied according to the programme being followed. All students had a contractual obligation to follow certain courses and fulfil certain requirements mostly in the main part of the day. Attendance was checked and collated across the week through electronic registers. Individual tutors followed up problems although average attendance figures had improved in each of the previous three years. Instances of school indiscipline had dropped considerably. Classroom incidents still occurred, and records of these were taken into account in each new phase of curriculum planning.

Debate about the school curriculum continued at local and national level. Broad agreements had been reached on the need for certain curriculum experiences to be common to all schools. A wealth of documents continued to arrive in schools from HMI and other sources. These, however, were less concerned with content, more with teaching methodology and the learning process.

The enormous extension of adult education, formal and informal, in the previous decade, in part because of the communication revolution, had influenced school organisation considerably. Many commented on the change in school atmosphere from an earlier period. Researchers were certainly able to point to improved levels of literacy and numeracy. The army of adult literacy experts could at last see the possibility of phasing out the programme. A minority viewed their findings with suspicion and suggested an alternative view of the future. Although still a political issue schooling did not excite the same sort of ideological antagonisms that had characterised the period of comprehensive institutional reform or, nearer the end of the century, the period of curriculum and organisational questioning. The clearly illustrated, socially divisive, outcomes of schooling still provided an important focus for both political and academic discussion. The debate, however, was more complex than a quarter of a century earlier. The previously separate worlds of education, work and training had become sharply less differentiated from the early secondary years onwards.

Managing staff development

The school and the classroom of the future could, within the same buildings and on the same site, become very different places than those we know today. The 'vignette' above is in no way all inclusive. Others would choose different perspective and different points of detail to illustrate an idea. It is, however, an attempt with which others can join to think beyond the often mundane and pressing everyday problems of schooling. A view of staff development that looks well into the future will create, not necessarily radically different, but certainly new focuses for discussion. School policies and, therefore, those of LEAs and providing institutions might well, for example, think carefully about the following.

1 The management of learning and the new technology

Not so long ago (perhaps they still exist?) teachers went on courses to learn how to use the 16mm projector. In some authorities access to the projector was impossible without certification. A little later the phrase 'resource based learning' tripped off the tongue of any aspiring in-service educator. Advisers for audio-visual aids were appointed, although these were some of the first posts to disappear in the post OPEC economic depression. With the notable exception of the ILEA, interest across the country dwindled. The methodology courses of the old teacher training colleges were rarely high status endeavours. It would be interesting to know whether, in the transformation of teacher education, teaching method posts have suffered at the expense of other interests.

It will be important to rehabilitate this aspect of initial and in-service teacher education. Computerisation to assist learning and as a valuable aid to the teacher's administrative tasks is an obvious example. The day will soon come, however, as the costs of technological equipment falls, when each classroom, workshop or laboratory will have available what previously was available in a much more limited way. The preparations for this should be in hand now. Greater understanding amongst teachers of classroom technology could bring forward the day when resources are provided. Airline pilots are trained on simulators. It might not be too far fetched to suggest that in many schools, and certainly in teachers' centres, colleges and universities, 'laboratory' classrooms should be set up on futuristic lines. The early abortive experience with teaching machines, video and computerisation have left an unfortunate legacy in the minds of many teachers. This needs dispelling if the benefits of third and fourth generation technological advances is to be realised.

In part, the reluctance to embrace technology comes about not because of resourcing difficulties nor through unsatisfactory experience with the early technology but because of a deeply ingrained attitude towards teaching. Learning in British society is imbued with the puritan ethic. The monastic, chilly classrooms of the nineteenth century public schools still have a place in the public consciousness. They still, of course, exist today. Carpeted, comfortable, well ventilated and properly resourced classrooms provoke guilt even amongst those who would benefit most. Amongst politicians they are viewed with suspicion. A few years ago one County Council barred the use of carpets in new schools. This was in the face of architectural evidence that the savings on sound insulation in the roof made this solution significantly more cost effective than vinyl tiles. To their credit staff in this school raised thousands of pounds to carpet the tiles in advance of the first new students. There is, therefore, a historical tradition that needs challenging when we look at modernising the teaching environment.

2 <u>Student centred assessment</u>
Individual, diagnostic and student centred assessment is now beginning to have a very significant impact on teaching methodology. Again it is useful to look at the background to this before outlining the implications for future policy. It will be much easier to refurbish our monastic classrooms than change thinking about assessment. Sir Cyril Burt has a lot to answer for. The majority of secondary school teachers received their initial training in a time when the validity of IQ went unquestioned. In many schools just about any test available is interpreted as an IQ measure! The concept of fixed unchanging intellect underpinned the introduction of selective schooling. IQ inevitably became linked to the scholastic and academic curriculum of the grammar schools which came to dominate the curriculum of the new comprehensive schools. From selection, backed by IQ, come those weary phrases that can be heard in staffrooms up and down the country. The 'high ability or low ability child' and, perhaps most demeaning of all the 'average child'. The 1963 Newsom Report was already bringing this into question. Edward Boyle's short introduction where he suggests

> all children should have an equal opportunity of acquiring intelligence, and of developing their talents and abilities to the full

puzzled many teachers at the time. And from the report itself one quotation would still today provide the grounds for a good staffroom debate

> We had difficulty with our terms of reference. "Average" and "below average" are full of pitfalls. The words themselves are useful enough, as ways of trying to identify in broad terms two large groups of pupils; but unluckily they often carry emotional overtones: the idea of "below-average ability" easily suggests "below-average people", as though the boys and girls so described were being regarded as generally inferior and in some way less worth educating than their "above-average" brothers and sisters. There can be no question of regarding

> one human being as less valuable than another, but though distinctions are difficult, some have to be attempted. Anyone involved in the job of teaching knows that the range of capacities to be encountered among the pupils of even a single school is very wide, and that to fail to take account of this is neither realistic nor likely to be in the pupils' own interests. (Newsom Report, 1962)

Rarely, if ever, is the word "ability" qualified by reference to a particular range of skills. Implicitly it refers to high or low ability in relation to the scholastic curriculum (most often described in terms of eight or nine subject titles). In a comprehensive school 'all in' generalisations such as this are demonstrably untrue. Ability in the traditional school curriculum says nothing about skills in a whole host of other domains, the creative, practical, interpersonal and linguistic to name but four.

There is an increasing awareness of this. Most teachers now would recognise the difference between criterion and normative assessment. The conversion of one Secretary of State to the former has had an important affect on educational thinking. The new GCSE examination industry is grappling, sometimes with bizarre consequences, with the need to shift thinking. Developments in Further Education, an area free to a degree from the historical legacy of schools, have increasingly impinged upon schools. Records of Achievement for each school leaver are now a feature of activity in most education authorities. MSC and TVEI may well be the Trojan horse inside the secondary school curriculum.

The teacher, therefore, will, again, ironically following the idealism of some teachers in the 1960s, be focusing on individual potential in relation to a wider range of skills and achievements than previously. The early staff development work in places like London and Oxford has shown this to be rewarding but complex. The implementation of the Oxford Certificate of Educational Achièvement in four areas, Coventry, Leicestershire, Oxfordshire and Somerset, has provided an indication of the benefits and problems of this approach. Records of achievement and GCSE will eventually involve every secondary teacher in similar development activities. It requires unpicking the common sense simplicity of the assumptions that link ability with student ranking.

In part this requires a change of attitude. Equally, however, there is a technical challenge to monitoring and facilitating progress in an inevitably more detailed, less hit and run style. It must, however, promote individualism. Secondary teachers, unlike their primary colleagues, despite years of lip service, will find this less familiar. Markbooks, for example, will become very different documents than those that exist today.

3 Teachers in teams

Negotiations about teachers pay and conditions have recently begun to make mention of teacher teams. In some schools this is beginning to mean much more than a subject department and advocates of a much more collaborative approach to teacher development are numerous. Yet again, as anyone familiar with secondary schools will know, this is a challenge to tradition. Even sharing worksheets is problematic, let alone more ambitious undertakings. To work in this way, common-place now in many areas of industry and commerce, requires preparation and planning. It also requires accepting limitations on personal autonomy. Professionalism for teachers still includes a healthy respect for the importance of the 'amateur'. Planned approaches to team organisation, task definition and delimitation of responsibilities for example, make some teachers feel slightly embarrassed.

Great economies of time can be made by a collaborative approach. Planned teamwork releases energies every bit as creative as the gifted individualism of teachers. It is also functionally valuable. Take one example. Over the next decade or more, given a relatively stable teaching force, there will be an increased need for updating in a number of curriculum areas. This is not the new subject and information areas but those already established and likely to survive. Individual teachers could cover the range of new knowledge through reading, distance learning perhaps and the occasional course. It would be an ambitious undertaking. An alternative strategy, if teamwork was well developed, would be for groups of specialists to agree that each individual should pursue specific developments in the field. The collective sharing of accumulated knowledge could promote and enhance scholarship.

More radical in its implications might be attempts by groups of teachers to experiment with new styles of engaging parents in learning. In primary schools, the vital role of parents has been well illustrated. There has been little explanation or experimentation of the potential for class links in secondary schools.

The list of possibilities for teamwork are endless. Within schools, however, the conditions for teams to be successful need establishing. Most teachers at some stage in their careers have enjoyed the stimulus, and elan, that comes from membership of a successful team. Usually a chance combination of personalities and circumstances has brought this about. The expectations of a school staff, and school organisation, however, can create the conditions whereby this is more, rather than less, likely to happen.

New styles of relationships

Relationships, of all the issues, have the biggest single impact on the daily lives of secondary school teachers. Questions of control daily exercise the whole army of teachers who have responsibilities within the unfortunately termed 'pastoral' system. Heads of House or Year and some deputies spend vast periods of their working week mopping up the failures of the control structures. In some schools a perverse, and inverse, status comes from the degree of difficulty with which the school is perceived. Inner City areas and working class estates are seen as more problematic than suburbia or the rural countryside. Not by all, however, for even in the most salubrious of communities, teachers in the schools will be seeking to uncover some more hidden but equally problematic influence on their working lives.

Teachers in the school of the future could remove some of the structural impediments that inhibit relationships, such as the built-in and inevitable expectation of failure in the examination system; the tedious movement from one lesson to another with notetaking the dominant activity;. the lack of practical, applied and community or work based activities in the curriculum; the ubiquitous school bell (even hooters in some places) regulating the beginning and end of learning; and, the mass arrival and exodus at 8.45 am and 3.45 pm five days a week.

Important as these issues are, the way in which teachers relate in face to face situations with individuals or groups of students is still of over-riding importance. In nearly all other service occupations training of some sort is used to improve the quality of relationships between client and customer.

A high level of attention is paid to inter personal skill training in occupations close to teaching such as youth work or social work. Teachers, especially those in working class areas, are often apprehensive, even alienated by staffroom stereotypes of classroom behaviour. In a fairly explicit way this has come to light where established groups of teachers have planned activities such as racism awareness workshops. These, however, are not easy areas to explore. Teacher embarrassment, covered by staffroom humour, is a very effective block on initiatives of this sort. The protection of policy is, arguably, more important in promoting a new approach to inter-personal training than in any other area of staff development.

Planning policy

There is now a considerable literature around the theme of staff development. This collection provides a further example. Virtuous but dull is how one headteacher reviewer described a recent wholesome publication about secondary school INSET policies. Check lists, systems analysis, rather tentative dabblings with appraisal and high minded observations on deputy head (staff development) job descriptions do little to engage the imagination of teachers or those who control resources. For development to become central to teachers lives they must feel the sense of ownership, of having a personal stake in the whole undertaking. To achieve this everything will have to become much more controversial. Where controversy has existed it is in propagating a teacher deficit model of change. Politicians in particular have in recent years waxed eloquent on the shortcomings of teachers and, therefore, the need for new approaches to in-service provision. It is a course of action that is unlikely to motivate teachers any more than it would those in other jobs. Some ideas about appraisal come dangerously close to this.

A critical review of existing practice would be essential, however, if the focus of staff development was the overall improvement of the working lives of teachers. How could this be effected? The dominant, though now declining, model of development is still what could be termed 'top down fishing' approach. Providers, usually from outside the schools, search around for teachers to join in a random offering of courses. Occasionally the line-casting is less random, as local authorities seek out groups of teachers to promote particular policies. Overall, however, this strategy represents the classic way of minimising the influence of individual teachers on their own development. No amount of union representation on planning committees will compensate for this.

An alternative and complementary model would be to borrow an idea that has become increasingly important in management training generally in recent years. Namely the formulation of individually focused and flexible development profiles for every teacher. These would be drawn up in discussion and in negotiation with immediate colleagues and with the school and local authority administration. There would be no direct link to promotional expectations or appraisal schemes. In other words there would be no compulsion on teachers to follow particular pathways. The programme would contain short and long term objectives. It might contain elements that neither the schools nor authority administration would support for resource or other reasons but the teacher would still have the right to register a request.

An aggregation of these profiles would be made within schools and these could then be reviewed by education authorities and other providing institutions. Just as individual teachers might be unable to realise their INSET expectations so this could apply to schools in relation to a local authority; or at one stage further to authorities in relation to central government. It would, however, be a genuinely grassroots approach and it would engage every teacher in a review of the possibilities. The chart below illustrates one form that this could take.

In producing such a profile the teacher will have to clarify current personal interests and ambitions. Once agreed it would be the job of the school and authority administration to agree which requirements could be met. In many ways the example given here is not controversial. The requirement in the first year is sensible and in the interests of the school. Years 2 and 3 reflect more personal needs and, looking well ahead, the tentative secondment proposal could be of institutional and authority value. Some other teachers might put forward less relevant or less realistic proposals. Blank profiles would be inadmissable. The use of all forms of distance learning, including the Open University, would feature in many submissions. The development of such a profile would not imply a right of resourcing. It would mean, however, a personal statement around which a teacher would claim personal development needs and it would make providing institutions more responsive to these needs. It would in part become a political activity with groups of teachers agreeing to opt for similar submissions. It would threaten some and it could be controversial.

<u>Development profile 4-year plan</u> -

Name - <u>Teacher</u> ... Home Economics/Design area of curriculum - mid career 2 years in present school

---

Current academic	(A^1)	worth some updating on links between Home Economics and Science curriculum	approach made by adviser to local College of Higher Education
	(A^2)	application for two-day Summer Term course on Active Tutorial Work	

Year 2	(B)	Wishes to begin an Open University Advanced Diploma - funding required from authority (... school management and administration)	Open University tutoring provided by authority
Year 3		2nd year of Diploma	
Year 4	(C)	considering one term or year secondment ... current interest in links between practical subjects	Local University Departments

---

<u>Discussions noted</u>

(i) With Heads of Curriculum area ... (A^1) discussed in departmental meeting and three other teachers will be indicating similar need

___________ ___________ (dates)

(ii) With Deputy Headteacher (twice ... A^1, A^2 & B) and Headteacher re A^1 & ^{2}, B & C

___________ ___________(dates)

(iii) With authority adviser responsible for link with national Open University programme (B) ___________ (date)

(iv) Letter to authority and appropriate adviser indicating interest in secondment (C). Copy attached to profile.

<u>Signed:</u> <u>Teacher:</u> <u>Headteacher:</u>

Notes - to include resource or other reservations on entries still appearing (other discussions) profile

---

SUBJECT INDEX